I0800223

IMAGES
of America

BENTON COUNTY

IMAGES
of America

BENTON COUNTY

The Benton County Genealogical Society

ARCADIA
PUBLISHING

ISBN 978-0-7385-1814-5

Published by Arcadia Publishing
Charleston, South Carolina

Printed in the United States of America

Library of Congress Catalog Card Number: 2005922446

For all general information, please contact Arcadia Publishing:
Telephone 843-853-2070
Fax 843-853-0044
E-mail sales@arcadiapublishing.com
For customer service and orders:
Toll-Free 1-888-313-2665

Visit us on the Internet at www.arcadiapublishing.com

Contents

Photograph Credits

Benton County Public Library—BCPL
Collection of Ron DeBruce—RD
Collection of Jack Dashper—JD
Collection of Carolyn Warden—CW
Collection of Betty Davis—BD
Collection of Eunice Pierce—EP
Collection of Nola Nunnery—NN
Photographs by Jean Gilley—JG
Touch-up by Tony Robinson—TR

INTRODUCTION

The area west of the Tennessee River was purchased from the Chickasaw Indians by the treaty of cession on January 7, 1819, which opened the lands up for settlement by the whites. After the treaty of 1819, settlers flocked across the river, settling in the fertile creek valleys and rolling uplands. One of the earliest settlements was on Rushing's Creek by Willis and Dennis Rushing in 1819. During the next few years, the population grew quickly with new settlers arriving from surrounding counties and from North and South Carolina, as well as other states.

Benton County, Tennessee, was formed from the western section of Humphreys County by an act of the Tennessee General Assembly of December 19, 1835, which provided that on January 1, 1836, the new county of Benton would officially be created. Ephraim Perkins, Nicholas Brewer, George Hudson, and Amos Bruce proceeded to lay off the county into nine districts, convenient in size to allow for the election of county officials. A site near the community of Tranquility was selected for the county seat, and a one-room log courthouse was erected in 1836. The county court—made up of magistrates selected in the civil districts who elected their own chairman—was the governing body of the county.

Initially, the county was named for Thomas Hart Benton, an influential lawyer and politician of the era. Because of Benton's strong nationalistic and anti-slavery positions, locals under the leadership of Stephen C. Pavatt introduced a bill on February 4, 1852, which would allow Benton County to keep the name of Benton but to be named in honor of David Benton, a well-known citizen of the county, and not Thomas Benton. A respected yeoman farmer, David Benton (1779–1860) served in the War of 1812 and in Benton County Quarterly Court.

The economy of Benton County for most of its early years was an agricultural economy supported by small yeoman farmers, few of whom owned slaves. They raised tobacco, cotton, wheat, peanuts, oats, and livestock.

Following World War II, most of the county was electrified by the Benton County Public Utilities and several industries located in the area—lessening the dependence on agriculture as the primary source of income for the people. In the 2000 census, the population of Benton was 16,537 with only 5.2 percent listed as farm workers.

Benton County is fortunate to have had people who placed value upon preserving its history many years ago. The Benton County Archives is located on the lower level of the Benton County Library. Through those records we learn about those who came before us. We can better know where we are going when we know from where we came. Through the preservation of history and photographs, our ancestors live on with us.

Time changes everything. Businesses have come and gone, historic homes and businesses have disappeared over the years, early settlers have passed from us, but records and photographs have been left.

The faces of the towns in Benton County have changed over the years. Some buildings have been lost to fire or other disasters, but many others were lost to "progress." Two that come to mind are the old rock shelter that stood at Pilot Knob and the former courthouse, which was torn down to build the present one.

Big Sandy, in the northern part of the county, was once a thriving railroad town boasting a canning factory, cotton gin, stave mill, retail stores, bank, dentists, funeral home, two millinery shops, a hardware store, poultry house, cattle yard, and blacksmith shop.

The Holladay area of Benton County, referred to as The Upper End, is located in the south end of the county. During the late 1800s and early 1900s, it was a bustling community with stores, cotton gins, water mills, saw and stave mills, a bank, and one of the best institutions of higher learning in the area, Holladay Independent Normal. It was a degree-conferring institution with an average of 300 students from several states.

The town of Camden began in 1836 with the sale of lots in the town, with the courthouse to be located in the central part. Log stores and dwellings and a brick hotel were some of the early buildings. The railroad was built following the Civil War. Being the county seat, Camden had several young lawyers, and two of them, Alvin Hawkins and Thomas Clark Rye, went on to became governors of Tennessee. Saloons flourished until the people rose up and demanded their removal. One of the historic homes that still stands was known as "The House Whiskey Built." The Benton Male & Female Academy was incorporated in 1838. Around 1855, a tobacco factory was established in Camden.

Eva was home to the Archaic Indians and today is in the location of Nathan Bedford Forrest National Historic State Park. Two very high points in Benton County garner attention for being the "highest point" in the county. They are Pilot Knob in the Nathan Bedford Forrest State Park and The Round Top.

A portion of the photographs in this book comes from a project of the Tennessee State Library and Archives that was compiled for the Tennessee Homecoming 1986. The Benton County Library maintains a set of negatives from this project. They are from photographs that members of the community brought in to be copied, and they tell how Tennesseans lived in times past. Others come from a collection in the Benton County Library and some from personal collections.

In addition, Ron DeBruce has been collecting photographs of Big Sandy that he chose to share for this project; Jack Dashper offered his collection of photographs, mainly of churches, made in the late 1980s. Others contributors include Betty Davis, Carolyn Warden, Eunice Pierce, Jonathan Smith, Nola Nunnery, and Jean Gilley.

One

Religion

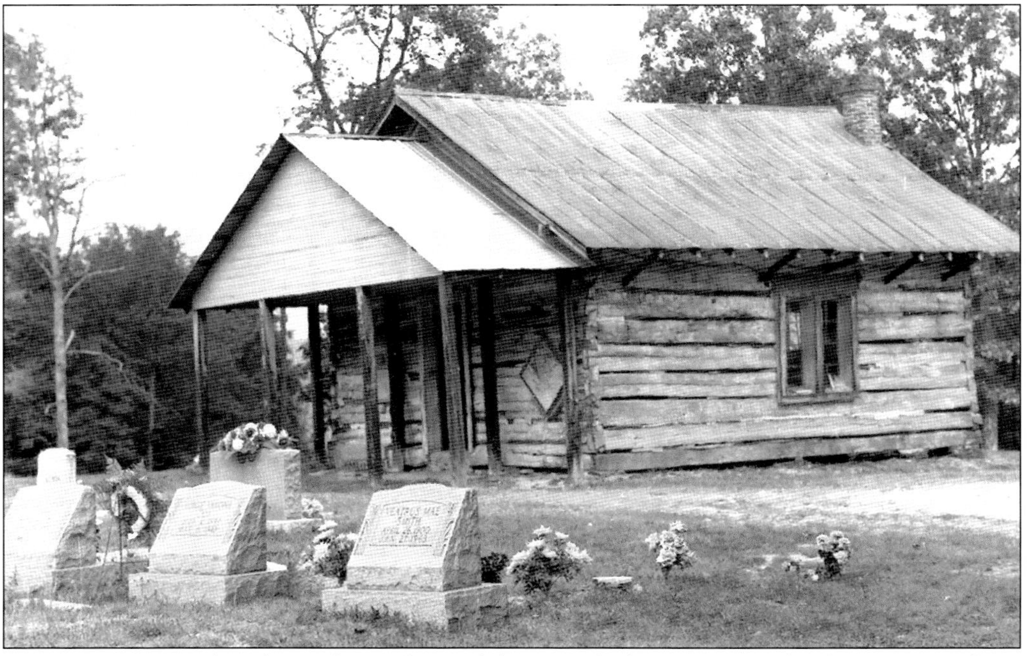

Mt. Zion Baptist Church was located at Sulphur Creek about seven miles from Big Sandy; it was built in 1812 (according to a plaque that was secured to the structure) and called Mt. Zion Meeting House. In October 1973, the church was entered on the National Register of Historic Places. It was destroyed by a fire on July 8, 1992, that was determined to be arson. (JD.)

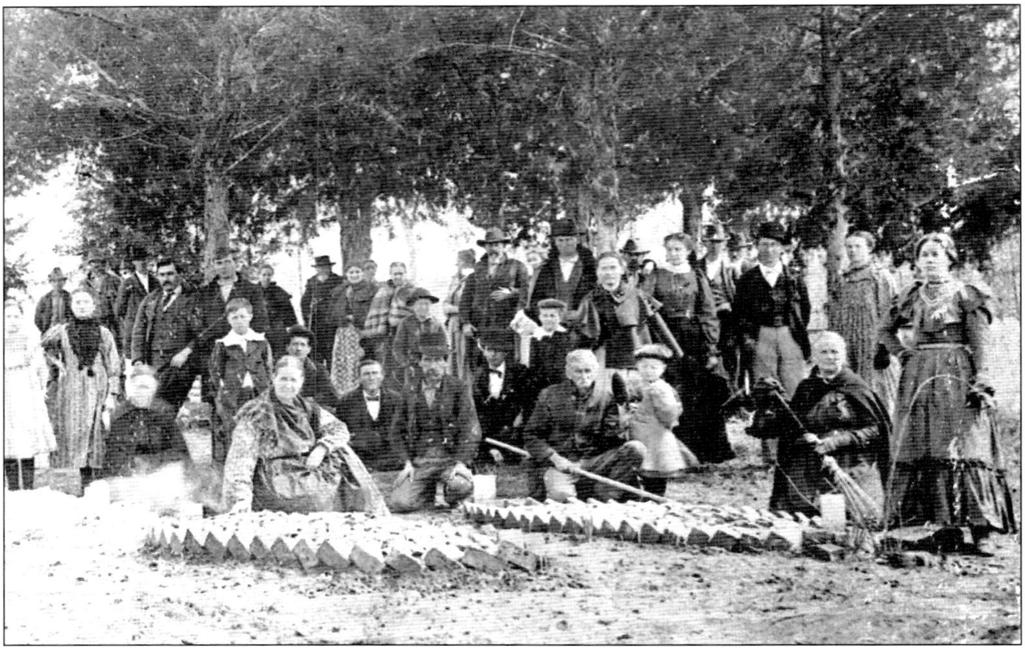

It was a common practice for families, friends, and church members to gather and clean the cemetery of their church or where their loved ones were buried. Pictured is cemetery cleaning day at Baker's Chapel Cemetery, near Big Sandy, around 1910 or earlier. Graves are shown in the foreground covered with mussel shells inside an outline of bricks. (BCPL.)

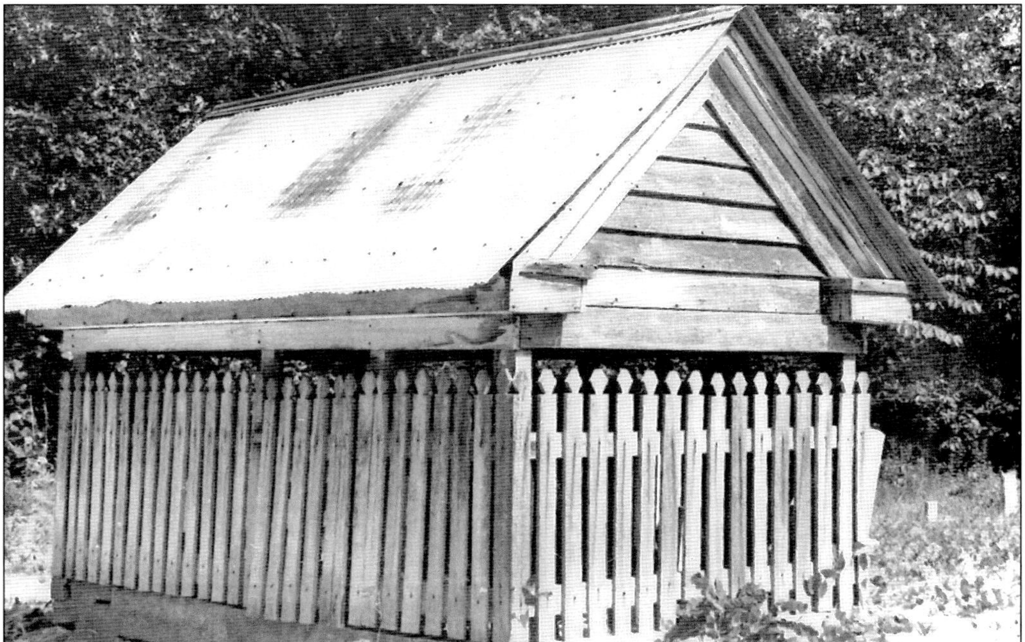

A watershed placed over a grave was a custom of the mid-1800s; this one stood over a grave in the old section of Flatwoods Methodist Cemetery. (BCPL.)

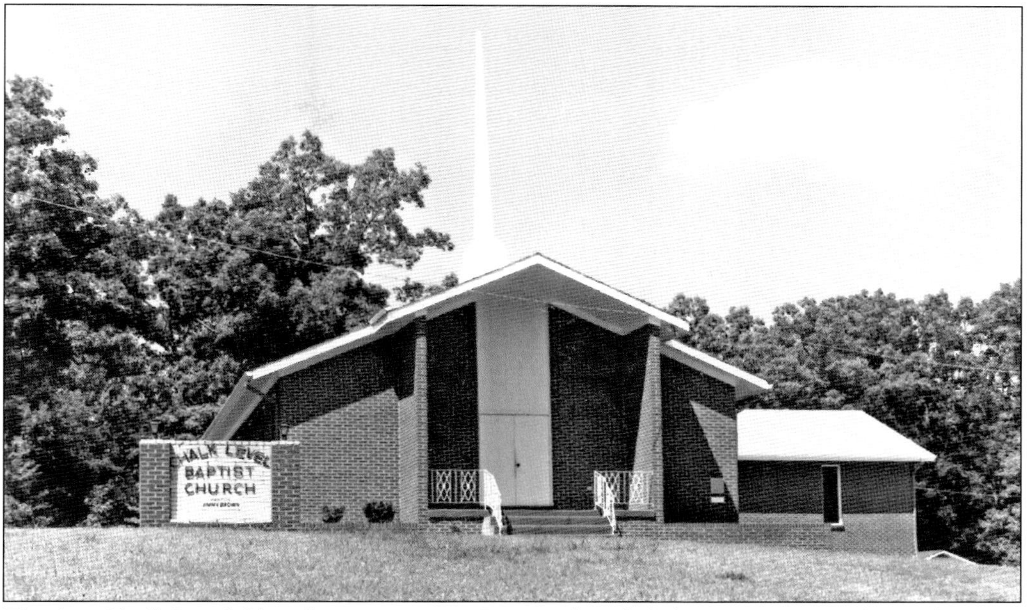

The first Chalk Level Church was Primitive Baptist, founded about 1830. It was located a quarter-mile west of the present church near the old Chalk Level Cemetery. In 1849, the church voted to become Missionary, and in 1882, a log building was erected. A frame building was erected in 1911 and a brick building in 1942. The present building was dedicated in 1971 and is located on Shiloh Church Road. (JD.)

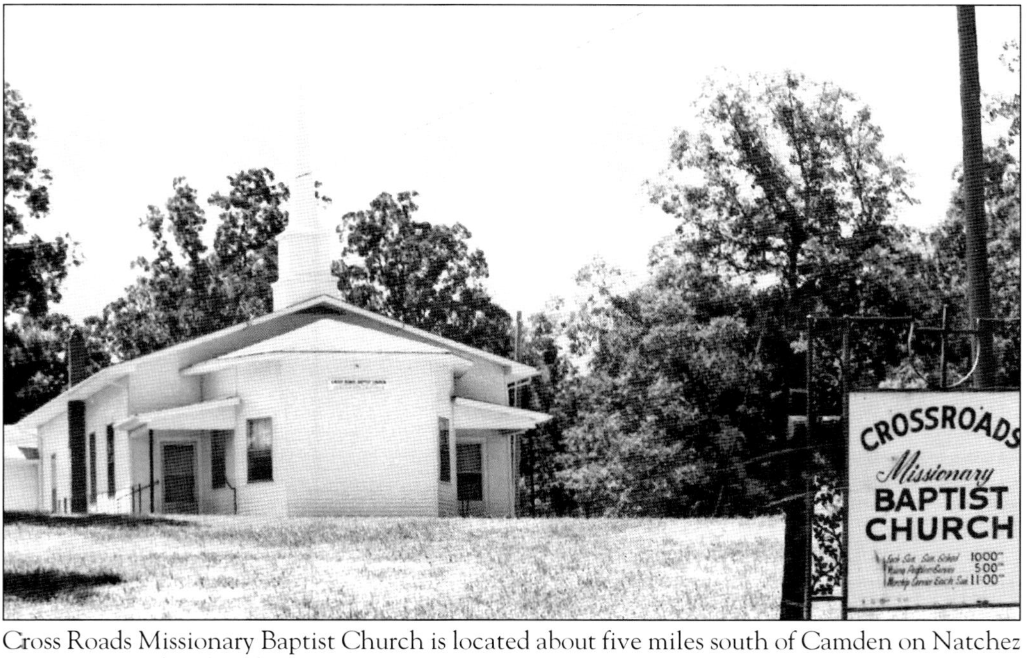

Cross Roads Missionary Baptist Church is located about five miles south of Camden on Natchez Trace Road. The church was organized in December 1849 by Elders David Quillan and Elijah Autry. The original church was a log structure, and in 1889, it had about 175 members. This frame building was constructed about 1918 and has been remodeled several times. (JD.)

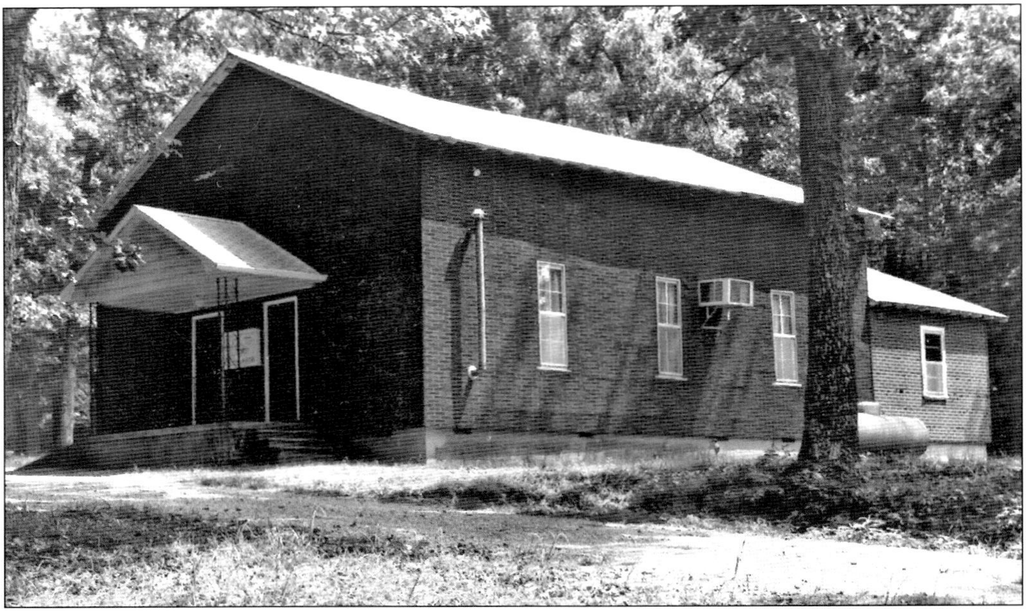

Eagle Creek Baptist Church was founded in 1887; the first pastor was Elder J.C. Park. First known as the Baptist Church of Christ at Eagle Creek, the church's first building slid off its foundation during services one evening in 1917. A new building was erected with a cemetery in 1917. In 1968, the building was remodeled, and three Sunday school rooms were added in 1971. (JD.)

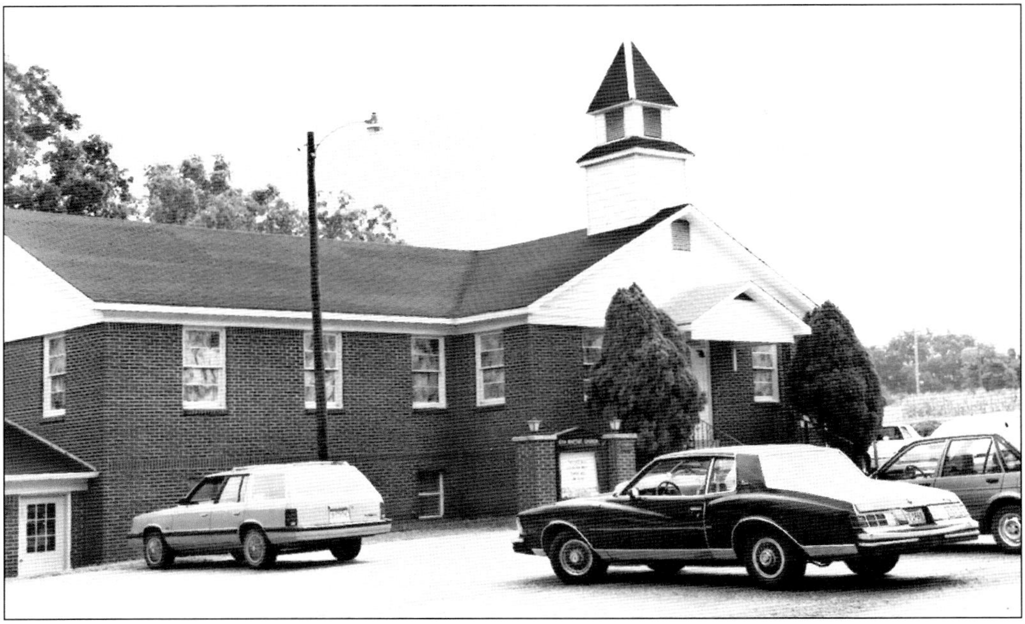

Eva Baptist Church was organized in 1917 by members of Chalk Hill Missionary Baptist Church. J.G. Hollingsworth gave land at the corner of what was then Camden Road and Depot Road. In 1932, the Eva Baptist Church affiliated with the Southern Baptist Association. The current building was constructed in 1956 and is located on the north side of Highway 191. (JD.)

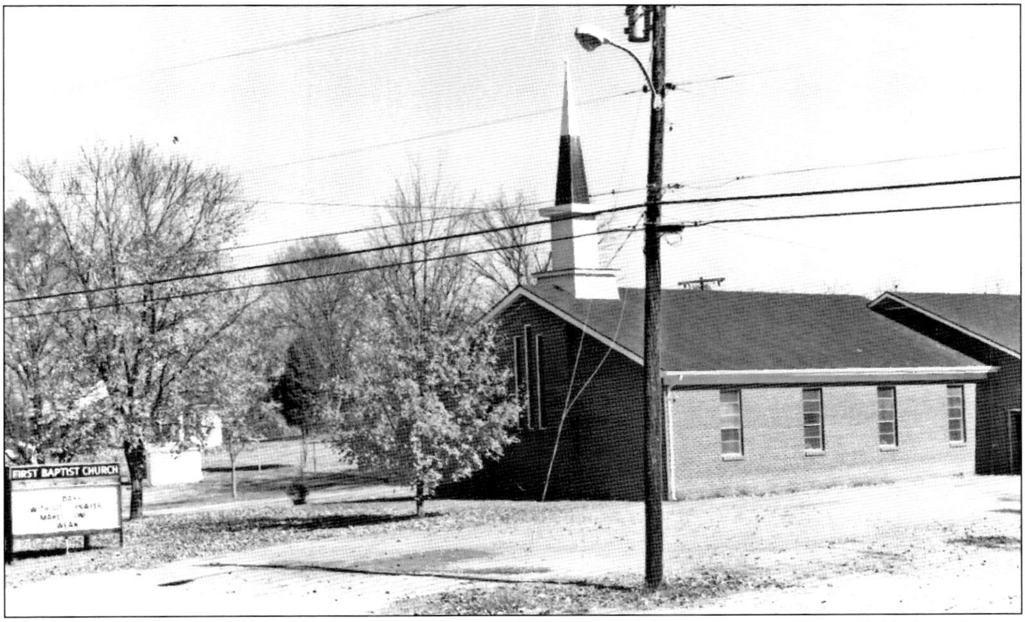

First Baptist Church at Big Sandy was organized on September 15, 1914. Rev. B.F. Smith was the first pastor; the church purchased an old school lot for a building site. The Sunday school was organized on March 18, 1917. After six years, the church was debt free. The name was changed to First Baptist Church in April 1959. The present building was constructed in 1966 and is located at 13510 Highway 69A. (JD.)

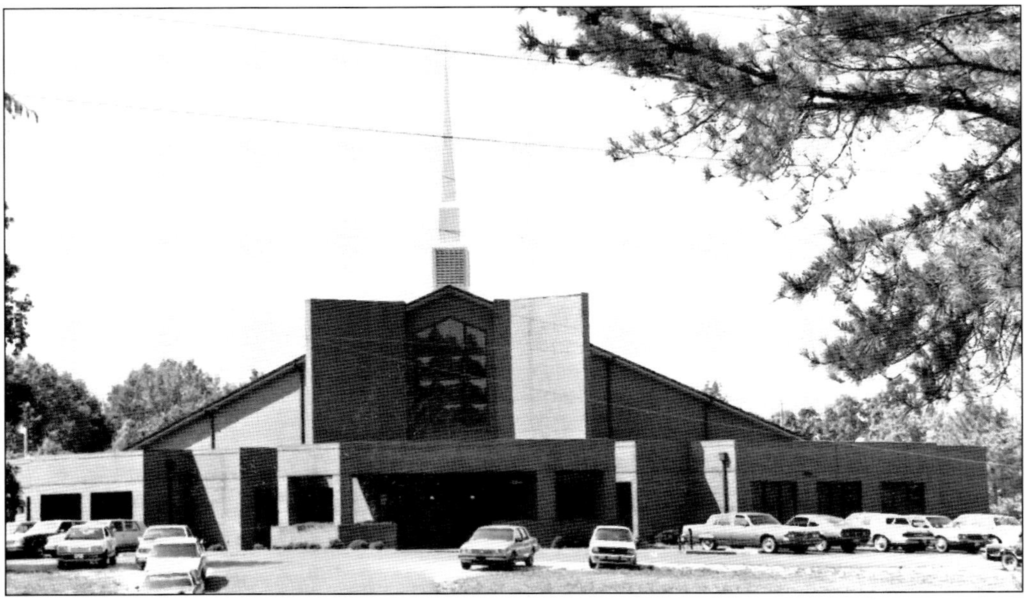

The First Baptist Church at Camden was organized in September 1896, and the first pastor was Rev. L.J. Leland. The congregation worshiped in the Presbyterian church building until 1904. The second building was constructed in the early 1940s. The first service in the current building, located at 269 Post Oak Avenue, was held on the first Sunday in September 1981, 85 years after the church was organized. (JD.)

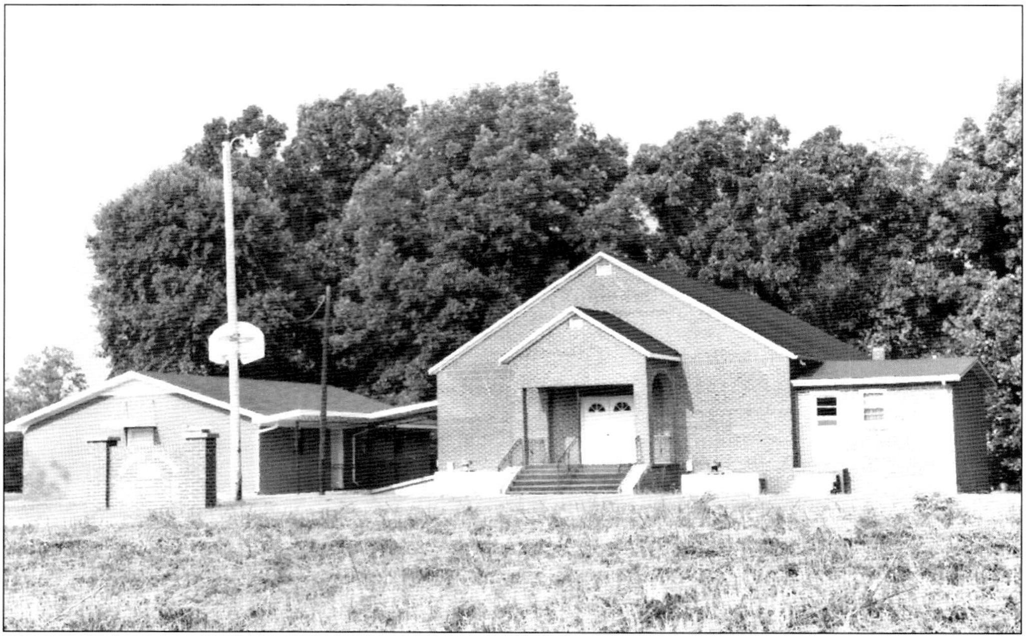

Flatwoods Missionary Baptist Church was organized on May 8, 1886. Several new buildings were erected over the years—one in 1913, another in 1941, and the present building was begun in 1953 and the outside bricked in 1954. (JD.)

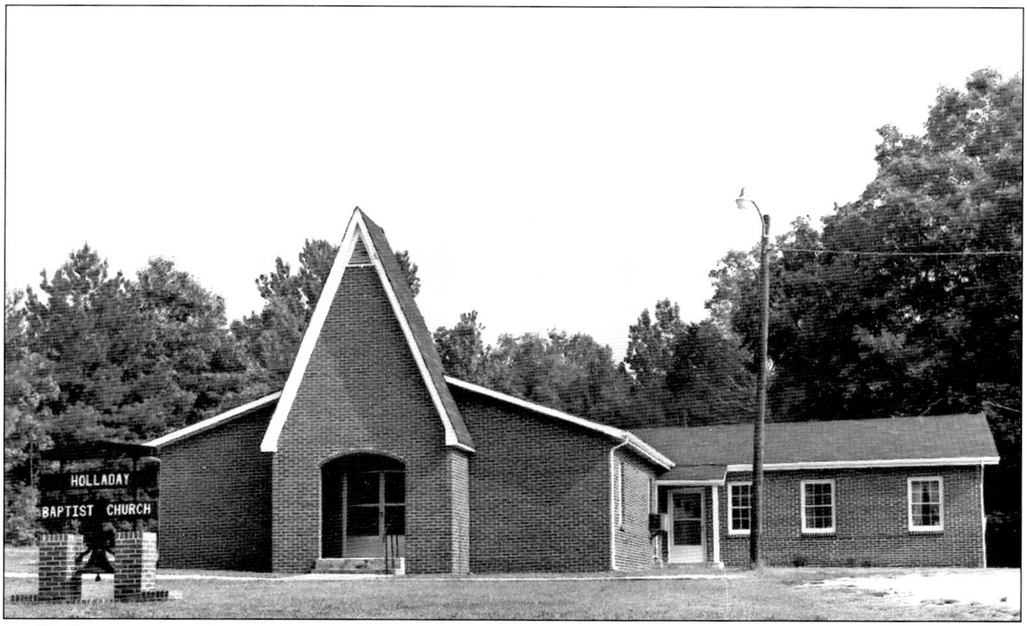

Holladay Baptist Church records date back to March 1899 and indicate it existed earlier. The first building was two-story construction with the first floor used for worship and the second story used by the Masons. In 1966, the Masons bought the land and constructed their own building. The present building was constructed in the 1960s and is located south of the center of Holladay on the east side of Highway 192. (JD.)

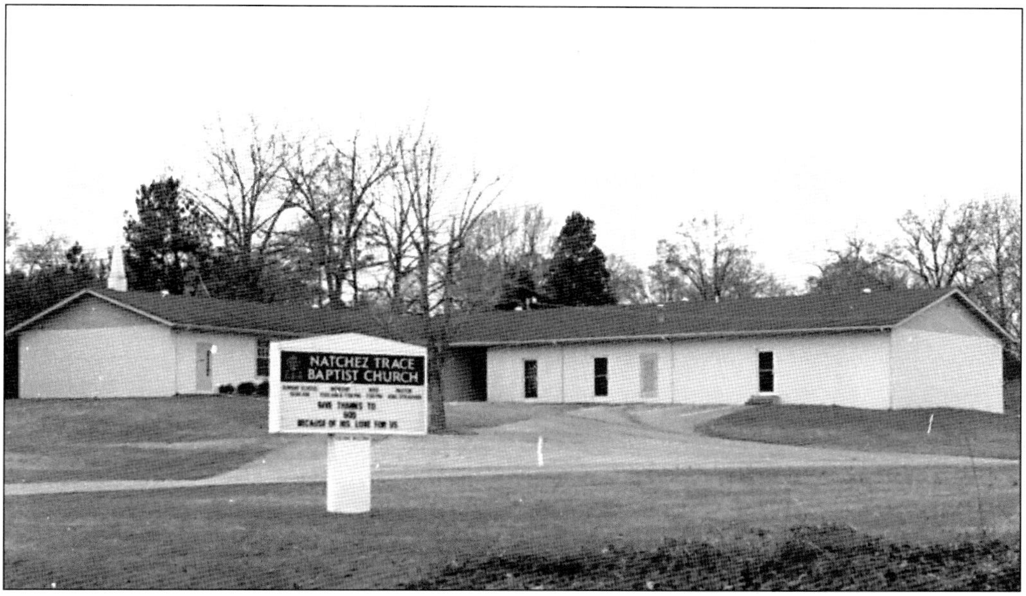

Natchez Trace Baptist Church was formed as a mission church of First Baptist Church. The first services were held October 6, 1963, in a log house with 16 people present. W.C. Drummond was the first pastor. They met in the log building until a new building was constructed, and the chapel was constituted a full church on April 23, 1972. The church is located at 278 Natchez Trace Road. (JG.)

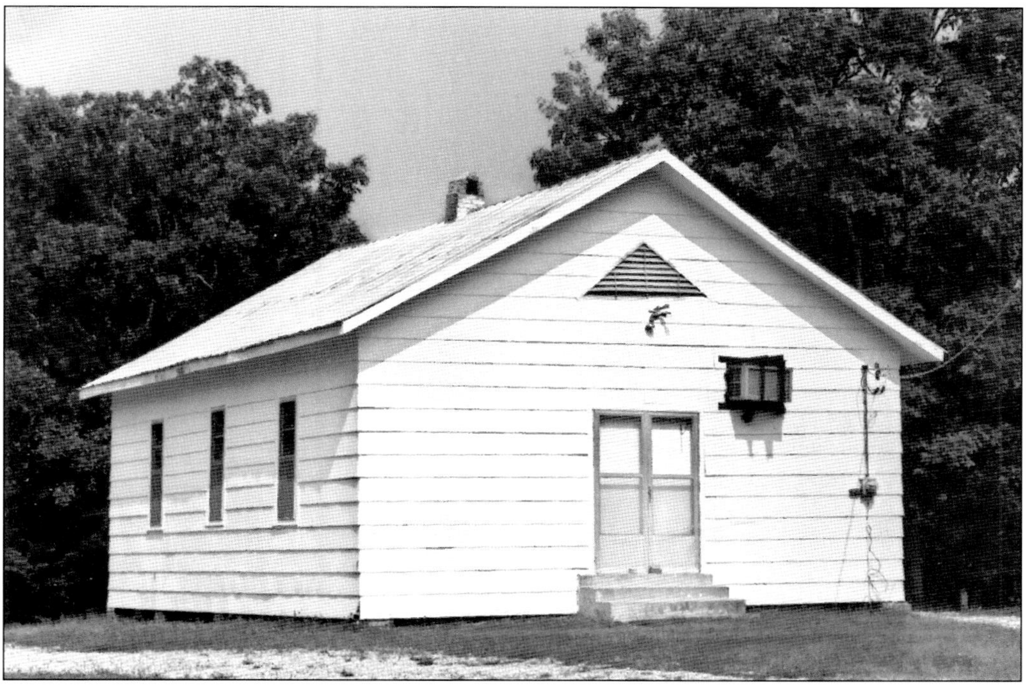

Old Union Missionary Baptist Church is located about two miles north of Holladay on Old Union Road. It was established by Elder Elijah Autry in 1857. In about 1939, the congregation erected a new building at the same location. (JD.)

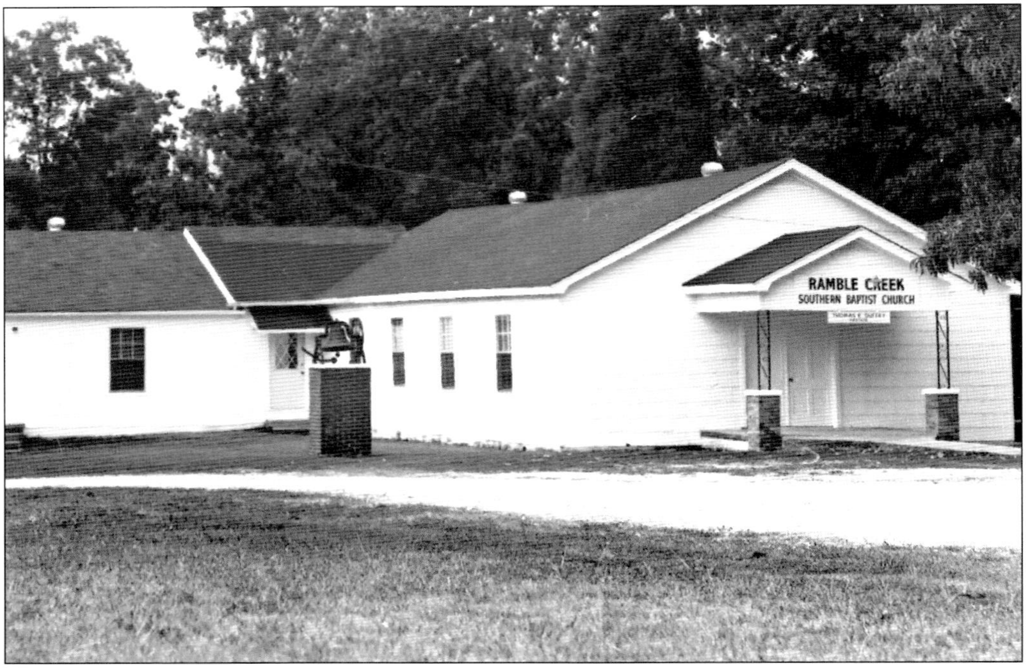

Ramble Creek Baptist Church was organized in June 1823 by Elder Jacob Browning. Through Isham Jones, one of its charter members, it received a land grant for 10 acres on which it was built. The present building was constructed and dedicated in 1959. (JD.)

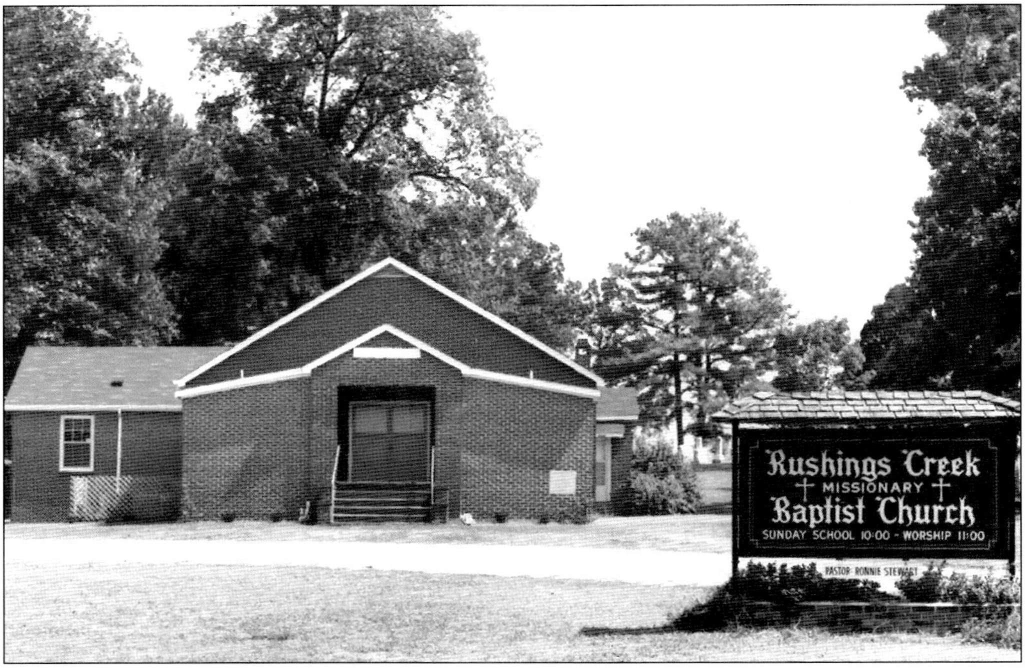

Rushings Creek Missionary Baptist Church was founded on May 7, 1825, and is located six miles north of Camden on Reynoldsburg Road. In 1952–1953, a new brick building was erected. Among the early organizers were Elder Jacob Browning and Elder John Horn. (JD.)

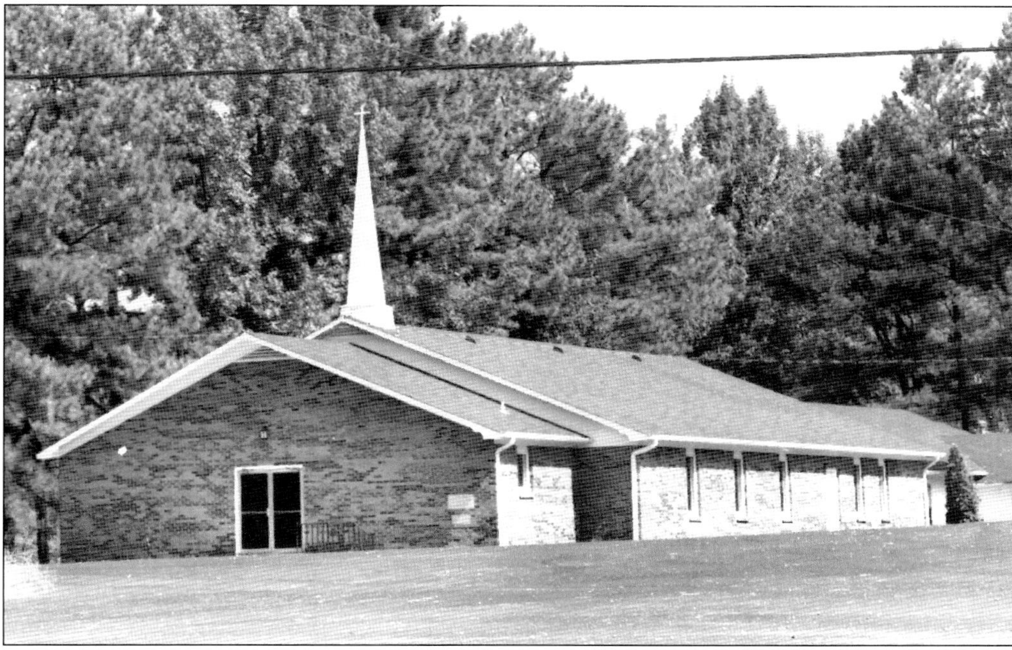

Sandy Point General Baptist Church is located on Highway 70 about three miles west of Camden. The church was organized in June 1946, and the first pastor was Bro. H.A. Douglas. (JD.)

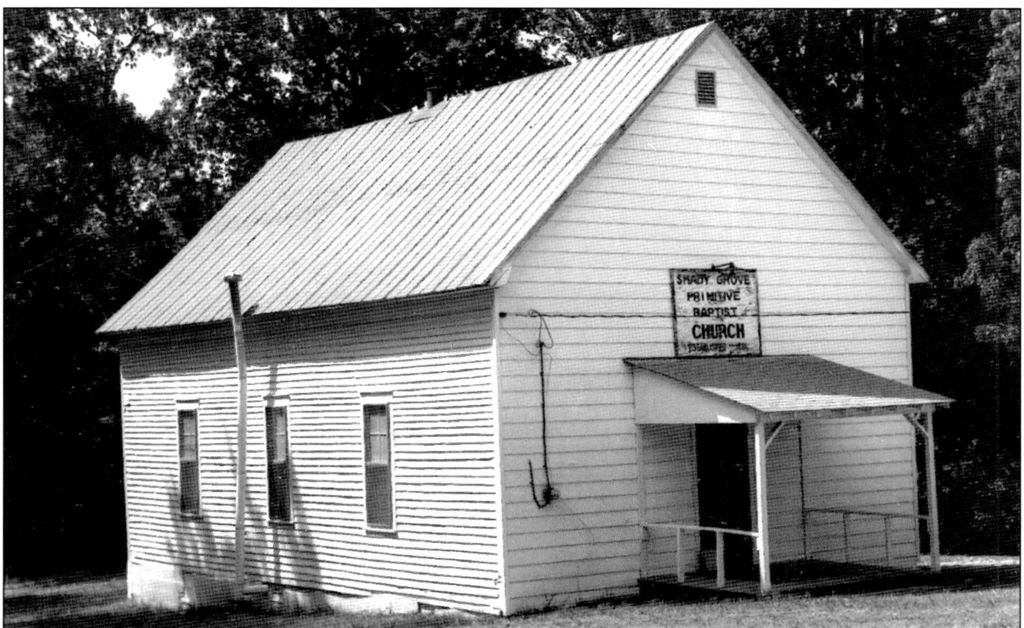

The Shady Grove Primitive Baptist Church was located five miles North of Camden on Highway 69 North. It moved to this building in 1911. The inside of the church was remodeled in 1969. The church is no longer active, and the building has been removed. (JD.)

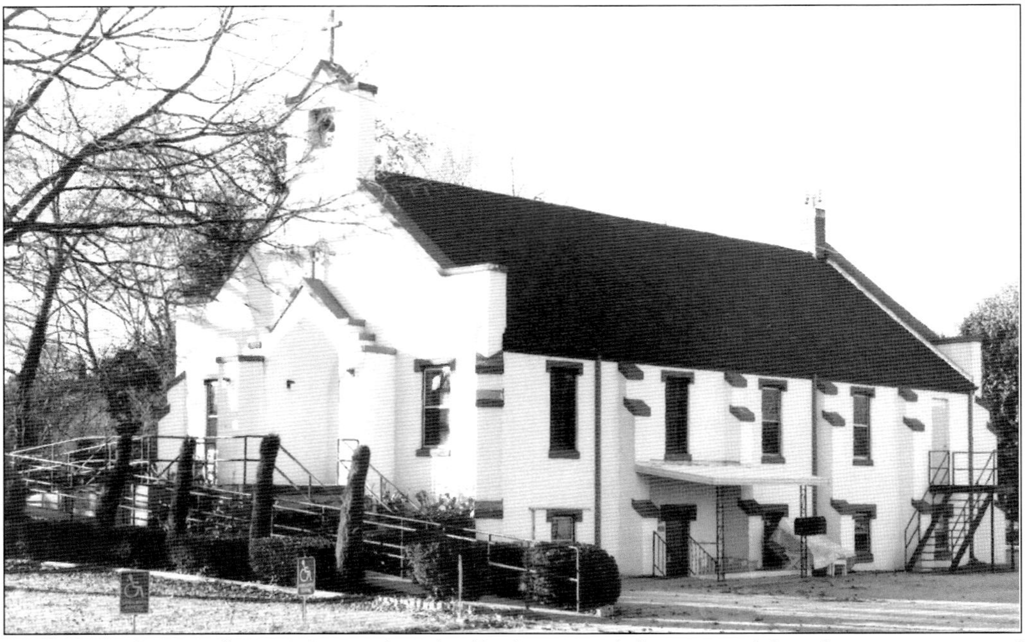

In 1948, Bishop William Adrian of Nashville designated the town of Camden as a mission of St. Patrick's Church, located in the town of McEwen. St. Mary's Catholic Church was built in 1950. In 1965, it became a mission of Holy Cross in Paris, Tennessee. On January 14, 1981, St. Mary's became a parish, additions were made to the building, and Fr. Richard Gantert was sent as its first pastor. A total of 14 priests have served St. Mary's. (JG.)

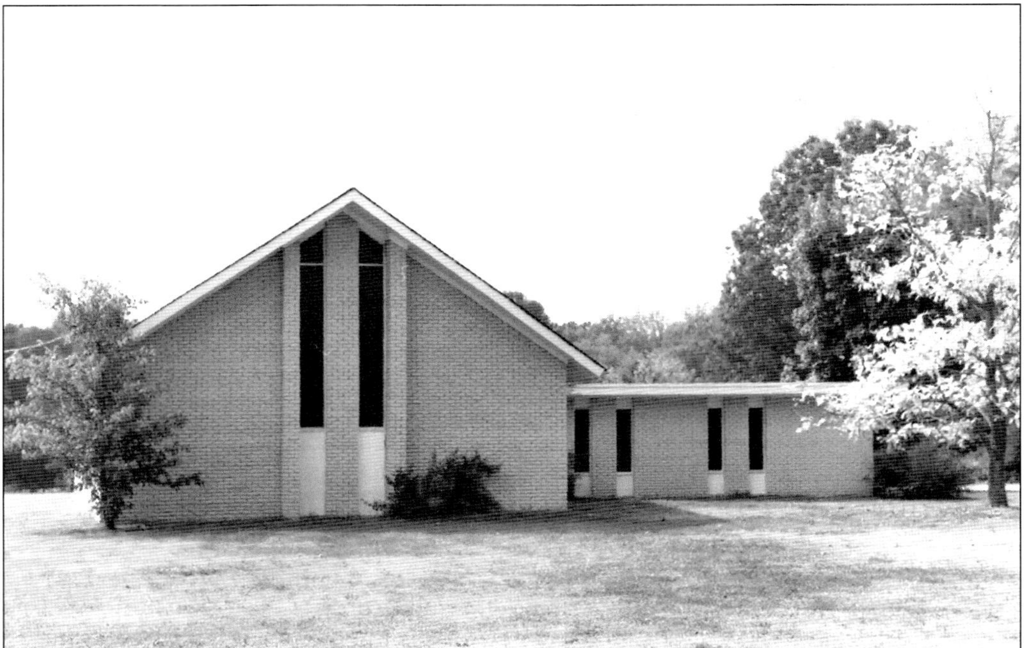

This photograph of Big Sandy Church of Christ was taken in 1987; the church is located on Highway 69A, next door to Big Sandy Schools. (JD.)

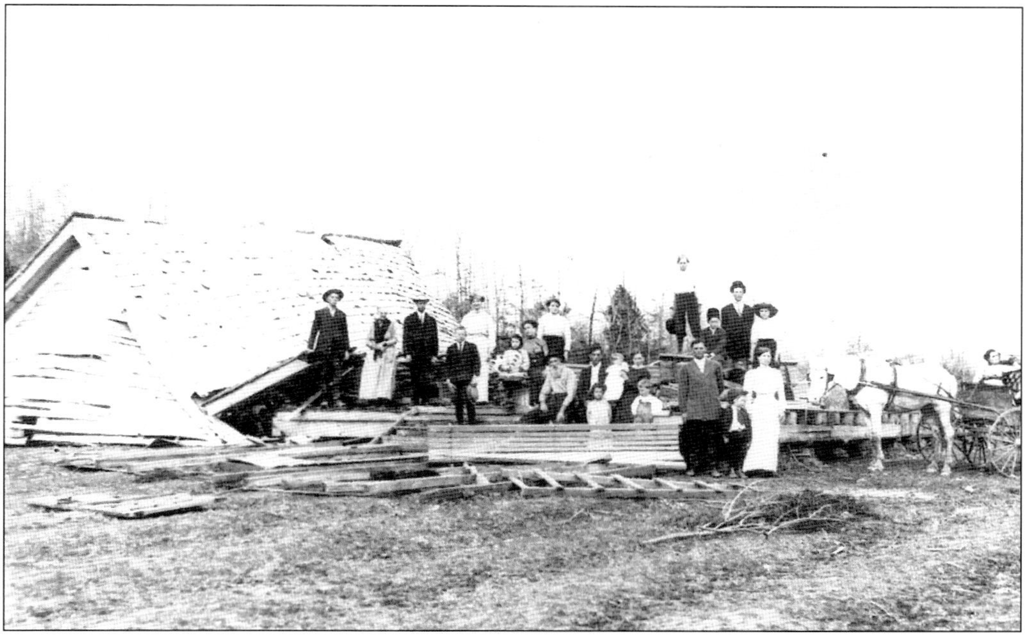

Beaverdam Church of Christ began on March 29, 1906. The land was deeded by G.T. Sarrett and his wife, Covy. The building was later used as a school and was destroyed by a cyclone on March 13, 1913. The church was rebuilt in about 1914. By 1957, the building was beyond repair, and a new building was completed in 1958 as the Eva Road Church of Christ. (BCPL.)

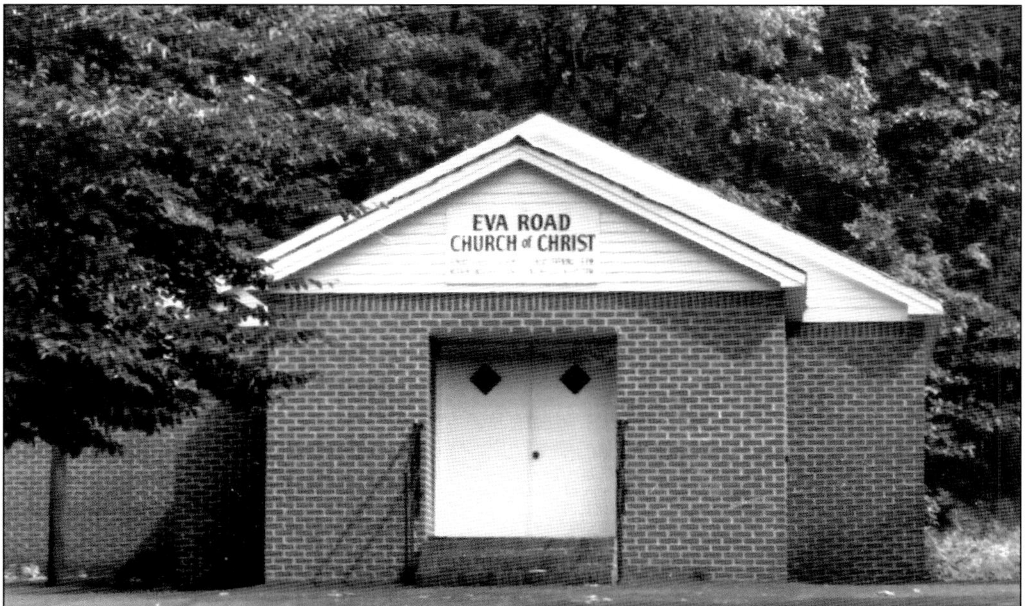

In 1957, Bob Walker deeded land for a new church building on Eva Road, since the old one was beyond repair. The Beaverdam Church of Christ congregation moved in 1958 to this new site and became known as the Eva Road Church of Christ. (JD.)

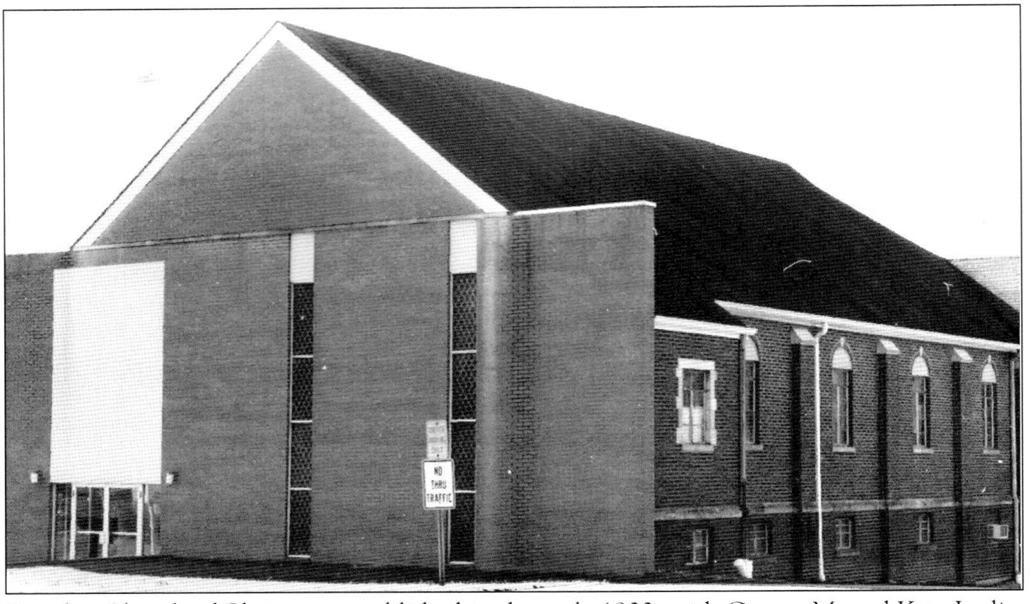

Camden Church of Christ was established in the early 1900s with George M. and Kate Leslie, Mrs. Tina Dodd and E.L. Dodd, Mrs. Delia Whitfield, Mrs. Mary Gibson, and Mrs. Anna Whitfield as members. A white frame building near the court square served the church until 1950, when a new building was constructed at 160 South Forrest Avenue. It was expanded in 1970, and plans are underway to build at a new location. (JG.)

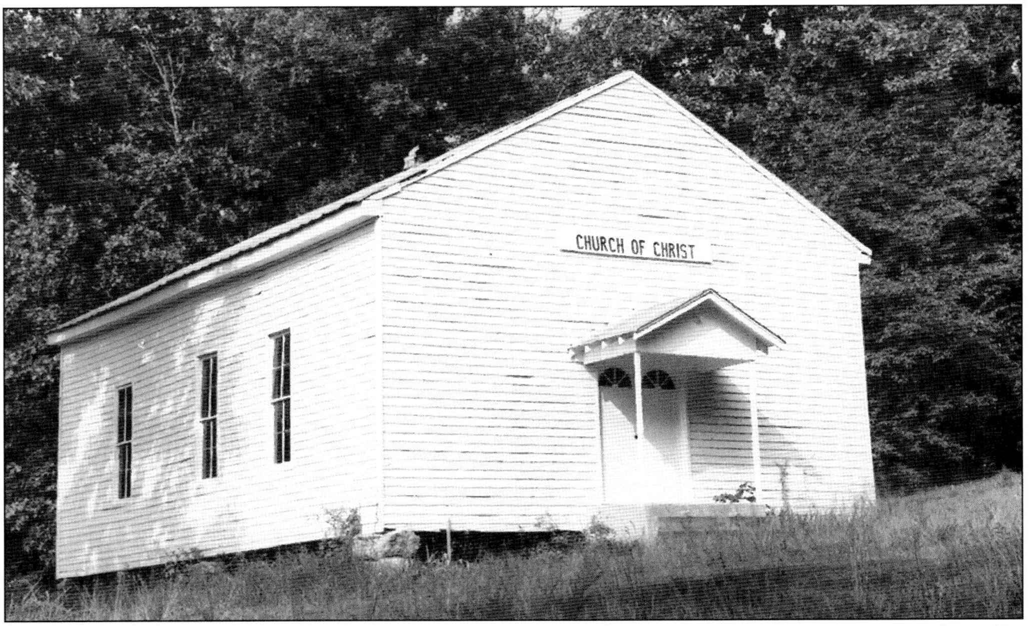

Cantrell's Chapel Church of Christ was established *c.* 1914–1915. William D. Cantrell, Mike Henry, George Bell, and a Mr. Newsom constructed the building on land donated by George Bell. William Cantrell's sons Carmack, Clint, and Ray and son-in-law Clifford Henry were leaders of this congregation for many years. It no longer meets, but the building still stands about four miles north of Sugar Tree, near Morgan's Creek. (JD.)

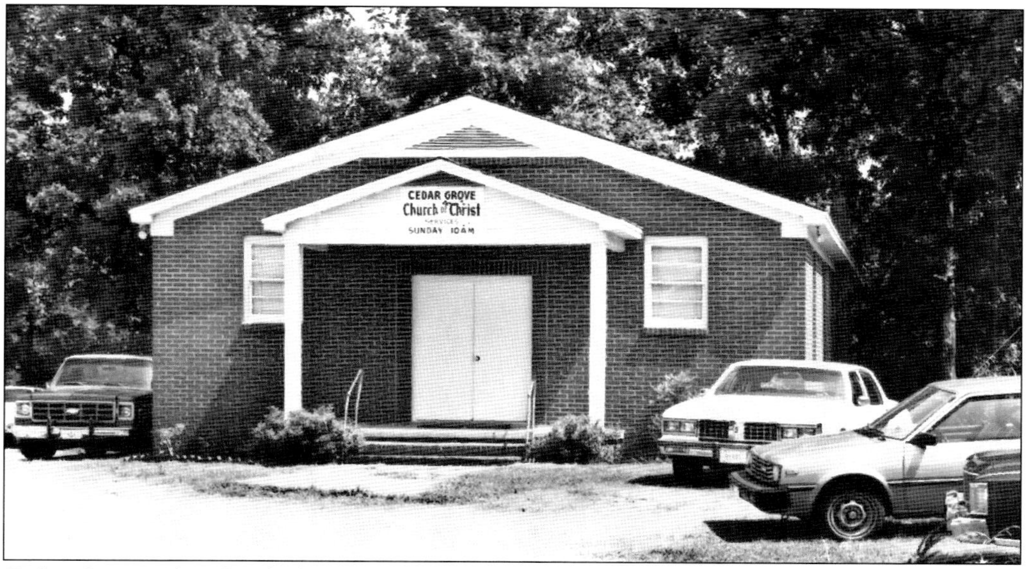

Cedar Grove Church of Christ held its first recorded meeting under a brush arbor in 1907; they later met in a large room of a log building. In 1911, a neat frame building was erected. After meeting in the frame building for over 50 years, the congregation erected a modern brick building. (JD.)

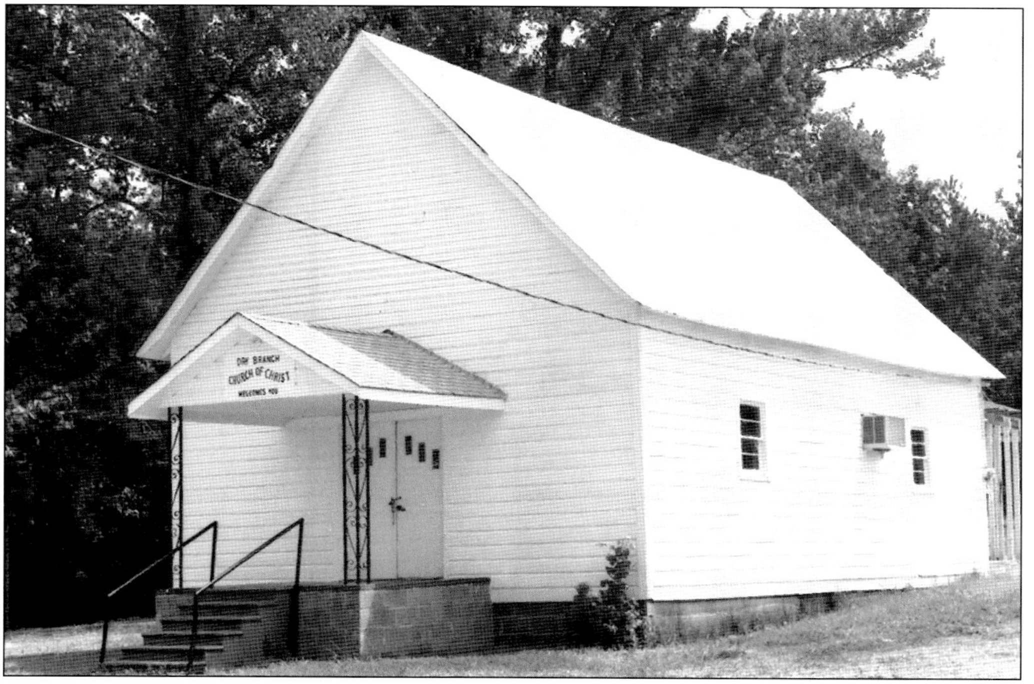

Dry Branch Church of Christ is located about three miles north of Interstate 40 on Highway 191. It was established before 1880. The first building was two stories with the upper floor used by the Masonic Lodge. The old building was demolished about 1980, and a one-story building now serves this congregation. Near the building is the old Dry Branch cemetery, in which many members of the church are buried. (JD.)

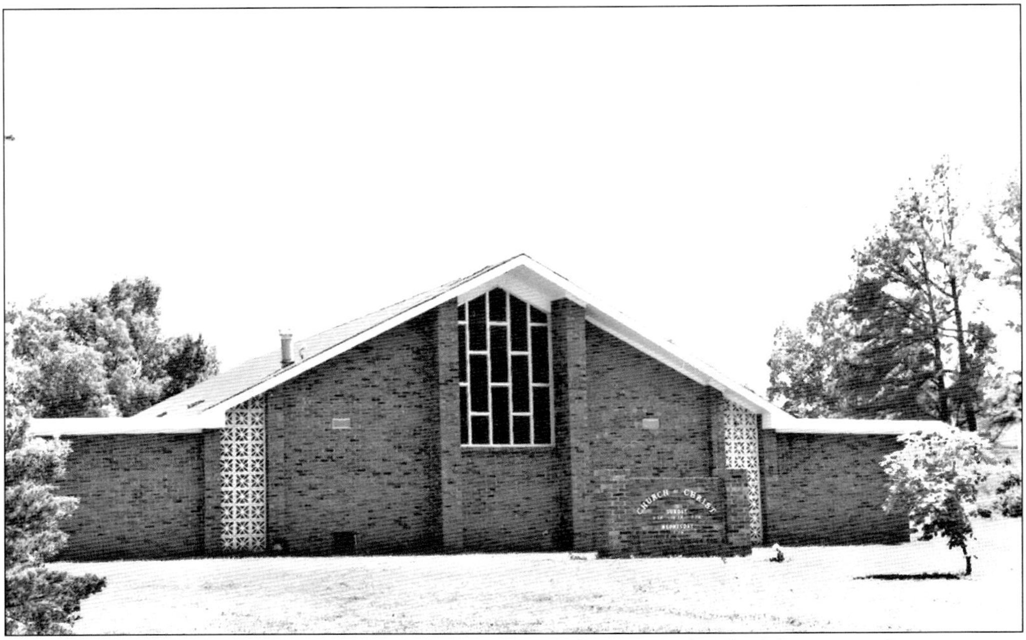

Holladay Church of Christ was organized in 1866 and met in a log building near the cemetery. In 1896, a building was erected on a lot in town, and the church met there until 1937. At that time, it was torn down and a new building erected. It served until 1968 when a new brick building was constructed. This congregation has never failed to assemble on the Lord's Day since its establishment. (JD.)

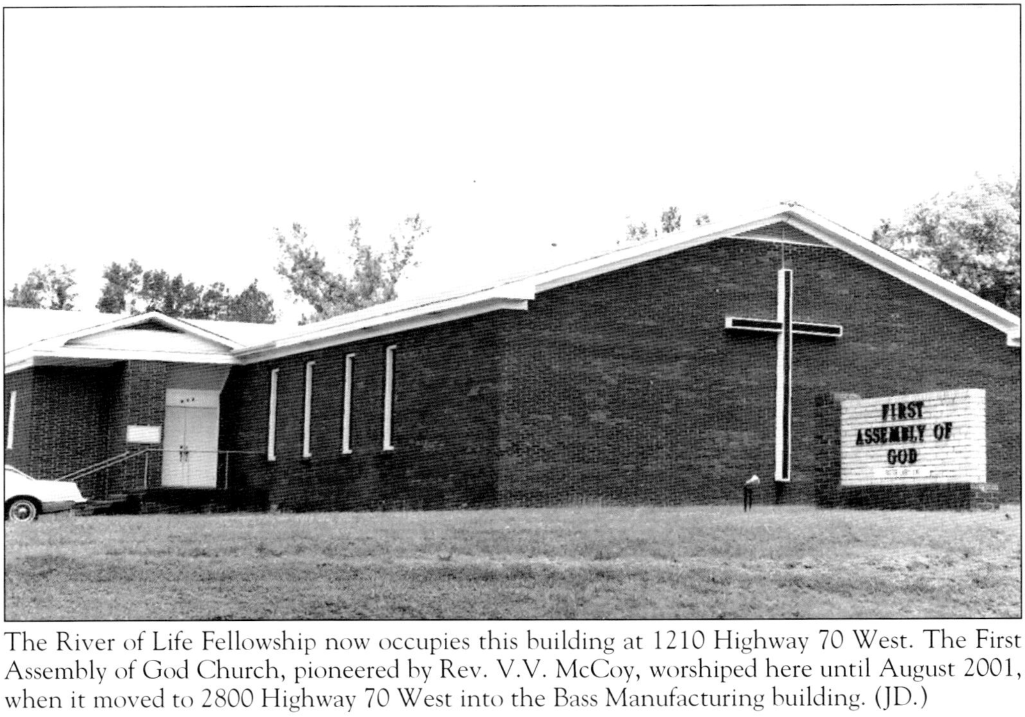

The River of Life Fellowship now occupies this building at 1210 Highway 70 West. The First Assembly of God Church, pioneered by Rev. V.V. McCoy, worshiped here until August 2001, when it moved to 2800 Highway 70 West into the Bass Manufacturing building. (JD.)

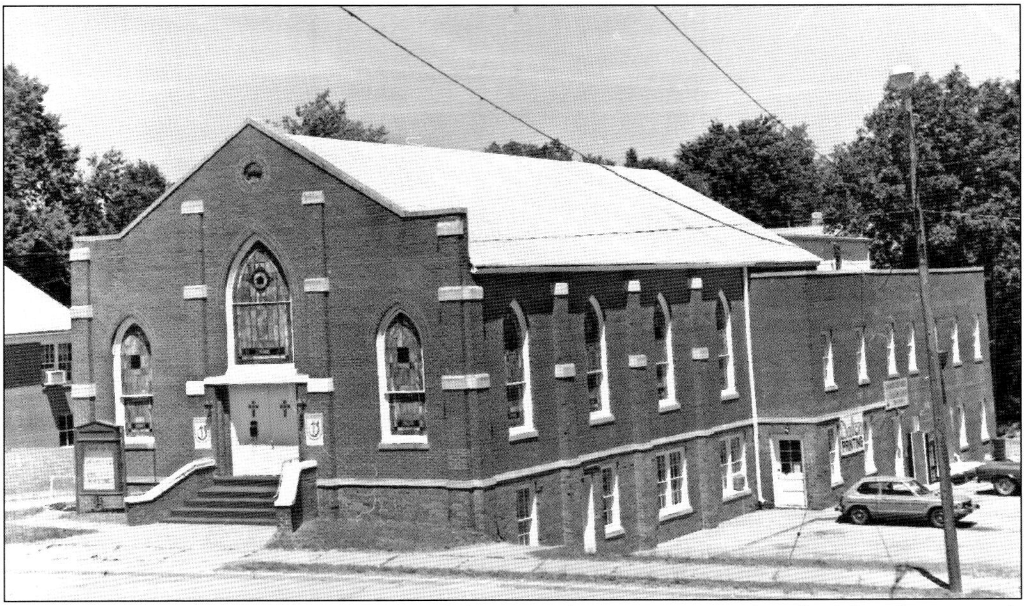

This building at 129 Forrest Avenue South began as the First Baptist Church. After they moved, the Church of God occupied it until about 1990; they also operated a day care and a thrift shop. The House of the Lord Pentecostal Church now occupies it. They were organized in March 1990, renting a building near Benton County Electric before locating to the present address. Rev. Ricky Jordan serves the congregation. (JD.)

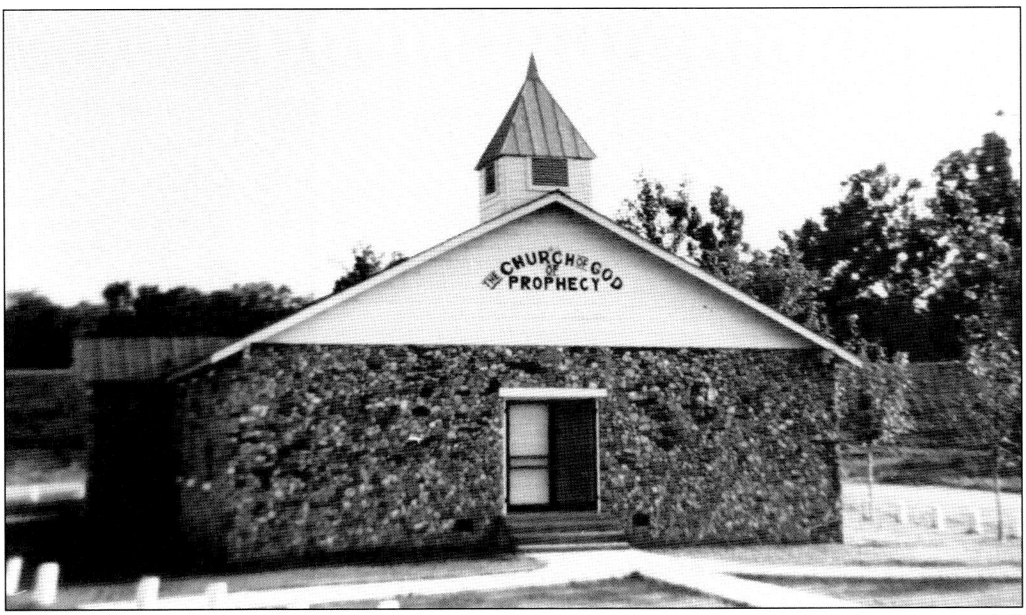

Church of God of Prophecy at Big Sandy was organized on August 2, 1935, by Rev. Virdell E. Stafford. Initially, the church had seven members. Early members hauled rocks from local creeks to construct the outside walls. Over the years, the building has undergone remodeling, but it has retained its rock design and is affectionately known as the "Little Rock Church." (RD.)

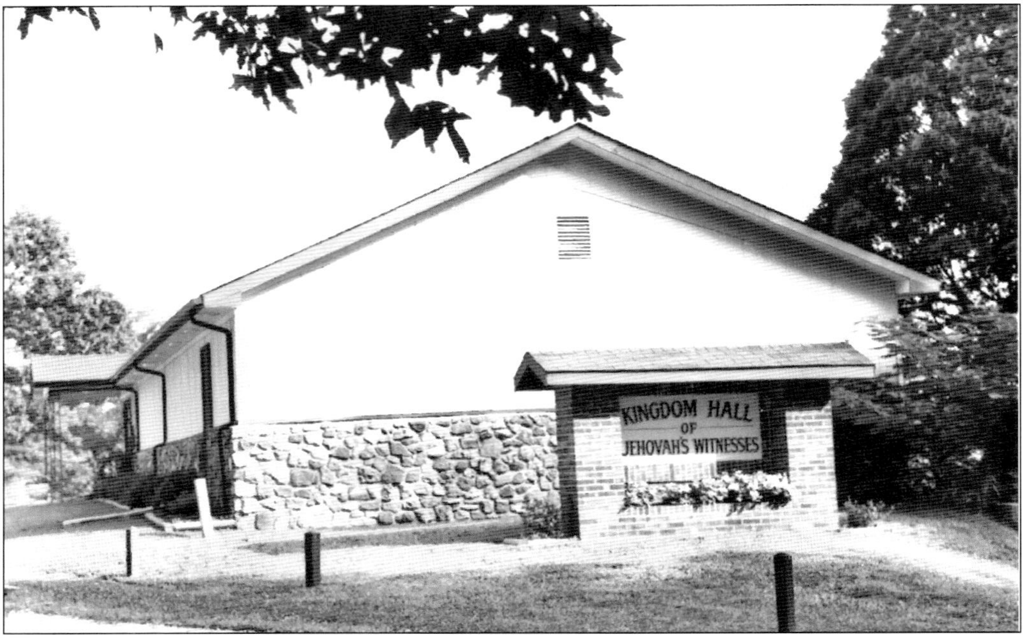

This photograph, taken in July 1987, shows the Kingdom Hall of Jehovah's Witness. It is located at 198 Schools Drive in Camden. The church was organized in 1975. (JD.)

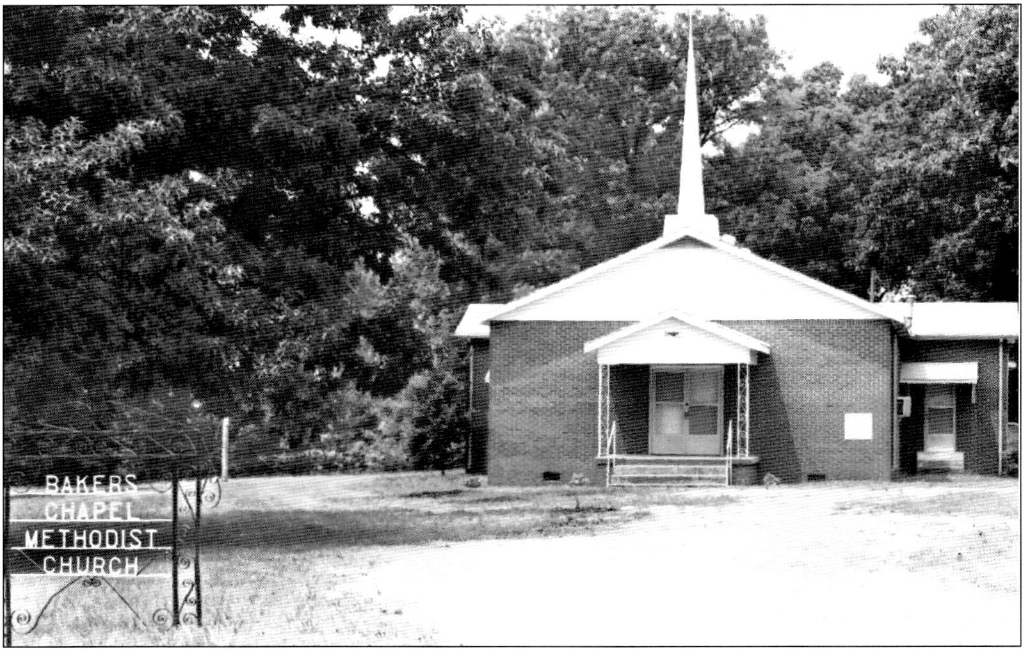

Bakers Chapel United Methodist Church is located six miles south of Big Sandy in the Baker's Chapel Community. It was established as the Methodist Episcopal Church South and named after Geb Baker. Land was purchased from J.N. Alsup in 1893, and a one-room building was constructed on a foundation of sand rocks. A new building was erected in 1957 when additional land was purchased. The cemetery adjoins the church property. (JD.)

Big Sandy United Methodist Church was originally called the Methodist Episcopal Church South. It came into existence in 1883 in Big Sandy. On October 27, 1902, W. Caraway deeded to the trustees the land where the present church is located, downtown in Big Sandy. The Masonic Lodge met in this building as well. The pulpit chairs and the lectern in use today have been used since 1902. The bricks used to construct the building were made on the site from clay found on the site. (RD.)

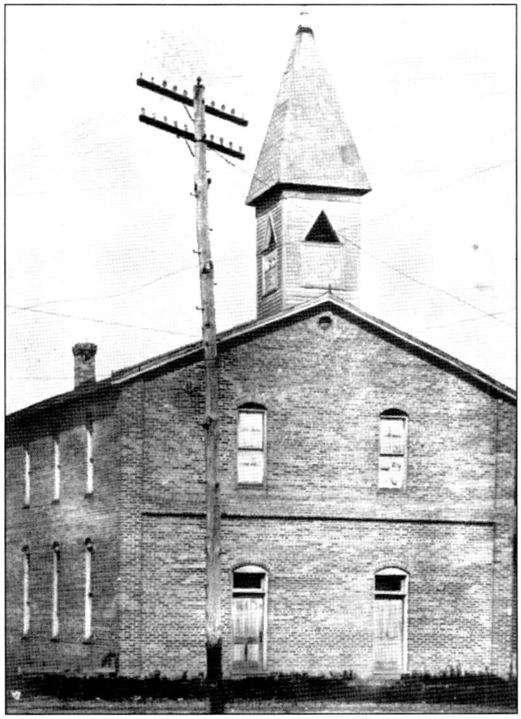

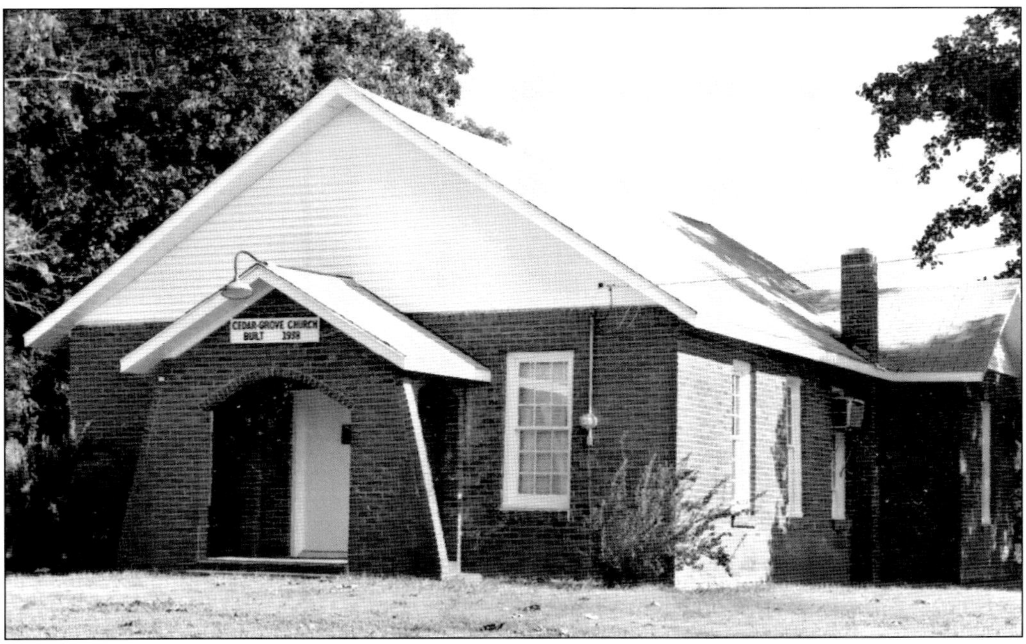

Cedar Grove Methodist Church was organized before 1800 in a log house about three-quarters of a mile southeast of the present church building. Sometime between 1886 and 1913, Mt. Zion changed the name to Cedar Grove Methodist Episcopal Church. Around 1887, a larger frame building was erected. It was damaged by a tornado in March 1913. The church still meets for services on the first and third Sundays of each month. (JD.)

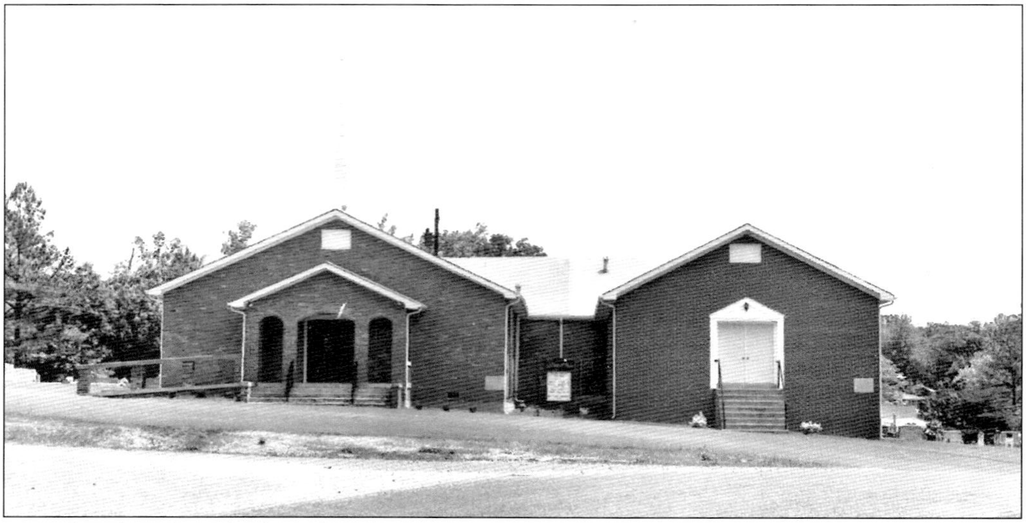

Cowell's Chapel Methodist Church was established when Benjamin Peeples and another circuit riding preacher named Garrett were sent by the Tennessee Conference in November 1820. It was the first Methodist church in Benton County. The first building was a log "chapel," and it was known as Chapel Hill. Later a small frame building had replaced the log structure. In 1938, the present building was erected. (JD.)

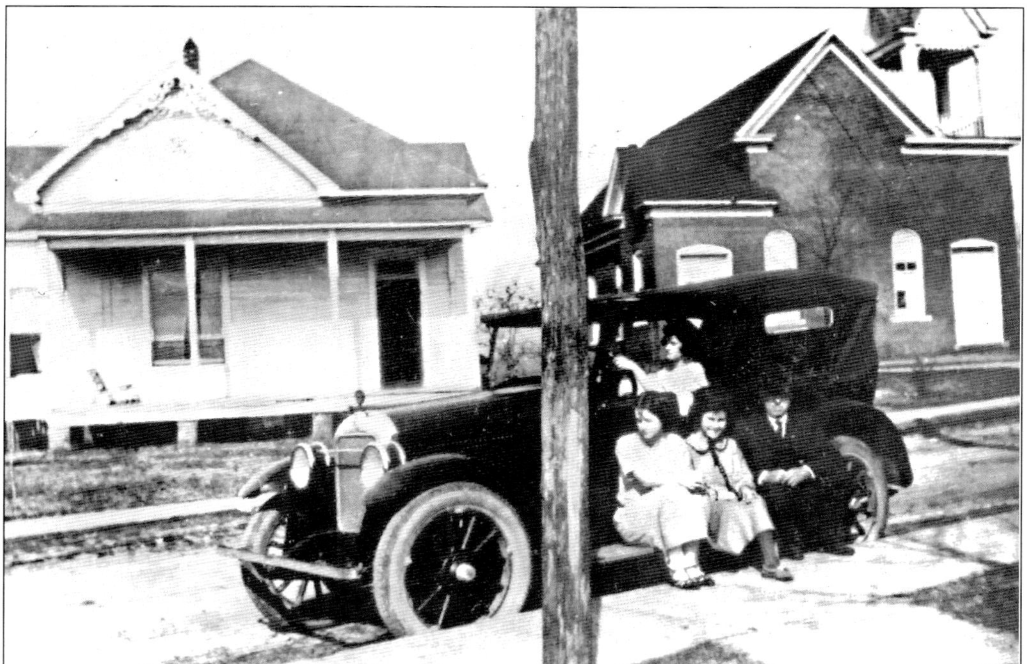

The Methodist Episcopal Church South was established before 1838 in Camden, and the congregation worshiped in the courthouse until about 1848. Over the years, they met in several locations. This church, built from bricks made on the grounds in 1901, and parsonage were located at the corner of North Church and Green Streets. Ruth Priestly (who later married Wyly Lockhart), Annie Looney, and friends are pictured on the old car. (JD.)

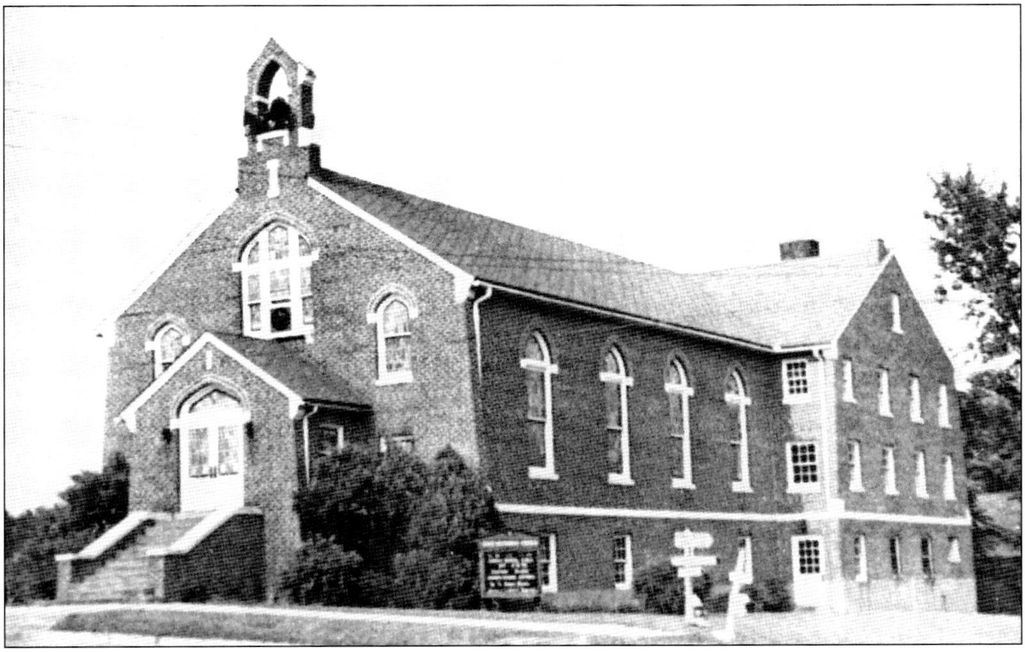

The Methodist church purchased property at the corner of Lake and Church Streets from G.G. Holladay in 1926, and fund-raising began. In 1929, the building was completed with the debt retired. Dedication services were held on November 7, 1934. The final worship service was held on Easter Sunday, March 30, 1975, and the building was then torn down. A new building was constructed in the same location. (JD.)

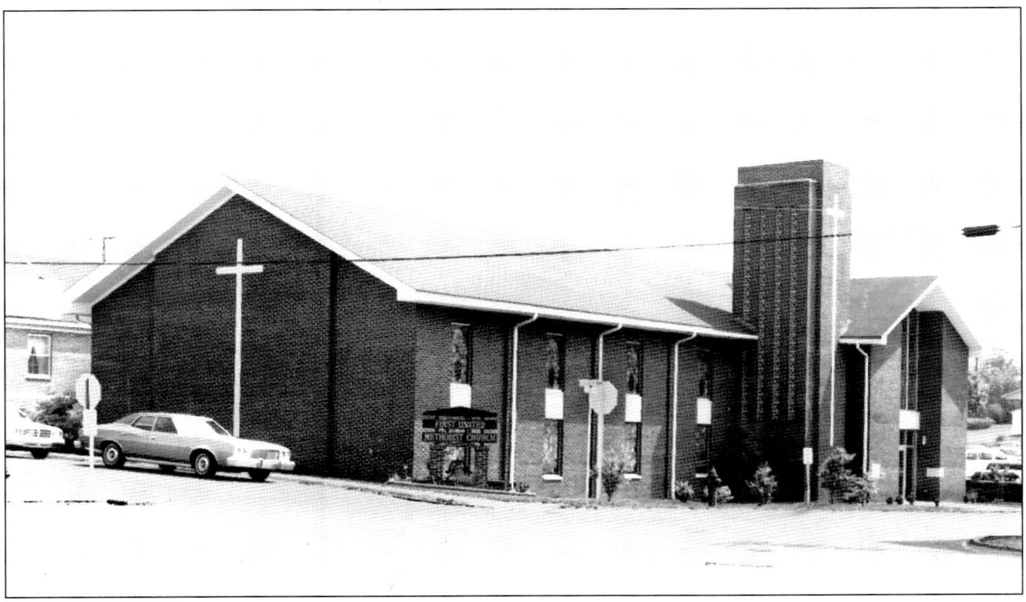

Groundbreaking for the present sanctuary of the First United Methodist Church at the corner of Church and Lake Streets took place on August 10, 1975. The congregation has worshiped in this building since its consecration on September 4, 1977. An educational unit, thrift shop, gymnasium, and Community Life Center have been added to the main building. (JD.)

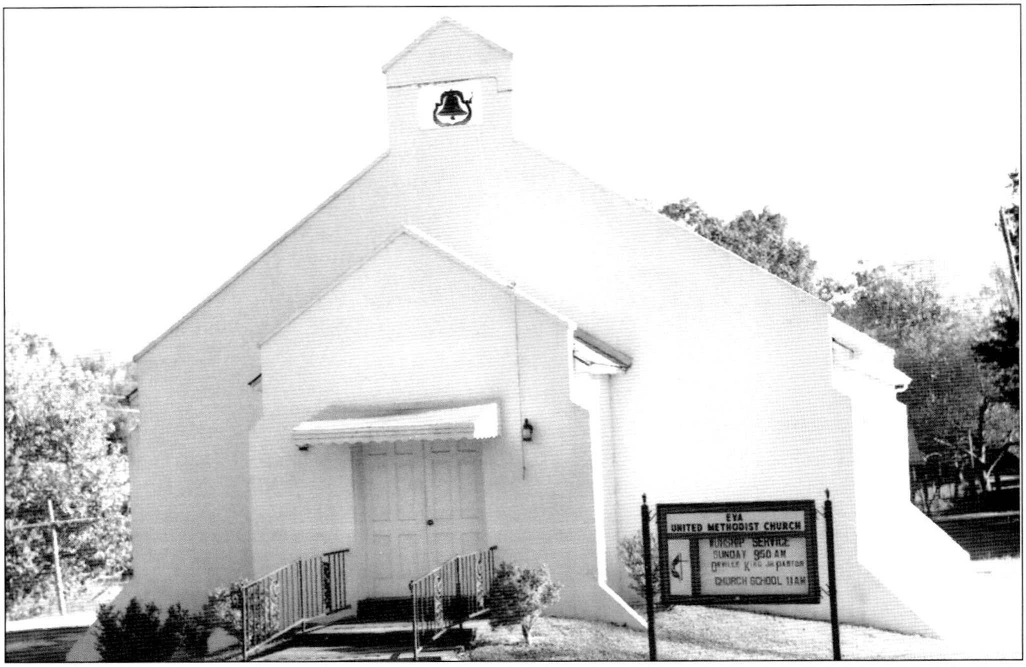

The first church in Eva was the Methodist Episcopal Church South, organized in 1913. The Eva Land Company gave land, and the community donated material and labor. It was located just a few feet from Eva Beach. The church moved to its present location on Highway 191 at the crossroads at Eva in 1951. (JD.)

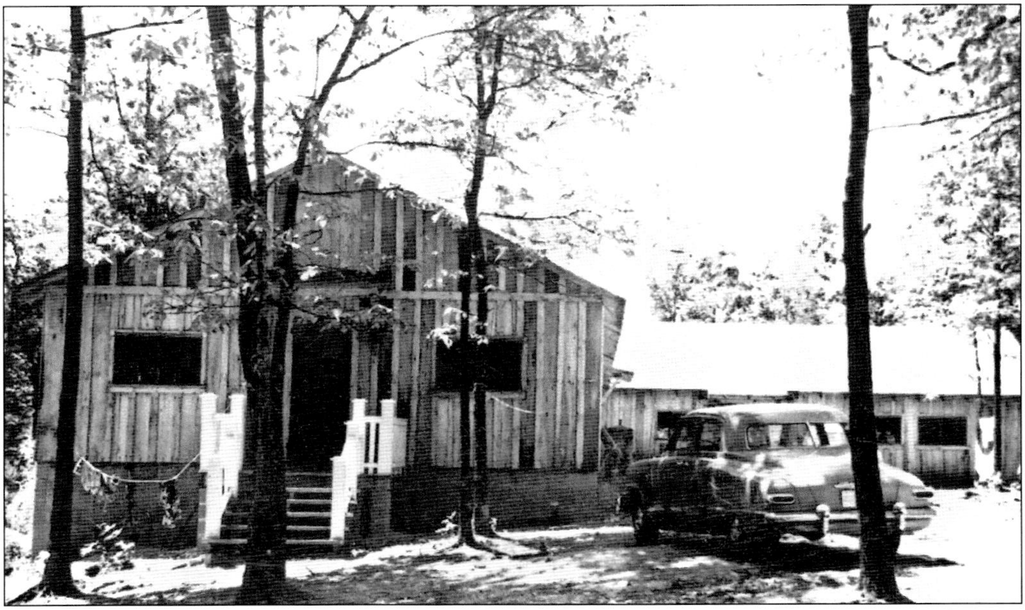

These rustic buildings are the dining room and main building at the Lakeshore Methodist Assembly grounds near Eva. A new building, used for camps and retreats, sits in a park near the Kentucky Lake between Eva and Nathan Bedford Forrest State Park. This picture was made in about 1950. (BCPL.)

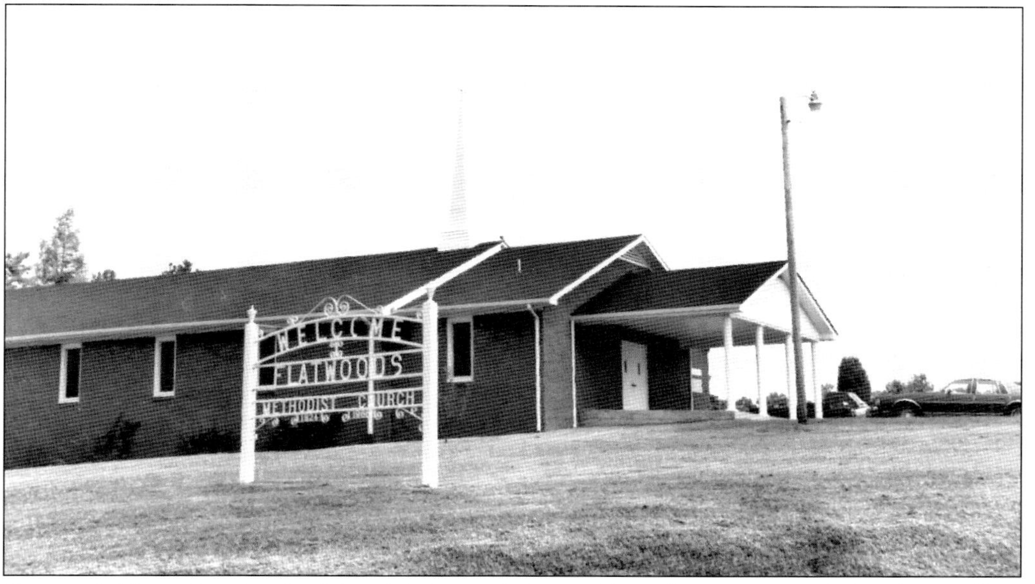

Flatwoods United Methodist Church is located about eight miles northeast of Camden on Flatwoods Road. It was organized in 1824 by Rev. John Pafford, even before Benton County was formed. This building was constructed in 1981 and is the fifth building the church has occupied since it began. There are two cemeteries associated with this church. (JD.)

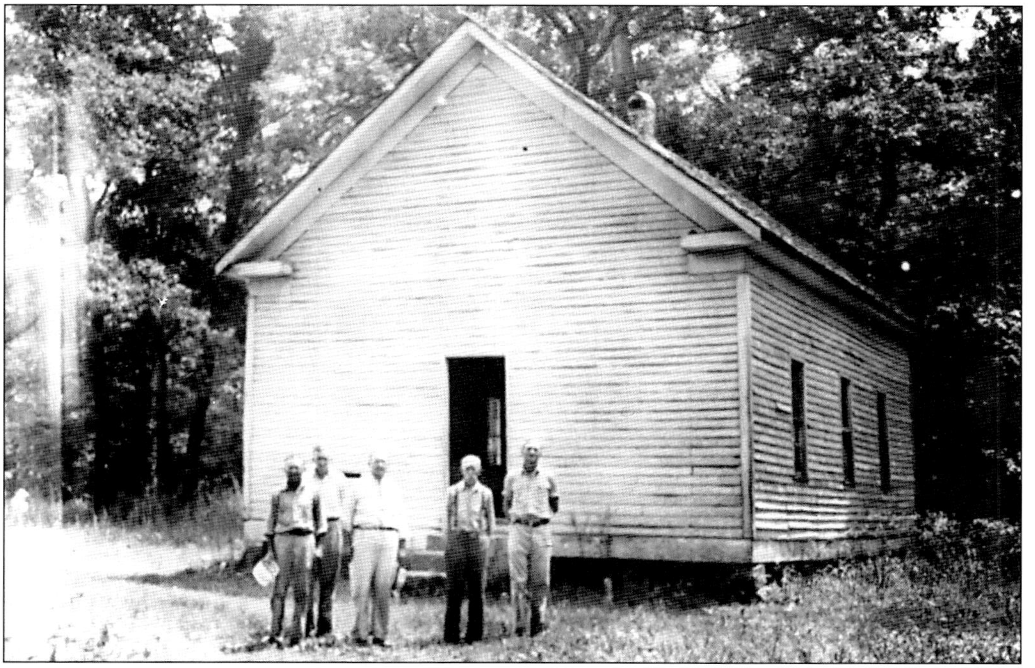

The land for the Harmon's Creek Methodist Church was part of a land grant given to Etheldred Melton; it was given to the church in 1869. The first building was made of logs; the second church was a frame building constructed in 1882. Those standing in front of the church, from left to right, are Walt Phifer, Joseph Melton, Roy R. Melton, Jack Melton, and Don McLin. A third building was constructed in 1947. The church is no longer active. (JD.)

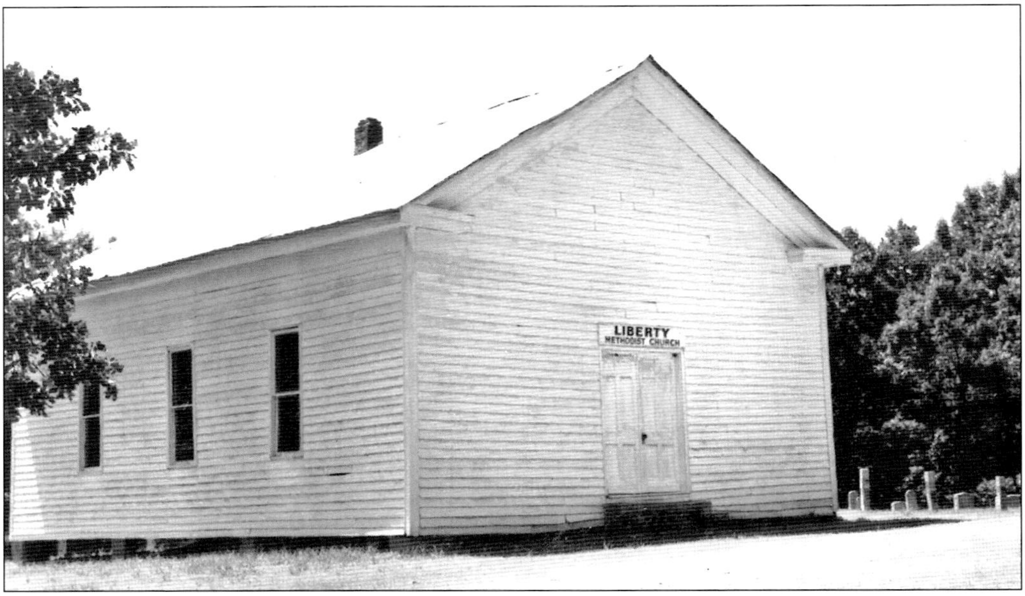

Liberty Northern Methodist Church was located about four-and-a-half miles northwest of Holladay on Liberty Church Road. It was established in the 1870s or early 1880s. The membership was made up of the Smothers, Barnes, Noles, Kirk, Ellis, and other families who lived in the neighborhood. To the rear of the church is a cemetery in which many of its early members are buried. (JD.)

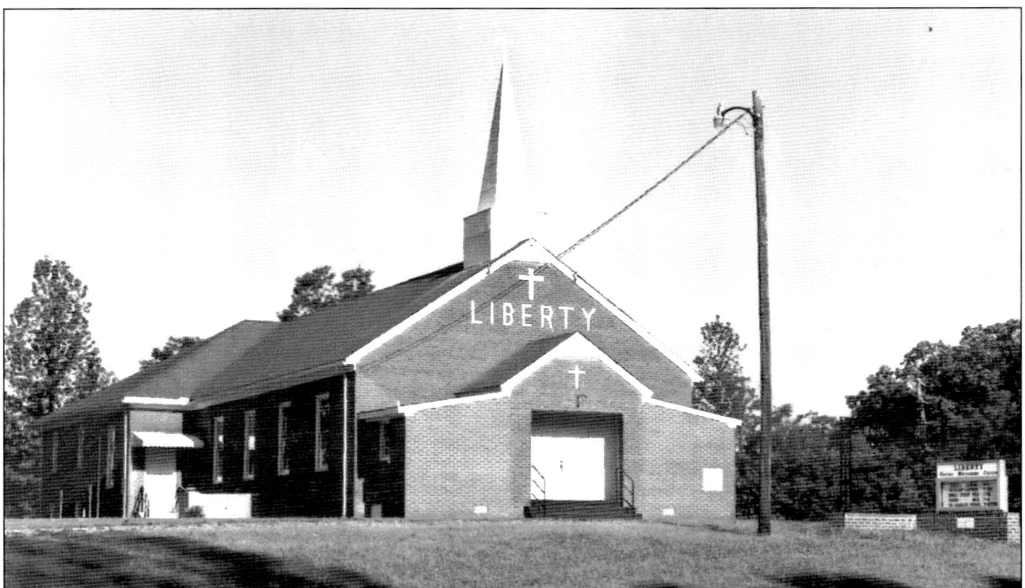

Liberty United Methodist Church is located three miles north of Camden on State Highway 69A. In 1858, G.W.L. Hudson donated the land, and a log structure was erected and called Liberty Meeting House. In 1893, a wooden frame structure was erected. In 1948, the brick building took the place of the former building, and in 1985, a fellowship hall was added. The cemetery adjoins the church property. (JD.)

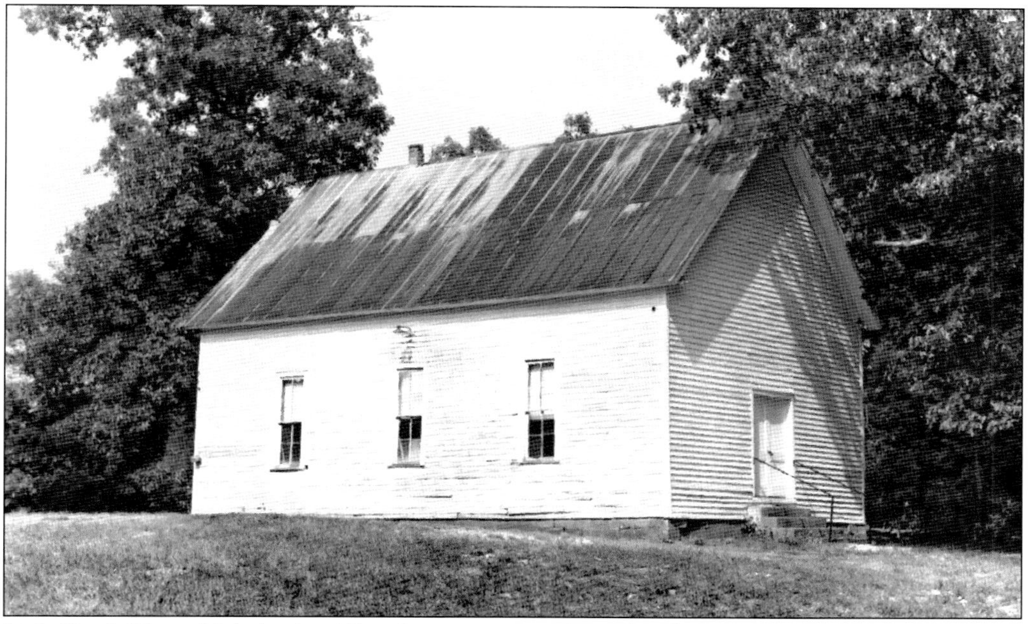

Lick Creek United Methodist Church was organized on October 19, 1896, when D.G. Stockdale and his wife deeded one and four-fifths acres as a gift to the Lick Creek ME Church South, of the Springville Circuit, for the purpose of ministry and divine worship. Trustees were J.W. Wright, Junior Young, B.F. Stockdale, E.J. Blunt, J.F. Cooper, and J.N. Beaton. This photograph was taken in September 1987. The building still stands. (JD.)

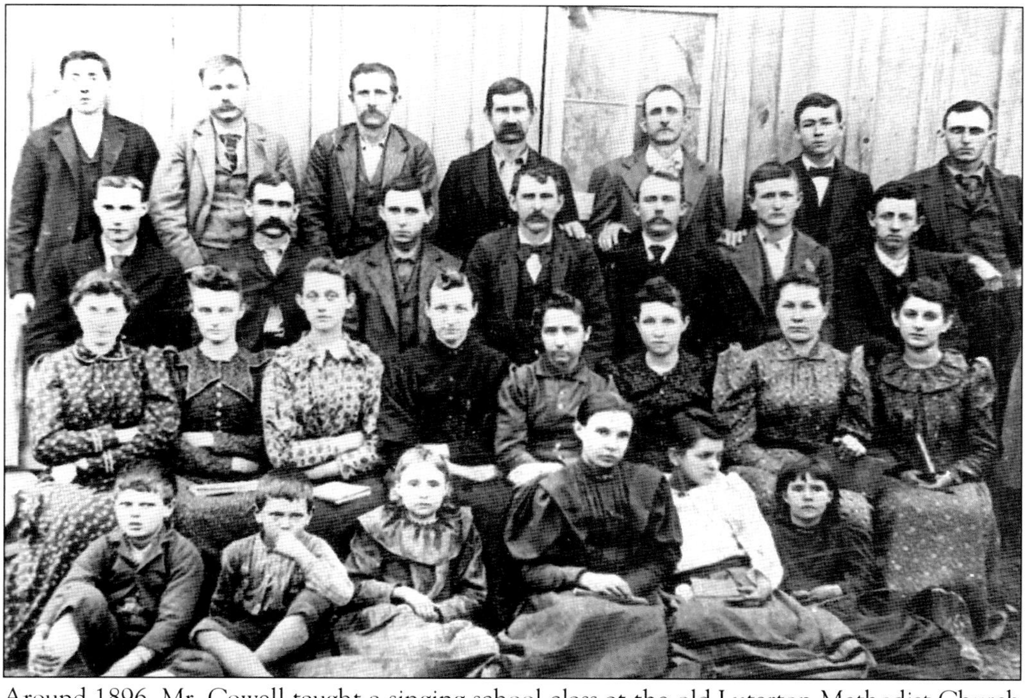

Around 1896, Mr. Cowell taught a singing school class at the old Luterton Methodist Church and School. (BCPL.)

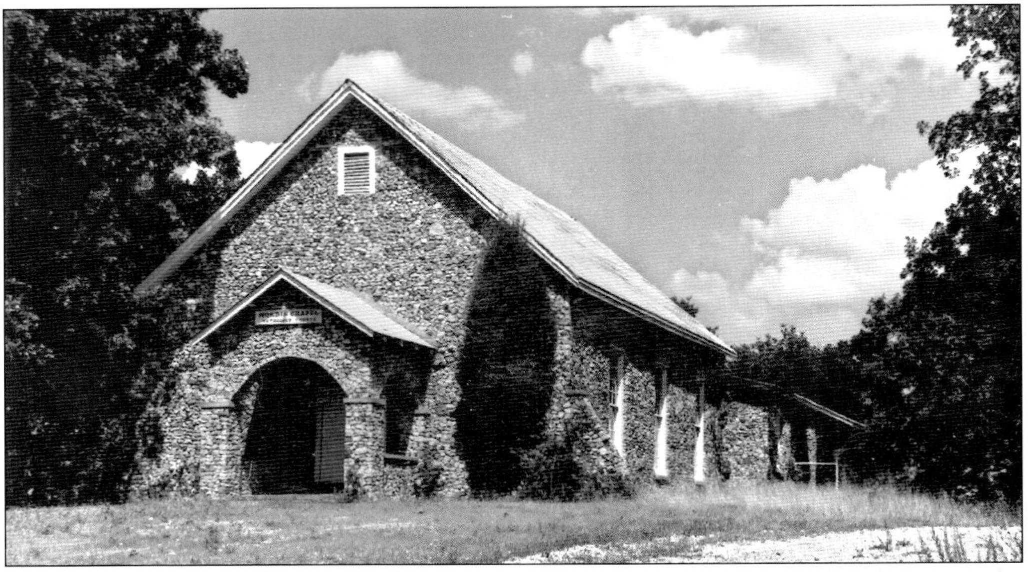

Morris Chapel Methodist Church is located five miles east of Camden on old Highway 70. The church had its beginning in 1883. It was used for a school until Sunday school rooms were added to the frame building in 1932. The native stones were collected by church members from the surrounding area. The church was closed by the Memphis Conference in the mid-1980s as the members died or moved away. The building still stands and has been used by various religious groups. (JD.)

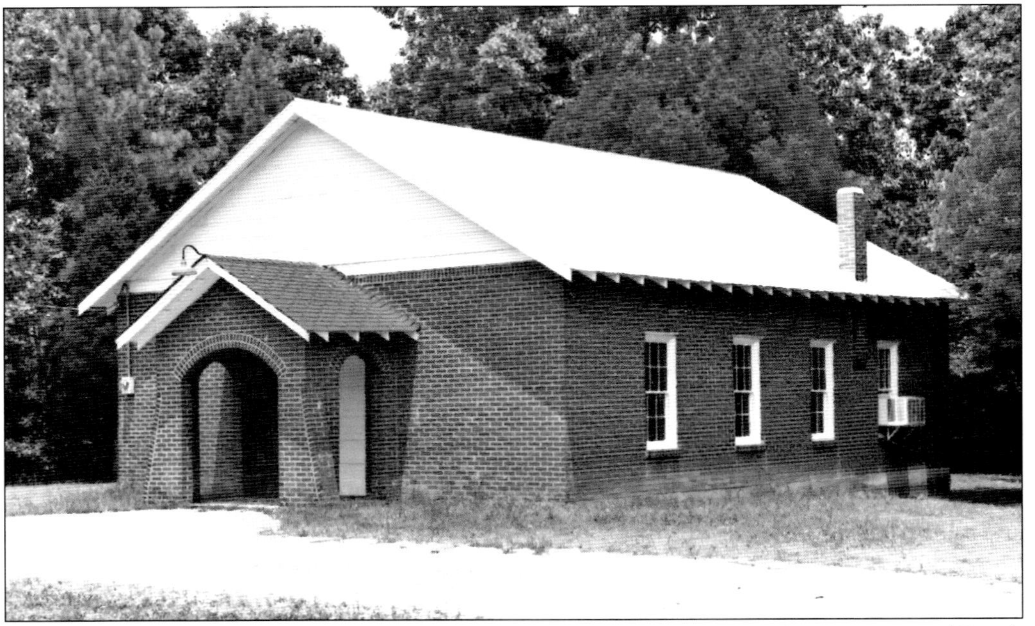

Mt. Carmel United Methodist Church was organized in 1854. It is located on Mt. Carmel Road, north of Sawyers Mill. A small, hewn-log building housed the congregation for many years. J.H. Williams, John Crossnoe, and J.W.H. Presson and his wife all deeded land to the church. Material, labor, and supplies were donated by members of the congregation. In 1901, the trustees acquired the graveyard area for a burial ground. (JD.)

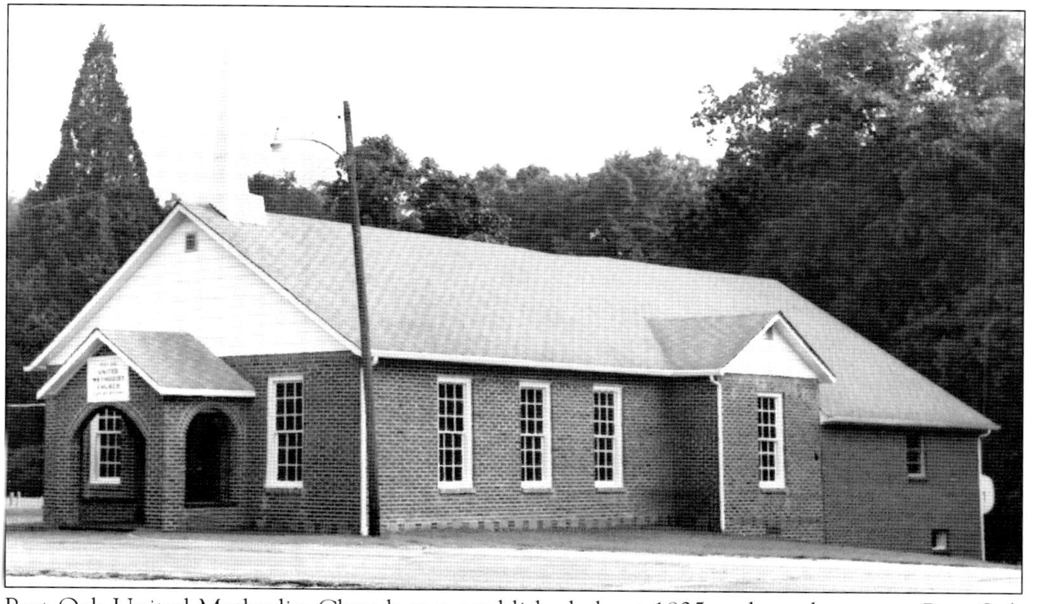

Post Oak United Methodist Church was established about 1835 and was known as Post Oak Grove. It was first a log church; then a frame building was constructed, which burned in 1912. Another frame building was erected and stood until 1932, when a windstorm damaged it. The brick building was completed and dedicated on October 5, 1938. Post Oak Cemetery adjoins the church property. (JD.)

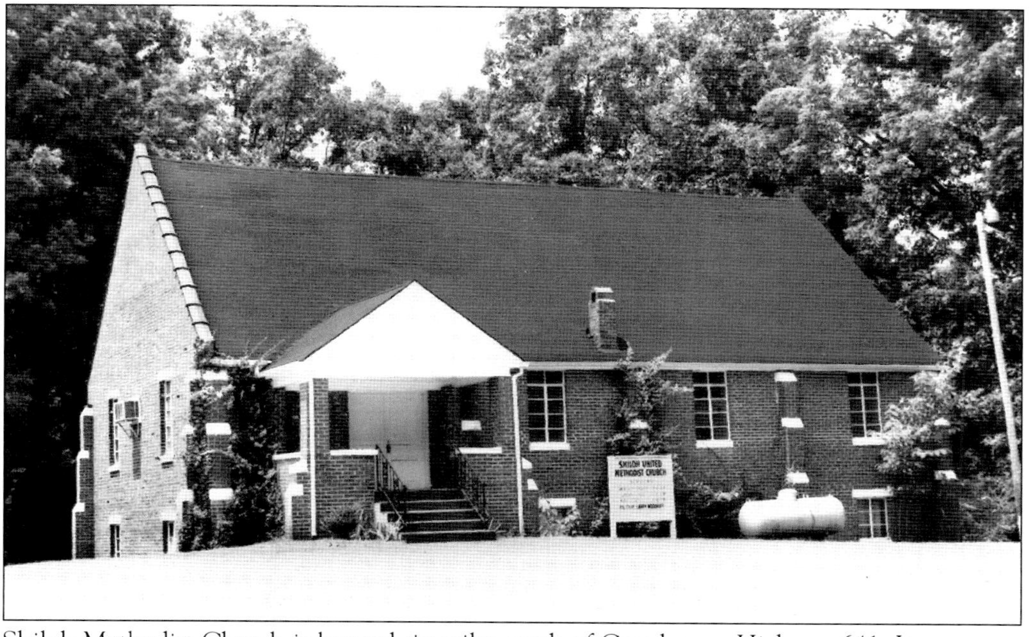

Shiloh Methodist Church is located six miles south of Camden on Highway 641. It was organized in the 1800s on land that belonged to Thomas Swindle. On August 26, 1867, he transferred this land to the church trustees. This congregation has had three buildings—the first was a log structure, which also served as a schoolhouse. Later a frame building was erected; the present building was completed in 1952. (JD.)

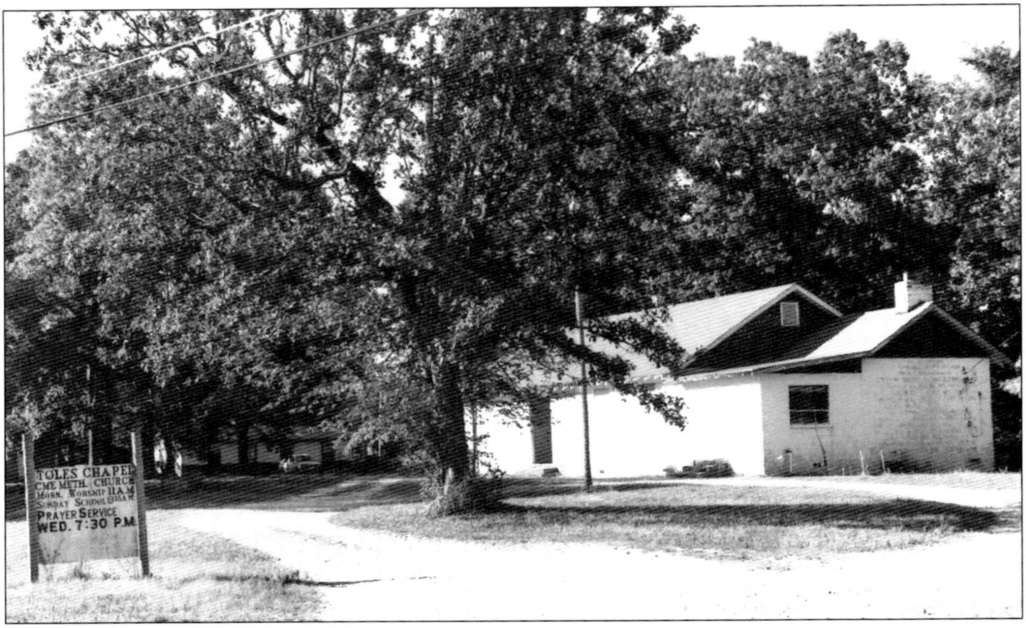

Tole's Chapel Church was organized in the 1800s and named for Arthur Toles/Towles. It was also a school and known to be one of the most important African-American schools in the county. The church is located in the northeast section of Camden, on Wren Avenue, at the site of the Calvary cemetery. It was once a Methodist church but is now non-denominational. This photograph was made in 1988 and shows the third location for Toles Chapel. (JD.)

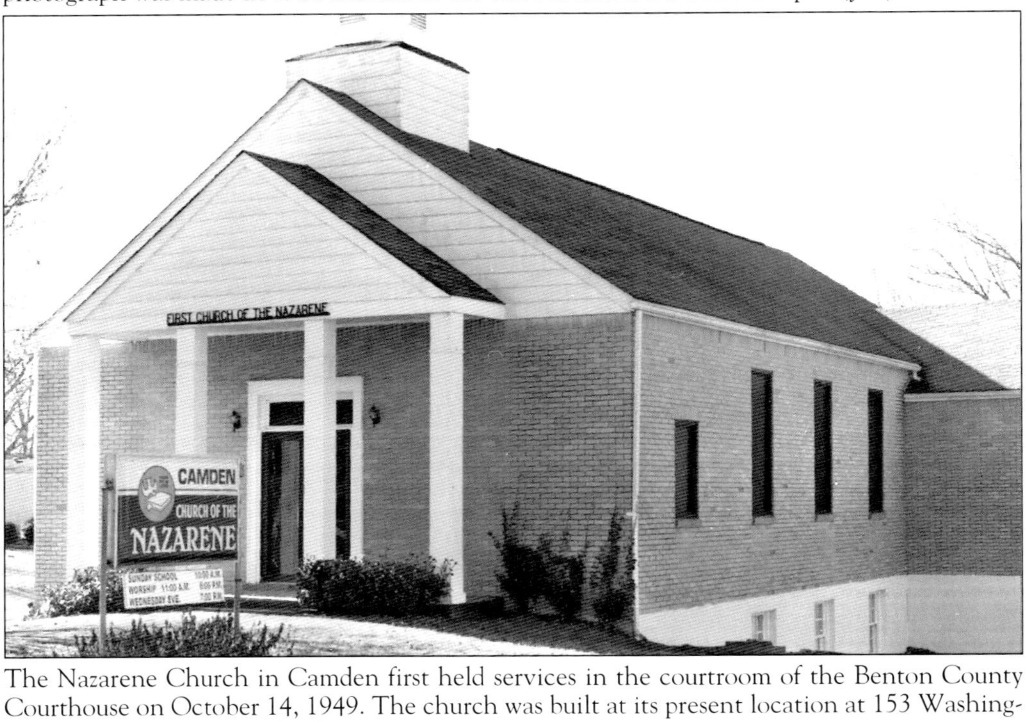

The Nazarene Church in Camden first held services in the courtroom of the Benton County Courthouse on October 14, 1949. The church was built at its present location at 153 Washington Street in June 1957. (JG.)

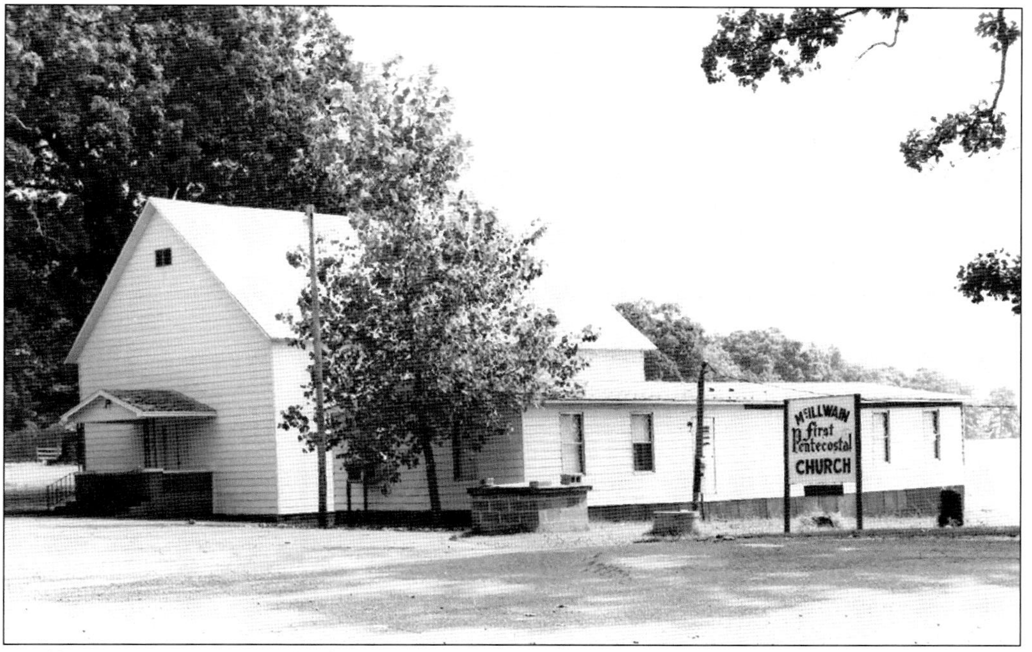

McIllwain First Pentecostal Church, pictured here in 1987, is located in McIllwain, a quarter-mile east of Highway 641 on the old Highway 69; it is still in use. The church was established about 1970 by Rev. J.T. Thornton. This was formerly the McIllwain Cumberland Presbyterian Church building, but the Presbyterians ceased to meet in the early 1960s. (JD.)

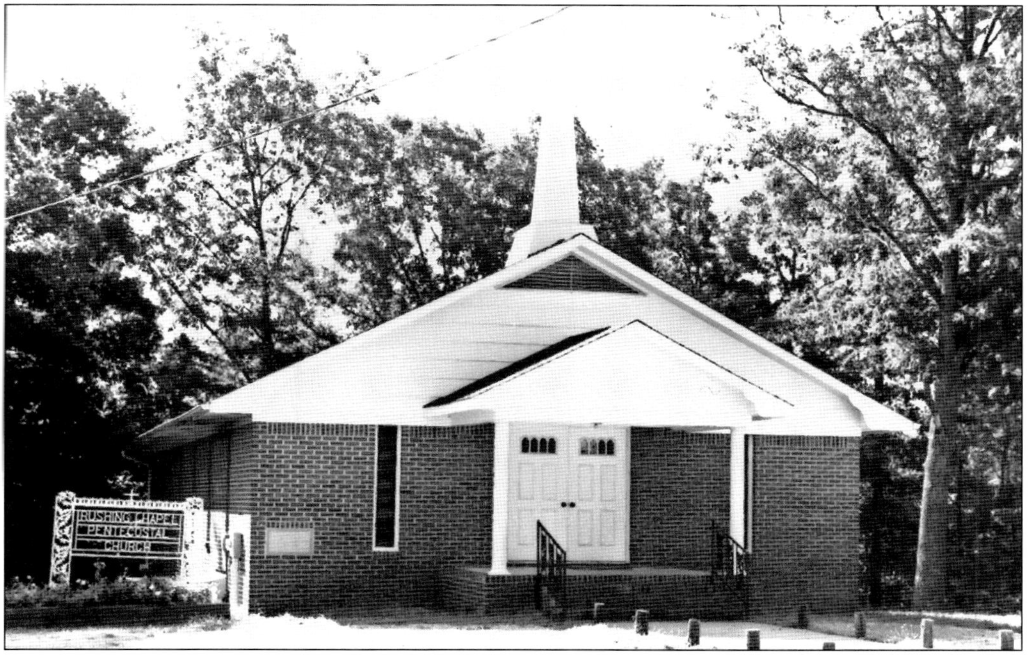

Rushing Chapel Pentecostal Church purchased the old Rushing Chapel Methodist building. They remodeled it several times and started the present building in December 1976. The first service in the new building was held on the first Sunday in February 1977. (JD.)

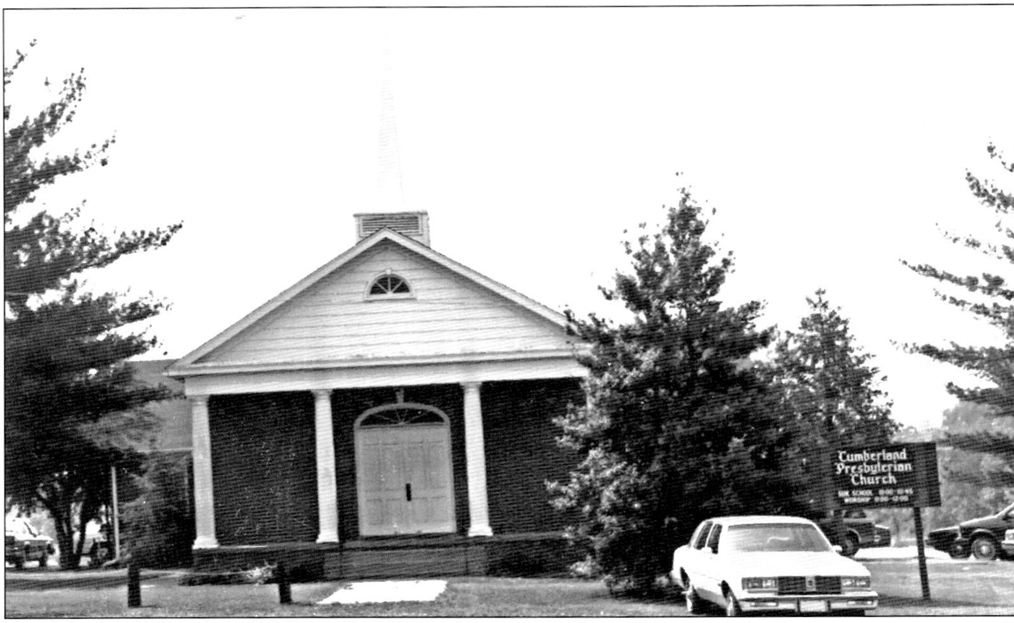

Cumberland Presbyterian Church was organized on August 16, 1842, and worshiped at 129 East Main Street for 30 years. Later they occupied the ground floor of a two-story building at 114 West Main Street, and the Masons occupied the upper floor. In 1955, the Masons purchased that building, and the church moved to a new building adjoining the Camden City Cemetery. The current building was dedicated in December 1955. (JD.)

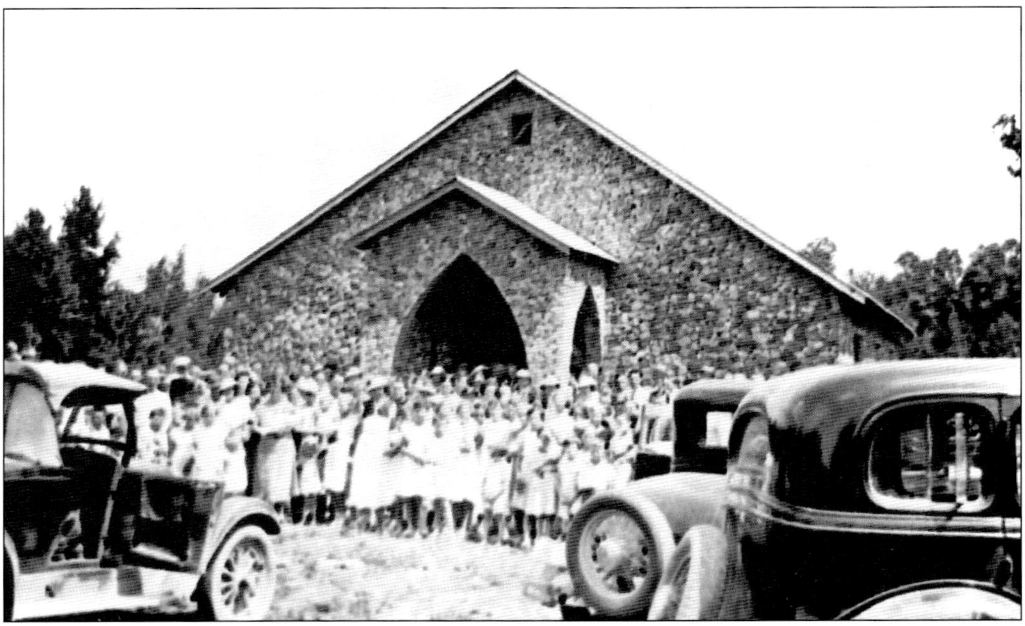

Halls Valley Cumberland Presbyterian, near Harmon's Creek, is pictured here in 1936. Members gathered rocks from fields and creeks to build the church. Then the members raised a crop of cotton to pay for this building. TVA flooded the area in 1942. Worship services are no longer held. (BCPL.)

Two

Education and Sports

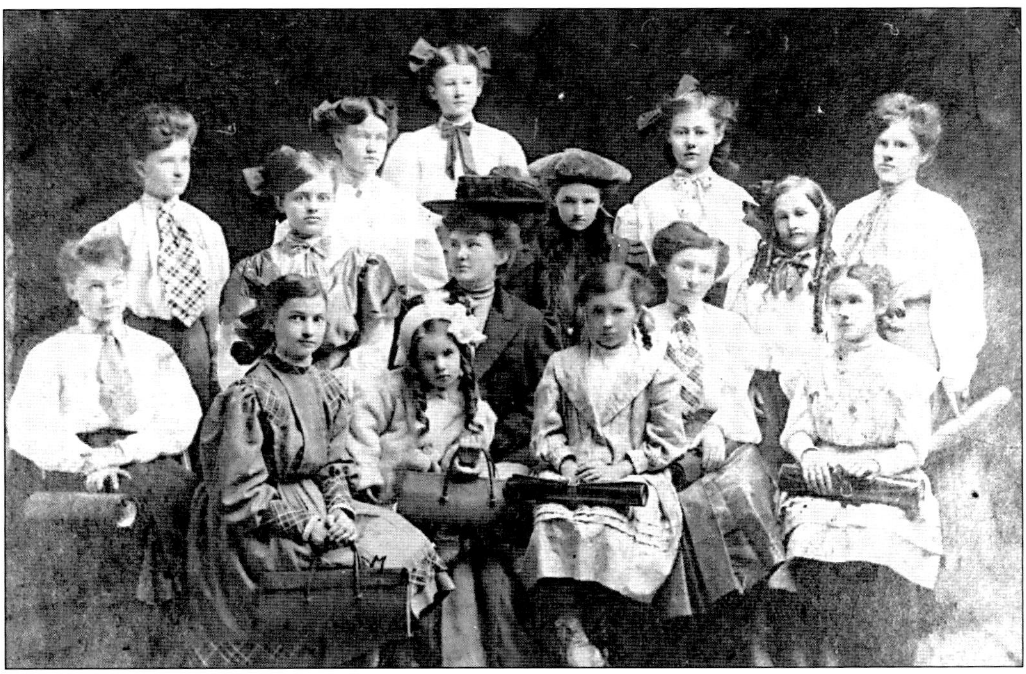

These students pictured here were participating in a music class on October 12, 1910. (BCPL.)

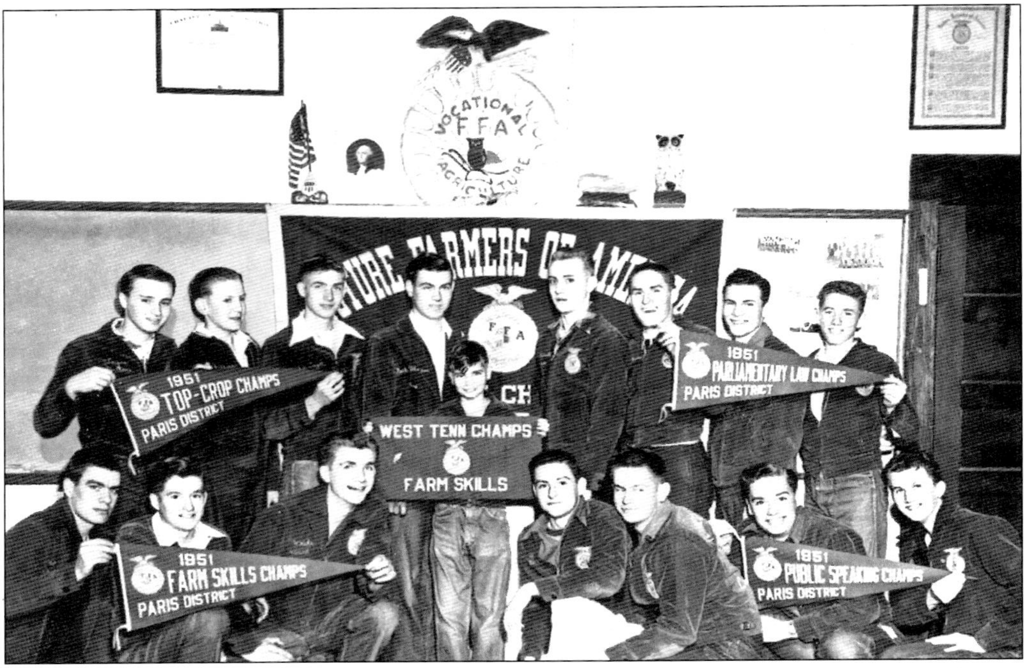

A group of Future Farmers of American (FFA) are holding banners showing the awards won by the Benton County FFA from Camden High School in 1951. Mr. Fred Armantrout was the instructor. (BCPL.)

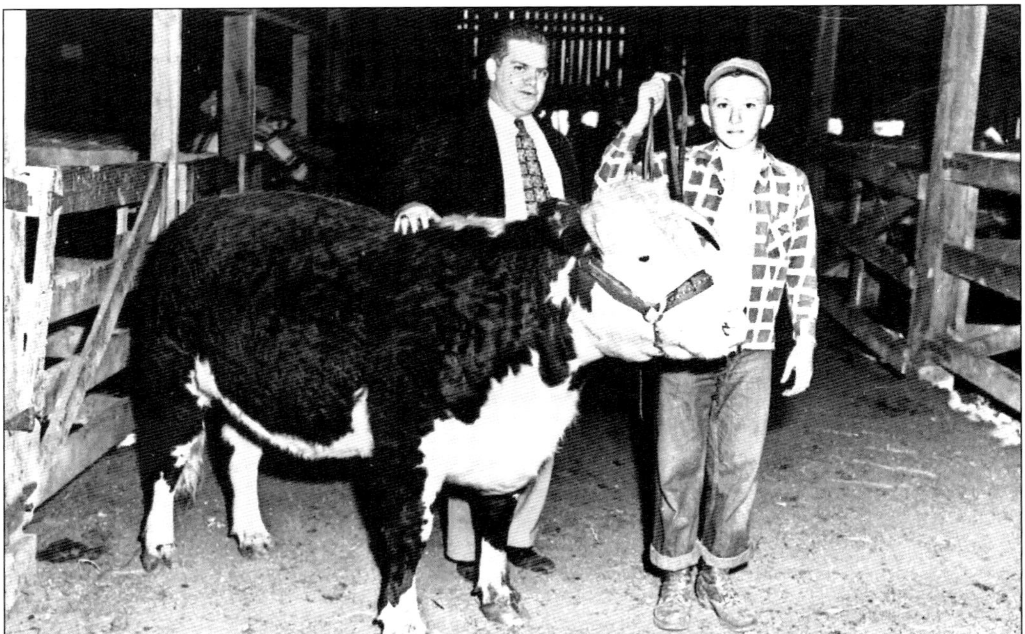

Harold Pettyjohn had a 4-H Club entry in the 1953 Benton County Fair. Shown with him is J.N. Jones, the leading grocer in Camden. (BCPL.)

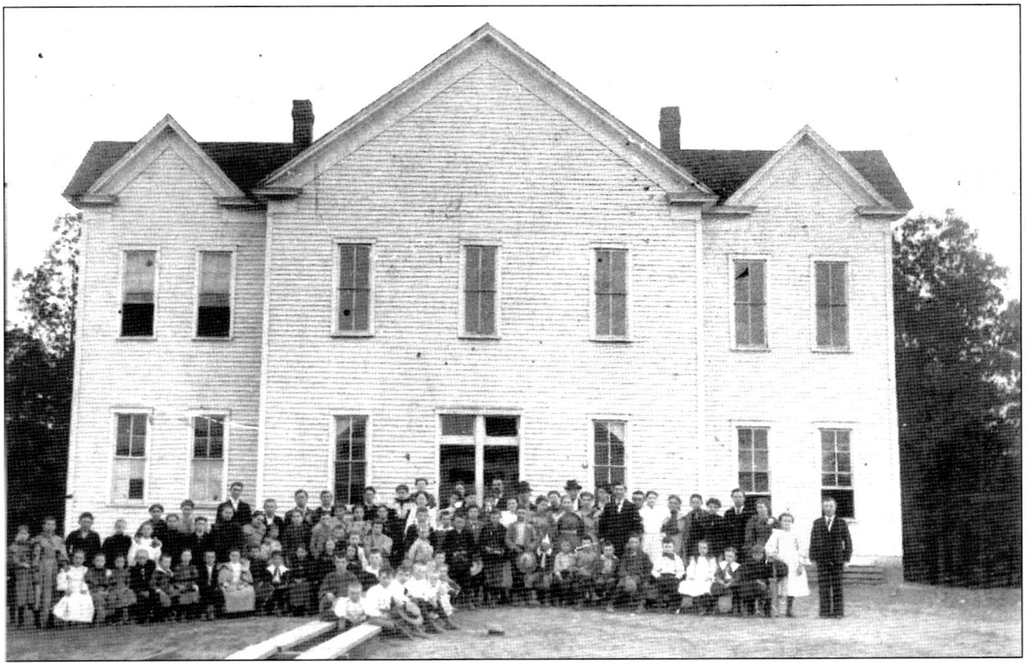

Benton County Seminary was a semi-private school built in the late 1800s and used until 1914, when it was restructured into a regular high school. It was located on Forrest Avenue on what was known as College Hill. (BCPL.)

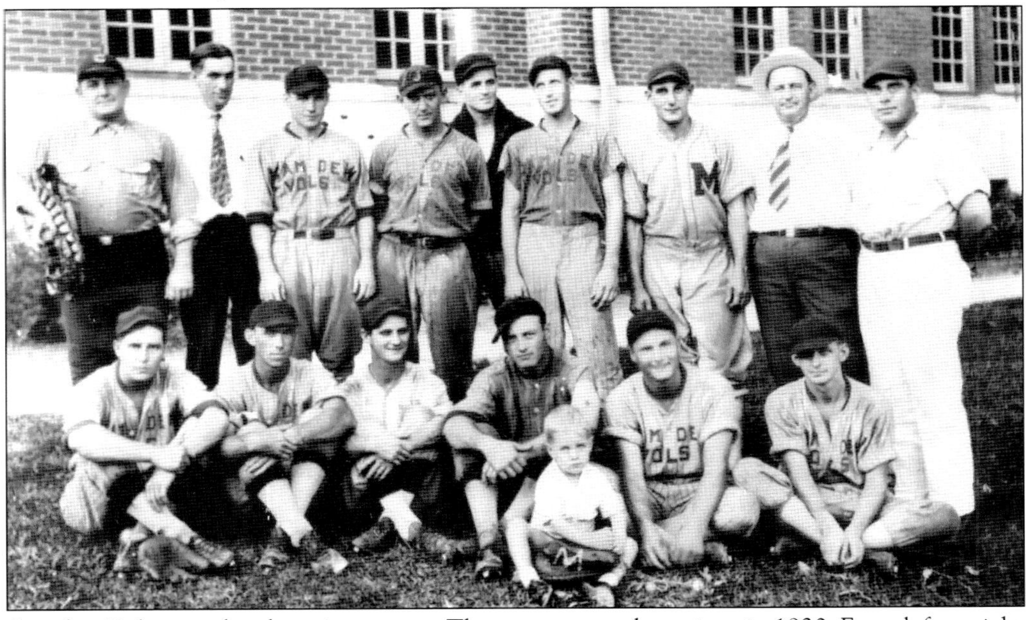

Camden Vols was a local semi-pro team. They were state champions in 1930. From left to right are (front row) Simmons, left field; Stark, pitcher; Hurt, shortstop; "Sausage" McEwen, catcher; "Lefty" Taylor, pitcher; A.V. Bowles, centerfield; and little Jackie Hurt, mascot; (back row) Cobb, ump; Miller, ump; Davis, second base; Jones, first base; Kain, pitcher; Dean, right field; Cirisi, third base; Roy Melton, sec; and John Wyly Lashlee, manager. (BCPL.)

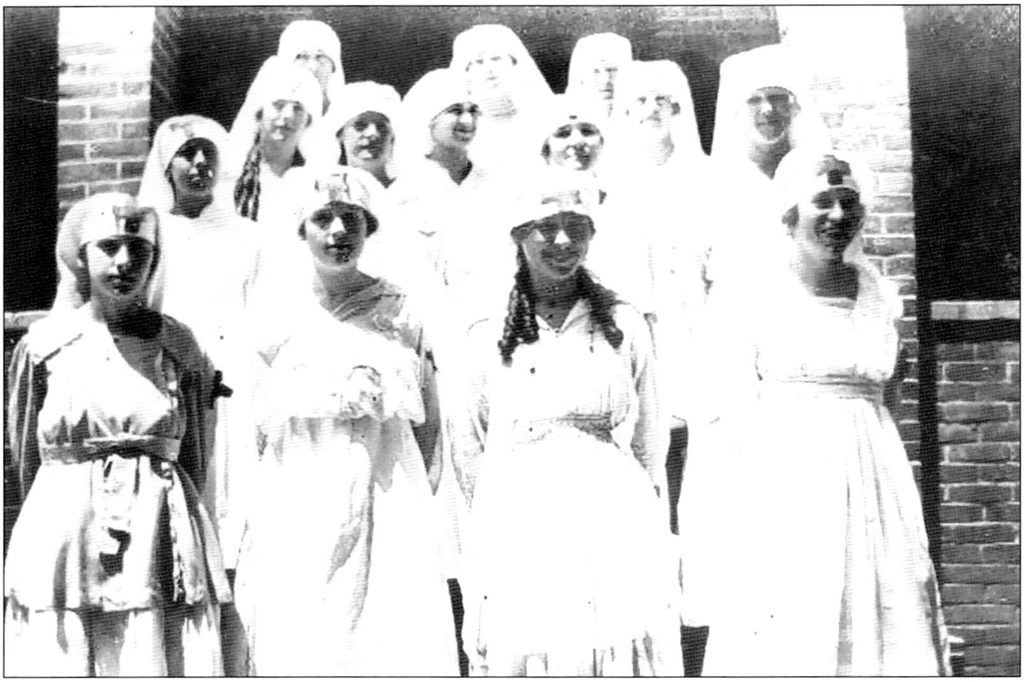

Student nurses are shown at Big Sandy School in their uniforms during World War I. (RD.)

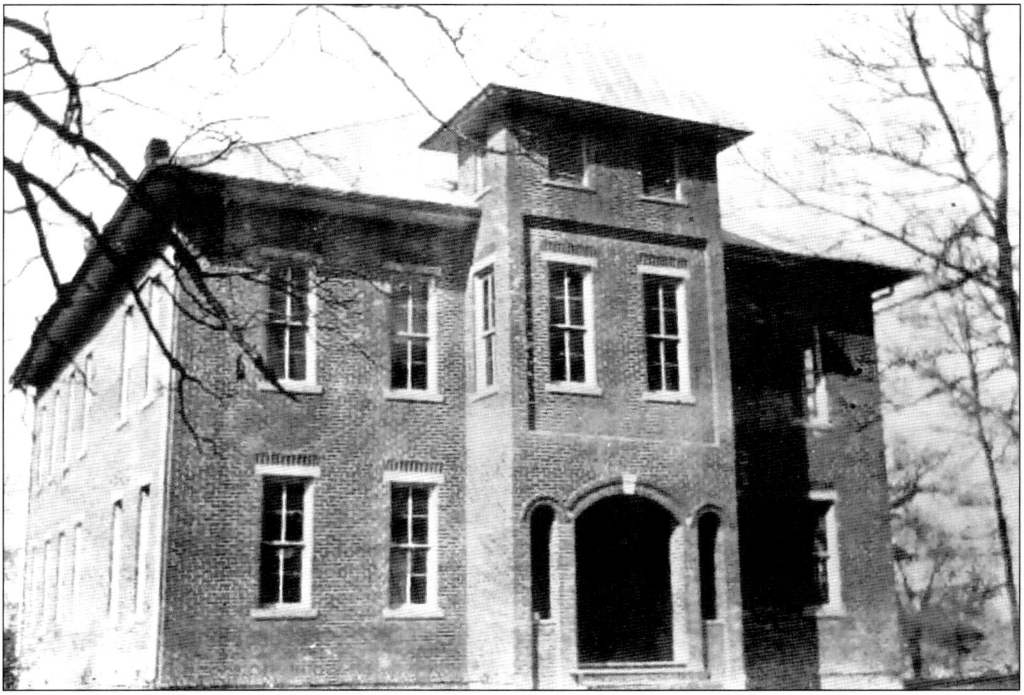

Big Sandy High School is seen c. 1915; the school was located at Big Sandy, Tennessee. (BD.)

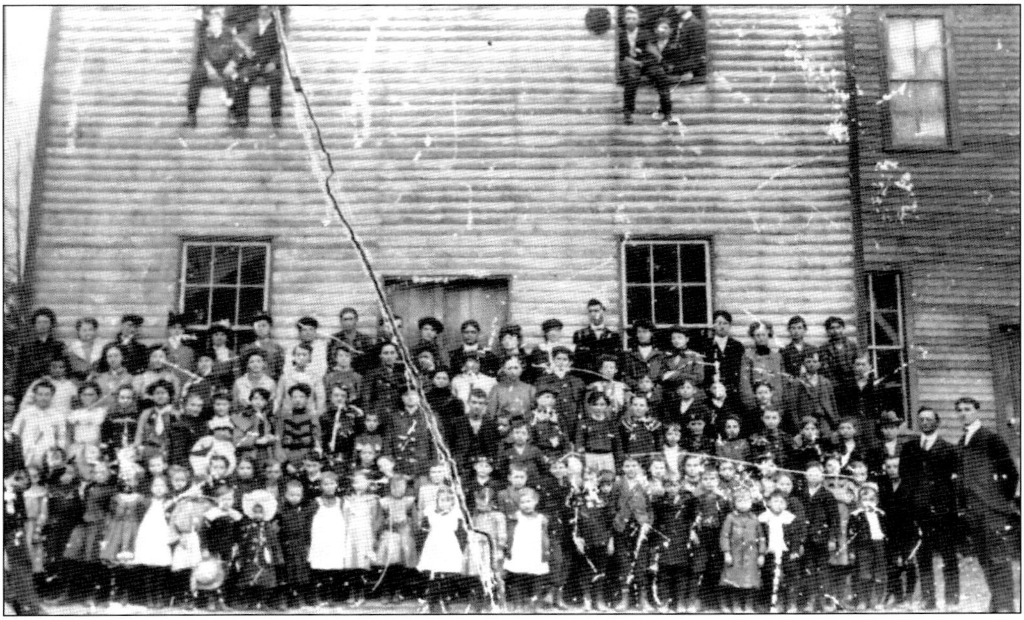

In 1903, J.R. Miller and W.H. Gingles opened the Big Sandy Normal College, offering a teachers' course. The school did not last long. The school in this photograph is the Miller Gingles Subscription School and was located where the present-day First Baptist Church is in Big Sandy. (RD.)

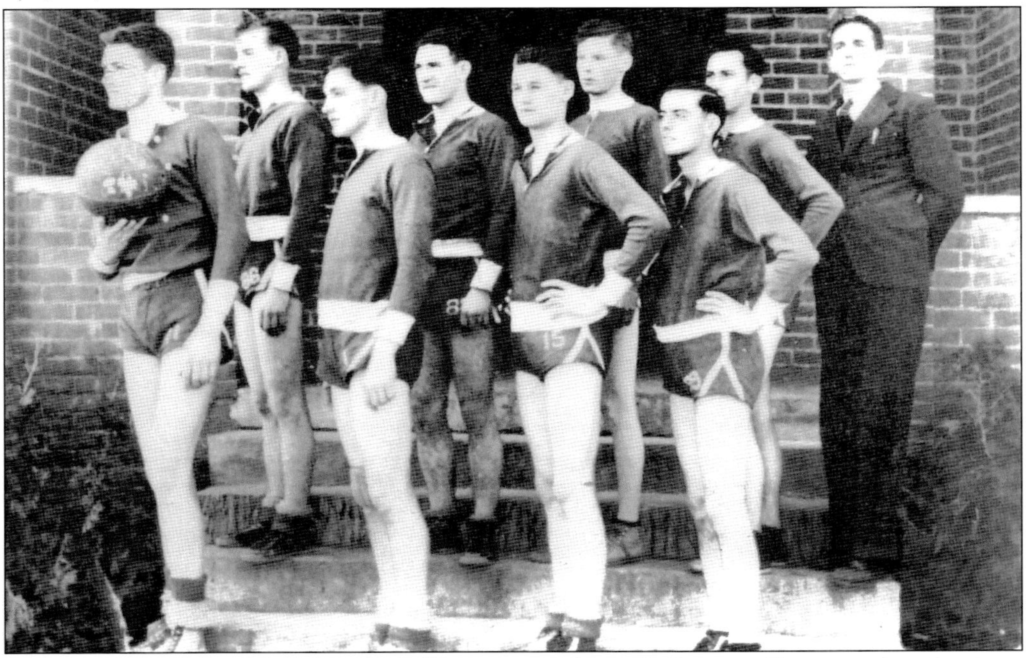

The Big Sandy High School Basketball team won the 19th District Championship for three consecutive years beginning with this team in 1934. Pictured, from left to right, are (front row) Price, Hall, Fleming, and Barnes; (second row) White, Bell, Derington, Rayburn, and Coach DeBruce. (BCPL.)

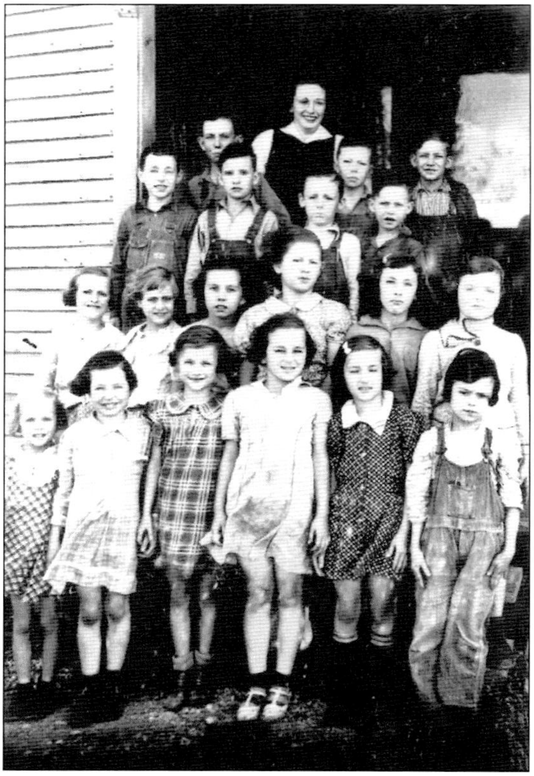

These Morris Chapel School students in 1938 are shown with Blossom Saunders, their teacher. Some of the students who are pictured, in no particular order, are Ophelia Weatherly, Ray Saunders, James Bryan Bivens, Randall Spence, Wynell Hatley, and Mary Sue Saunders. (BCPL.)

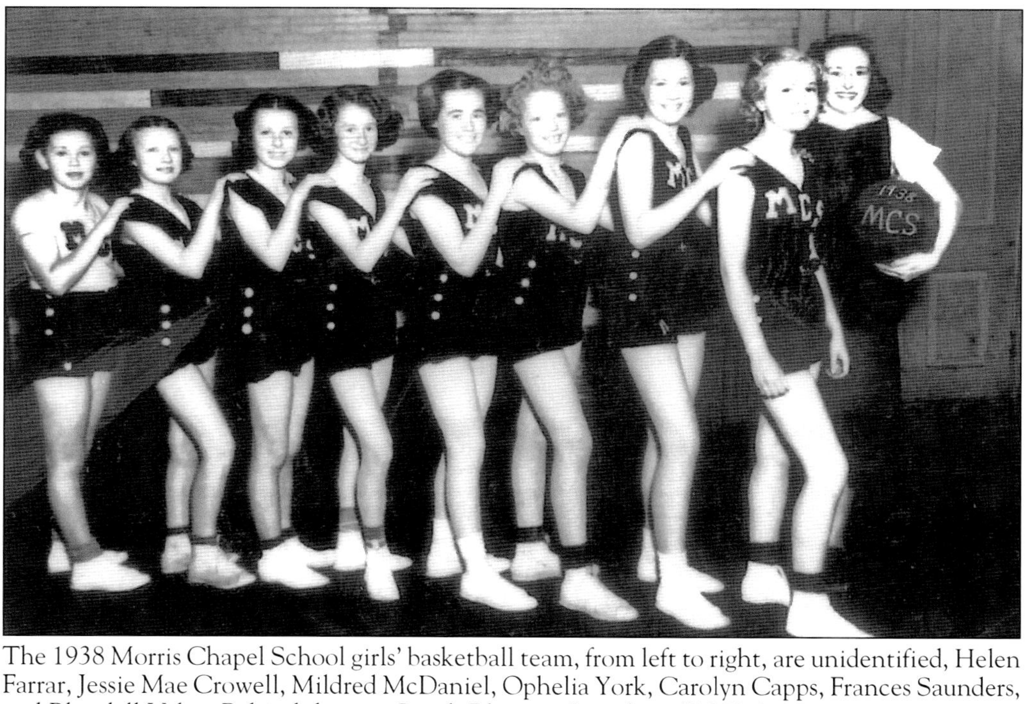

The 1938 Morris Chapel School girls' basketball team, from left to right, are unidentified, Helen Farrar, Jessie Mae Crowell, Mildred McDaniel, Ophelia York, Carolyn Capps, Frances Saunders, and Blondell Utley. Behind them is Coach Blossom Saunders. (BCPL.)

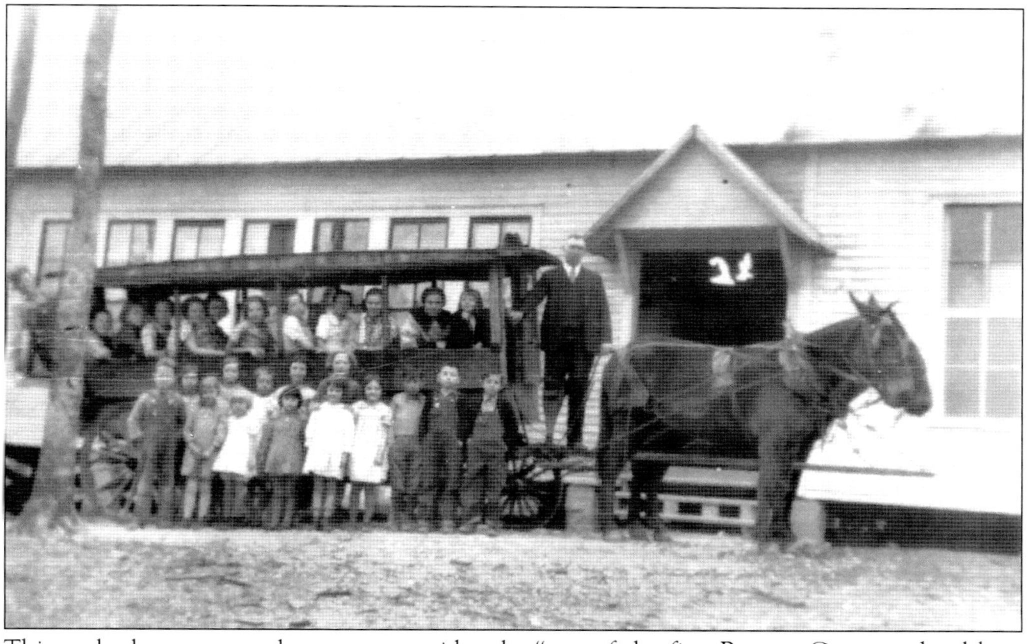

This mule-drawn covered wagon was said to be "one of the first Benton County school buses" providing transportation for children of the county. Morris Chapel School had its first school wagon in 1914. The driver was John Summers, and his two mules were named Bud and Nell. (BCPL.)

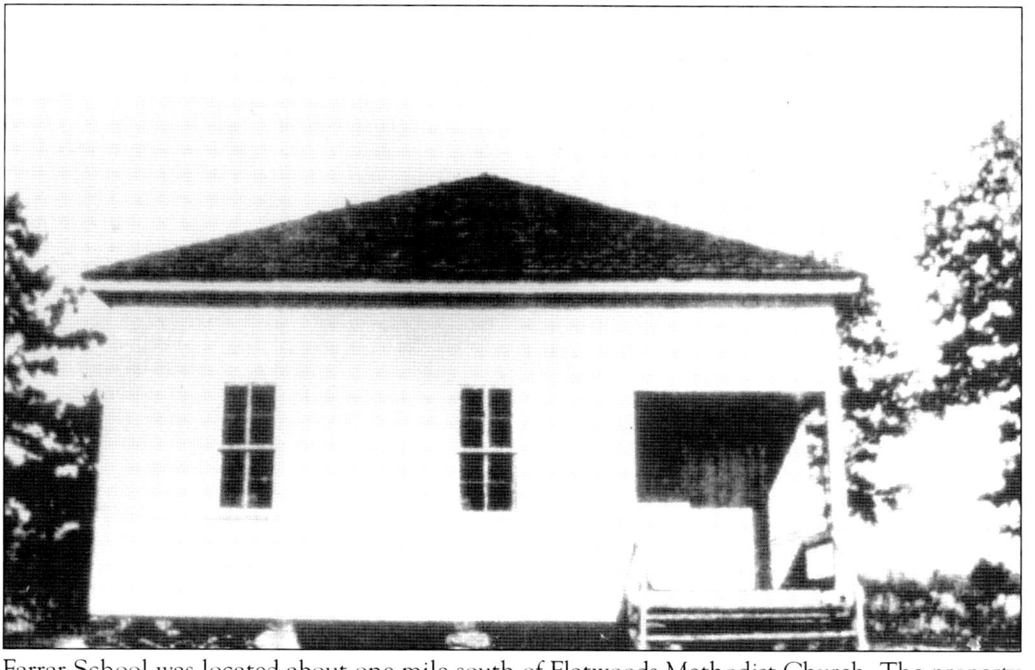

Farrar School was located about one mile south of Flatwoods Methodist Church. The property was bought by Leander Farrar from D.B. Holland, and two acres were reserved for a school about 1916. The school was built in 1920 and closed in 1953. (NN.)

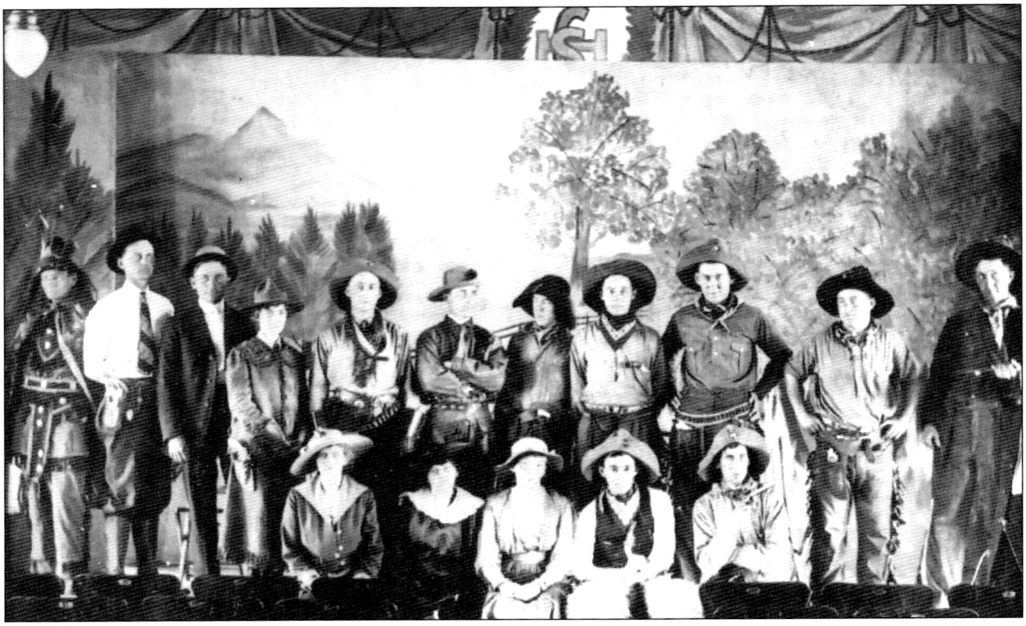

"Home Talent Players" were leading citizens who travelled the Tennessee River for about a week in 1915 or 1916 presenting a play at various landings. On the curtain above the stage are the letters "CHS"; it is believed to have taken place at Camden High School. The photograph is dated May 22, 1915. In the center front row are Maude (Weatherly) Dougherty and her husband, Dr. Lew Dougherty Sr. In the back row, second from left, is Joe Odle. Fifth from the left is Bob Davis. (BCPL.)

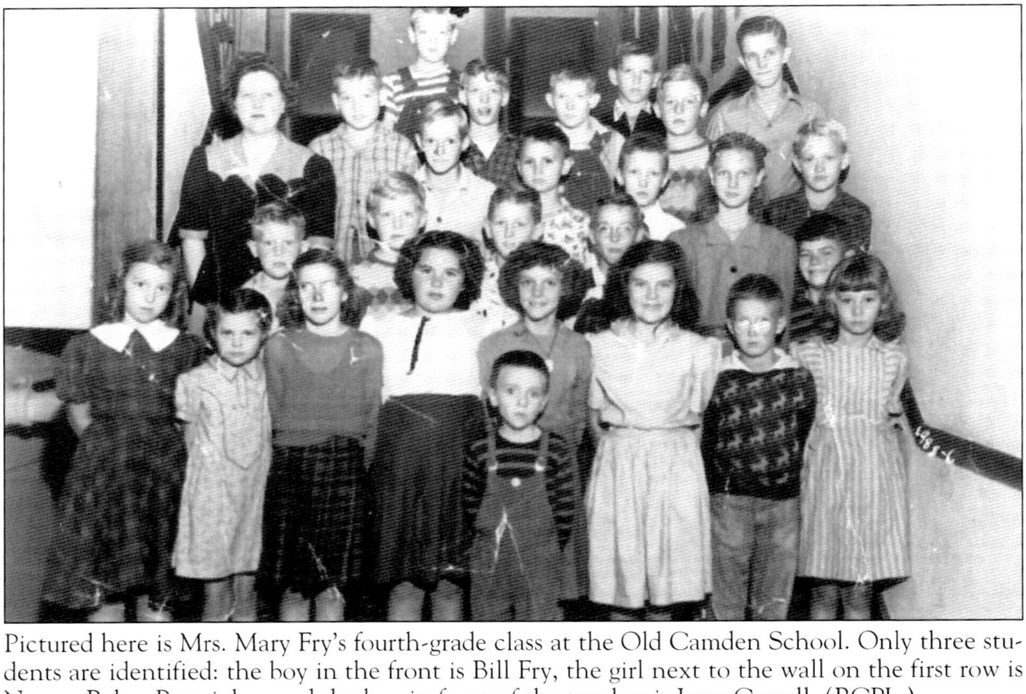

Pictured here is Mrs. Mary Fry's fourth-grade class at the Old Camden School. Only three students are identified: the boy in the front is Bill Fry, the girl next to the wall on the first row is Norma Baker Pettyjohn, and the boy in front of the teacher is Jerry Cowell. (BCPL.)

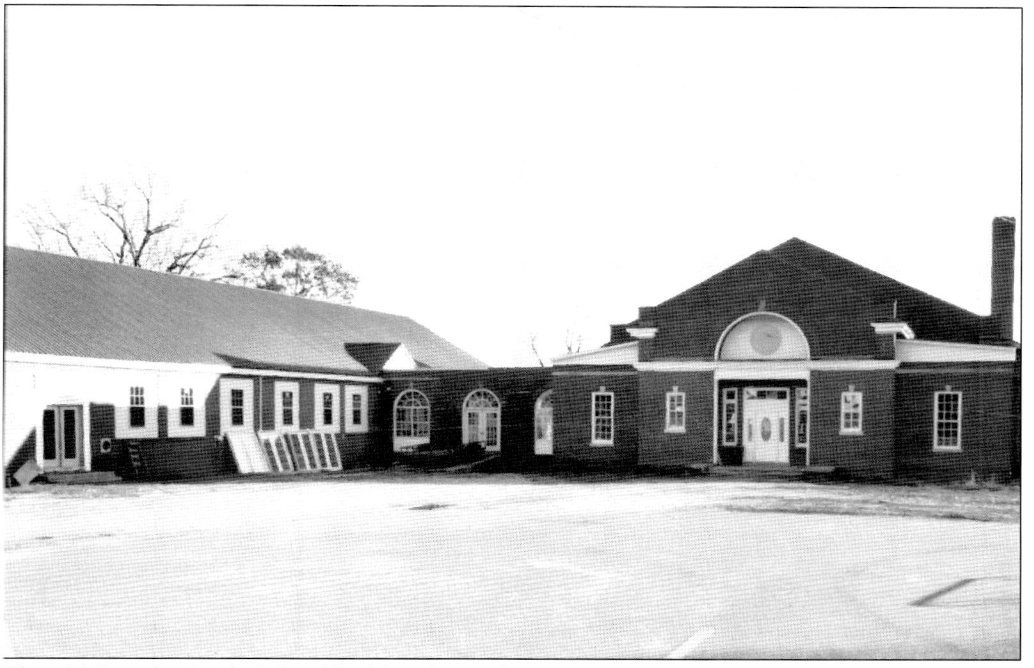

The old Camden High School building located on Forrest Avenue is now being converted into a civic center by New Beginnings Church of God. The gym is already in use, and future plans include specialty shops, a café, workout gym, and also space for senior citizens—something for all ages. Jeff McKee, the senior pastor, is very involved in the remodeling project, which may be another year until completion. (JG.)

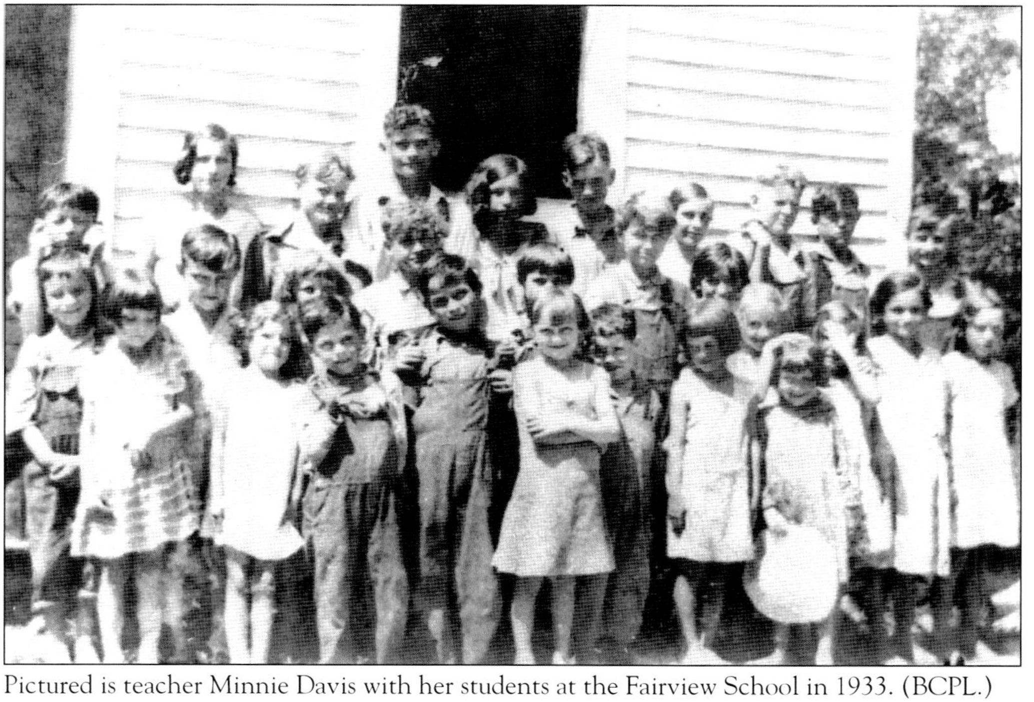

Pictured is teacher Minnie Davis with her students at the Fairview School in 1933. (BCPL.)

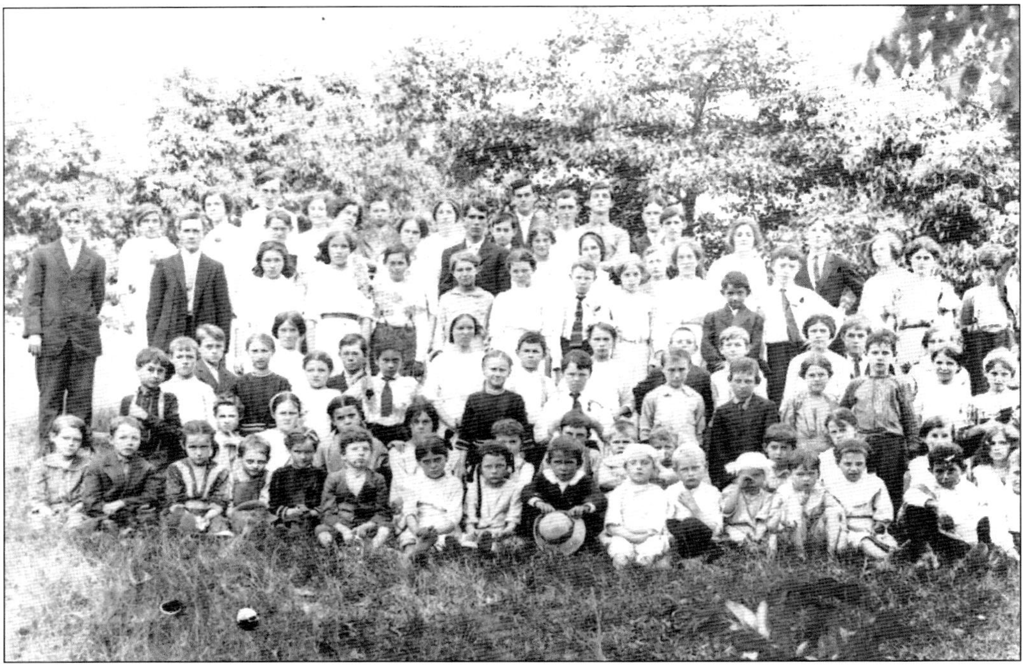

Students are pictured c. 1912–1915 at the Mt. Moriah School, which was located in the Birdsong community. (BCPL.)

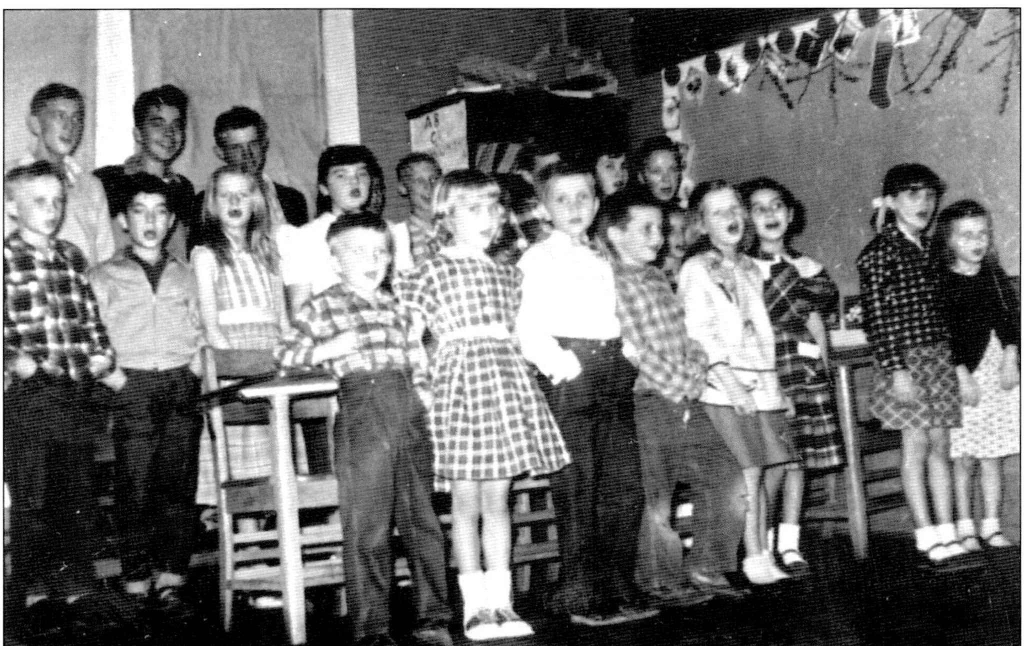

The students pictured here are from Mt. Moriah School in 1956. Mt. Moriah School was located in the Birdsong Community and was a one-room school with one teacher for grades one through eight. (BCPL.)

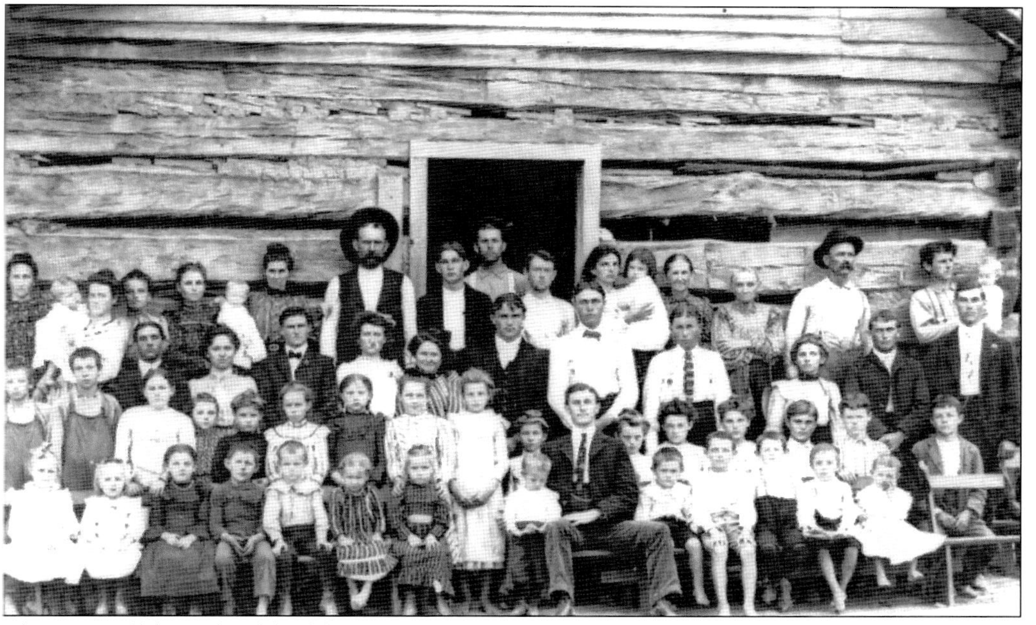

The Tie Hill log school building was located in the Shiloh Community. Albert Bell was the teacher. (BCPL.)

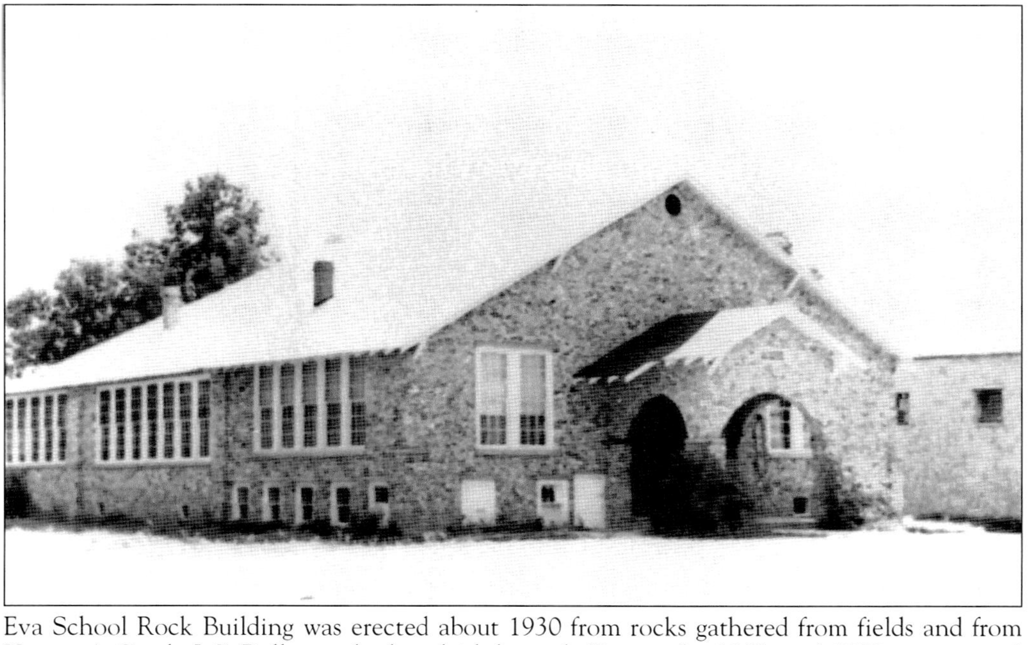

Eva School Rock Building was erected about 1930 from rocks gathered from fields and from Harmon's Creek. J.C. Bullen and others laid the rock. During the 1960s and 1970s, it was used as Benton County Kindergarten, and Jean Fry was the principal. It is now home of the Eva Volunteer Fire Department. (BCPL.)

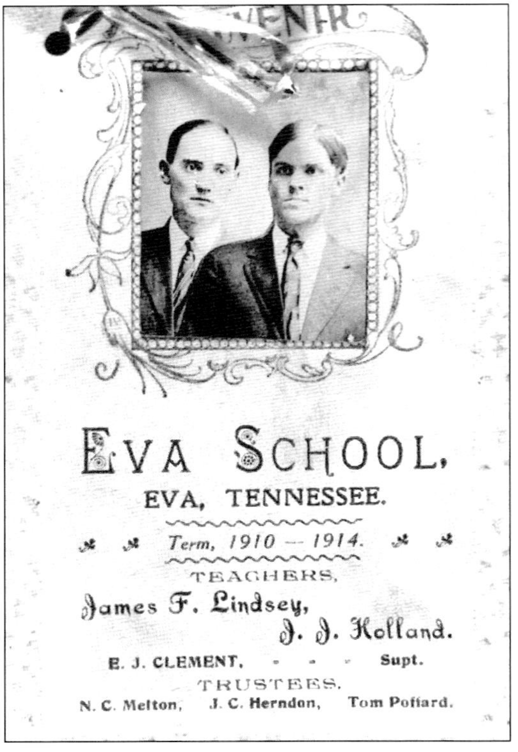

This Eva School graduation program from 1910–1914 shows James F. Lindsey and J.J. Holland on the front cover; the program was tied with a ribbon. (BCPL.)

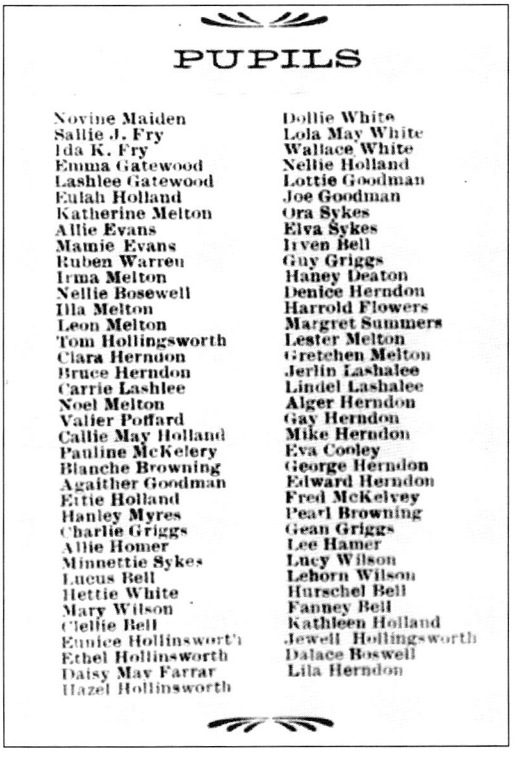

PUPILS

Novine Maiden
Sallie J. Fry
Ida K. Fry
Emma Gatewood
Lashlee Gatewood
Eulah Holland
Katherine Melton
Allie Evans
Mamie Evans
Ruben Warren
Irma Melton
Nellie Bosewell
Illa Melton
Leon Melton
Tom Hollingsworth
Clara Herndon
Bruce Herndon
Carrie Lashlee
Noel Melton
Valier Poffard
Callie May Holland
Pauline McKelery
Blanche Browning
Agaither Goodman
Ettie Holland
Hanley Myres
Charlie Griggs
Allie Homer
Minnettie Sykes
Lucus Bell
Hettie White
Mary Wilson
Clellie Bell
Eunice Hollinsworth
Ethel Hollinsworth
Daisy May Farrar
Hazel Hollinsworth
Dollie White
Lola May White
Wallace White
Nellie Holland
Lottie Goodman
Joe Goodman
Ora Sykes
Elva Sykes
Irven Bell
Guy Griggs
Haney Deaton
Denice Herndon
Harrold Flowers
Margret Summers
Lester Melton
Gretchen Melton
Jerlin Lashalee
Lindel Lashalee
Alger Herndon
Gay Herndon
Mike Herndon
Eva Cooley
George Herndon
Edward Herndon
Fred McKelvey
Pearl Browning
Gean Griggs
Lee Hamer
Lucy Wilson
Lehorn Wilson
Hurschel Bell
Fanney Bell
Kathleen Holland
Jewell Hollingsworth
Dalace Boswell
Lila Herndon

The inside of the Eva School graduation program has a list of students of Eva School in 1910–1914. (BCPL.)

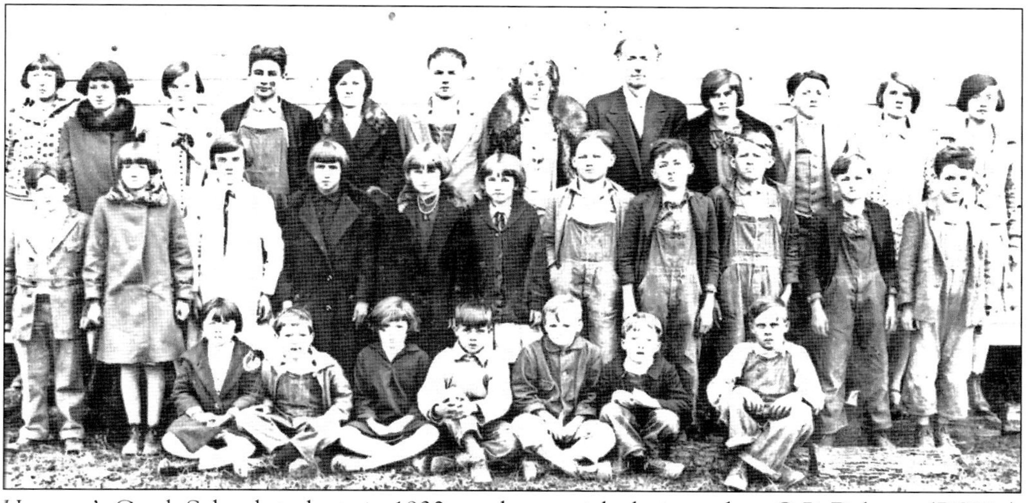

Harmon's Creek School students in 1930 are shown with their teacher, O.P. Dobson. (BCPL.)

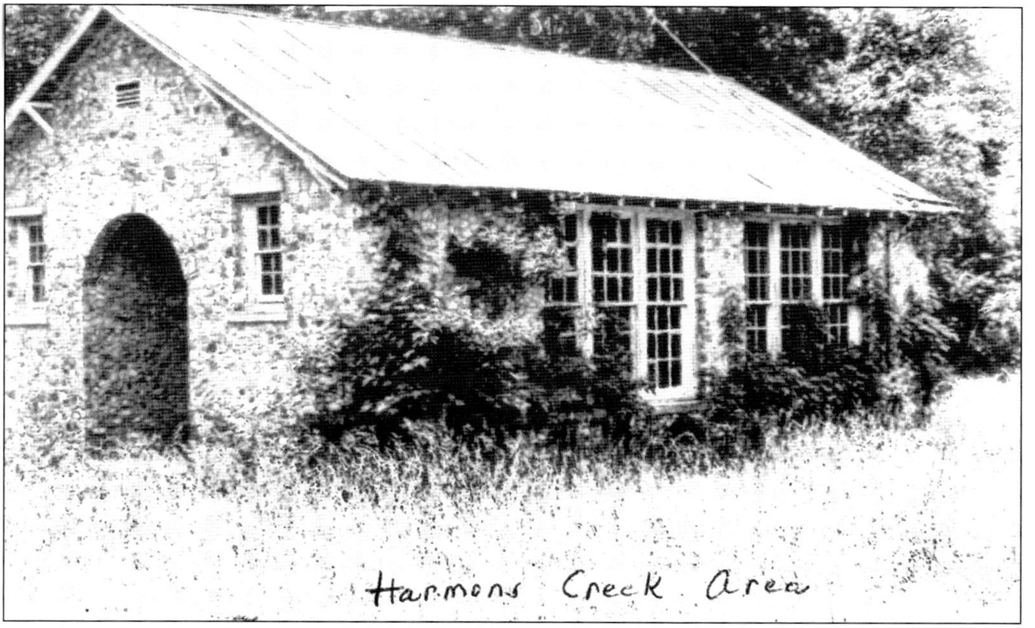

The first school at Cherry Grove was established before 1899. Later a frame building was constructed at another site in 1914; it burned on August 17, 1939. After the fire, the children went to schools in other locations until the 1940–1941 term opened in this native rock building. Cherry Grove consolidated with larger schools at the end of the 1956–1957 school year. This building still stands in the Harmon's Creek area. (NN.)

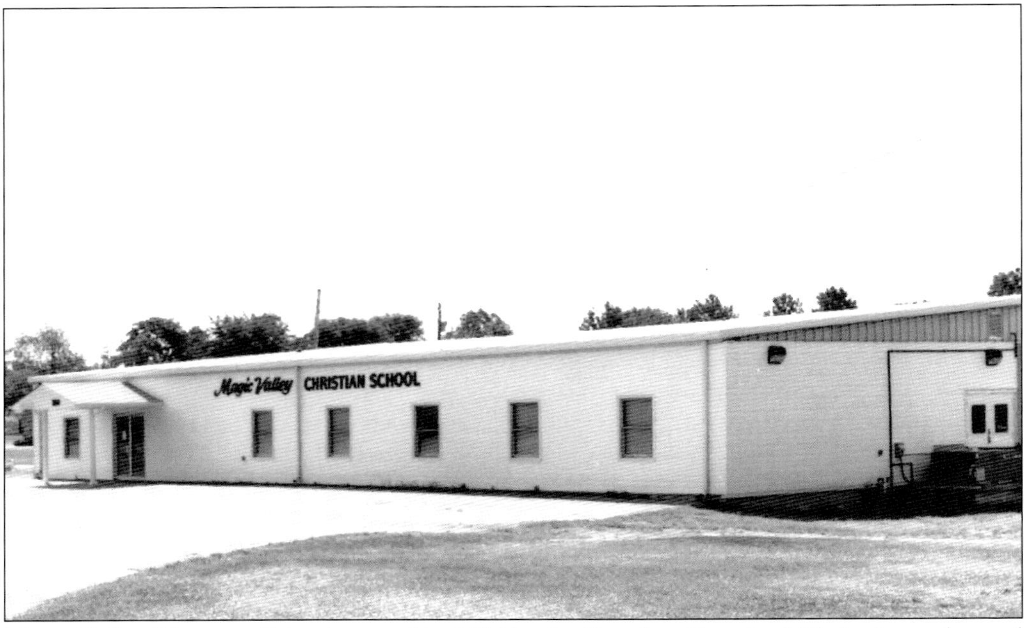

Magic Valley Christian School opened in 1986 by the Camden Church of Christ. It was located on Overhead Bridge Road, south of Camden, and served students from kindergarten through eighth grade. The Bible was taught, along with the state-required subjects. The school operated for a number of years. The Church of Christ sold the property to the state, and it opened in 2004 as Magic Valley Headstart School. (JD.)

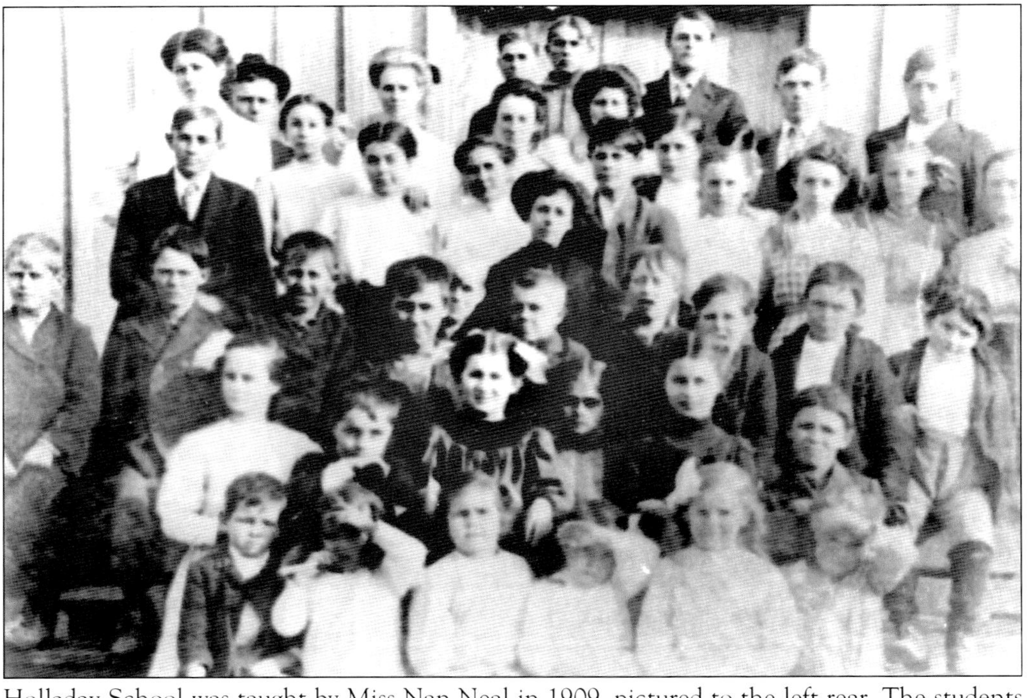

Holladay School was taught by Miss Nan Neal in 1909, pictured to the left rear. The students are unidentified. (BCPL.)

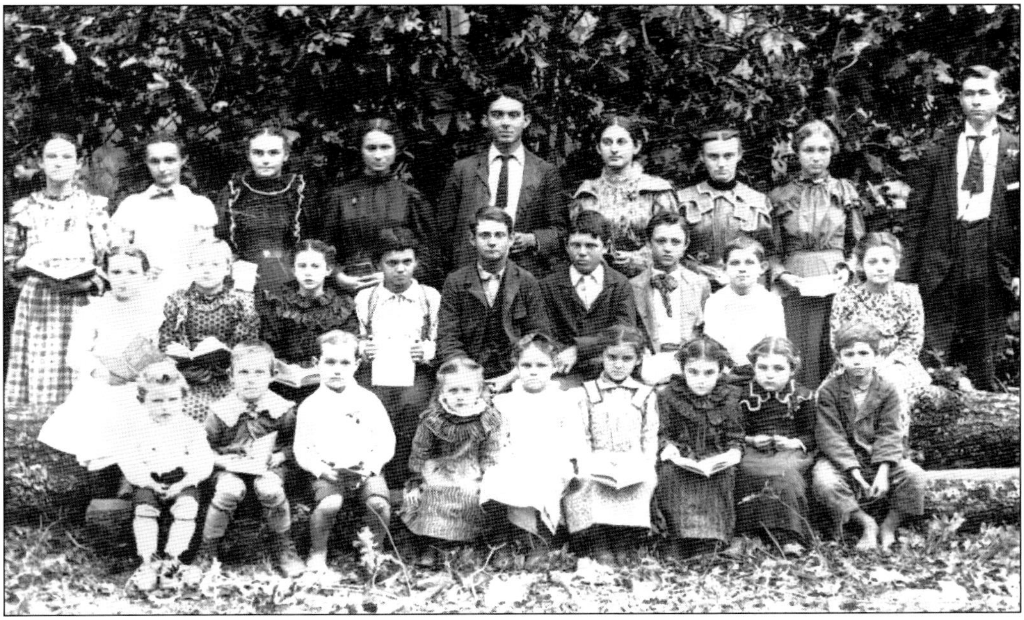

Students of Luterton School, east of Big Sandy, are pictured with their teacher, W.F. Pafford. (BCPL.)

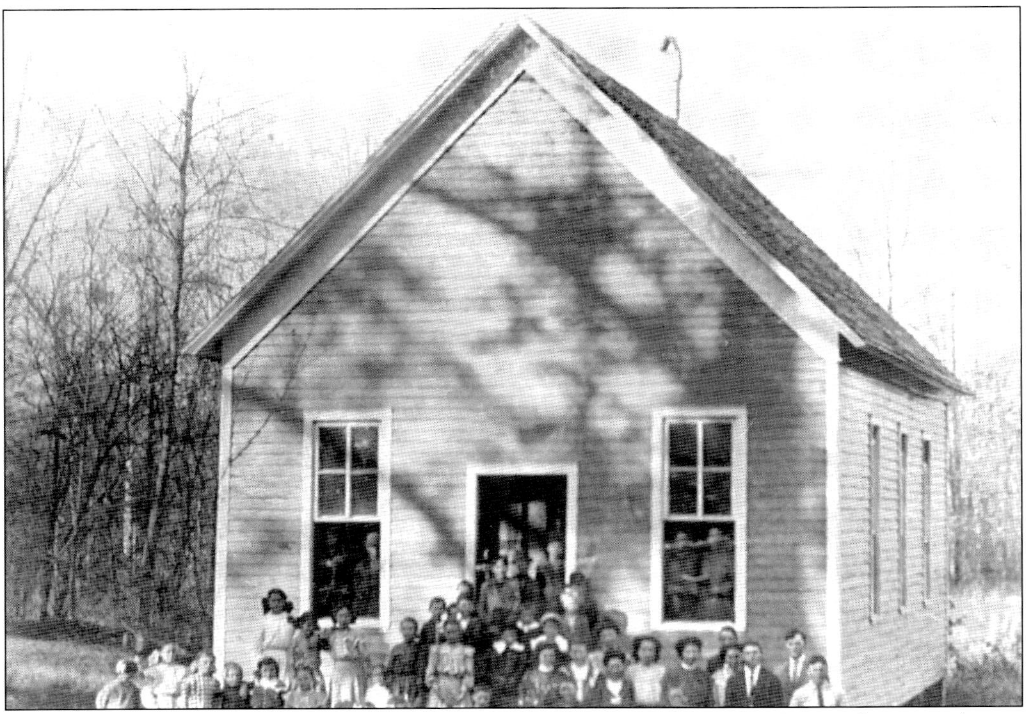

The Crooked Creek School building had one large classroom and a cloakroom for coats, boots, and lunches. This photograph was made about 1908; the building burned in 1920 or 1921. School was held in the church until a new building was erected. The fourth child from the left is Ocie Eulah Robbins, who was born May 25, 1901. (EP.)

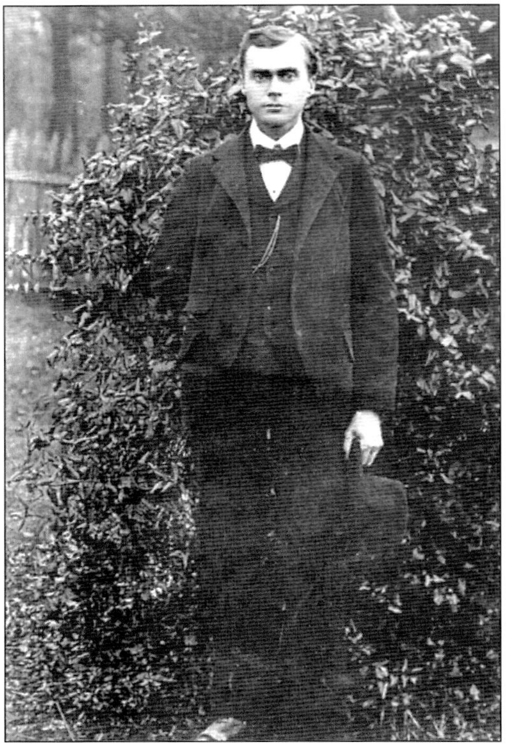

William Lemuel Thompson (1871–1918) was a Benton County school teacher. He taught in several schools throughout the county and was a member of the Masonic Lodge. (JKTS.)

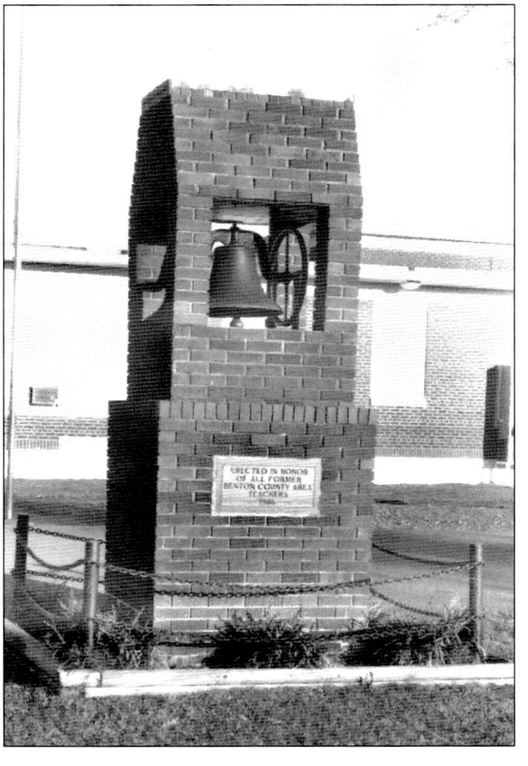

This bell was erected in honor of all Benton County area former teachers. It is located on the Camden Elementary School premises. (JG.)

Three

BUSINESSES

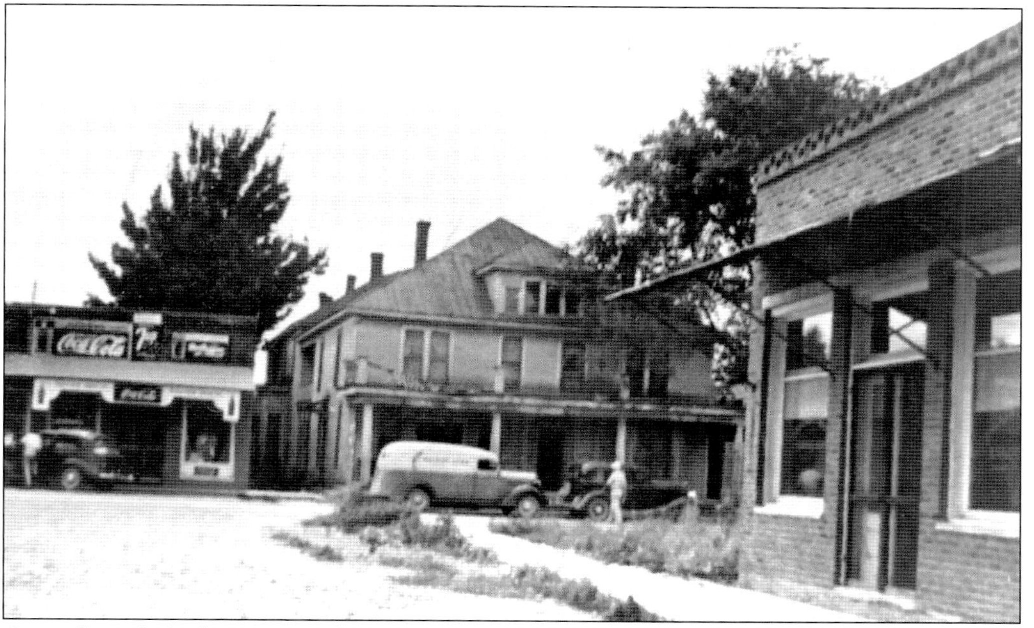

Cantrell and Graham Funeral Parlor, which later became Graham's Drugstore, is shown on the right of this photograph of the west side of the square in Big Sandy. The Dowdy Hotel is shown in the middle of the photo. The building on the left was Harvey Cantrell's Drug Store, where a soda fountain was located. The building on the right is now the Big Sandy Library. (RD.)

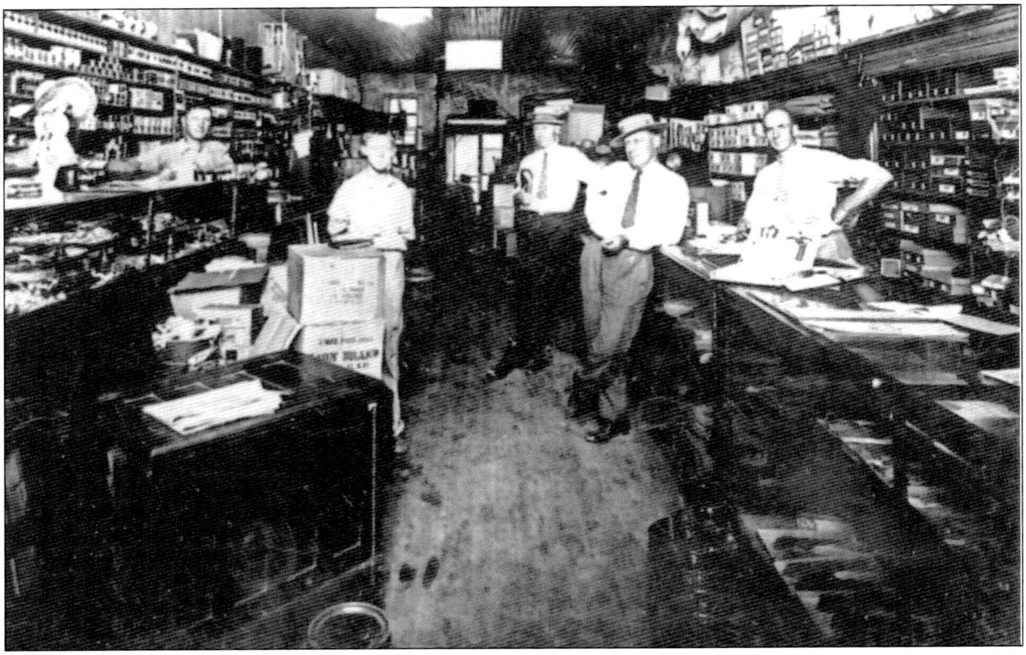

Shown in Graham's General Store in Big Sandy about 1930 is Ralph Graham, in front, with Emmit Graham on the far right. (RD.)

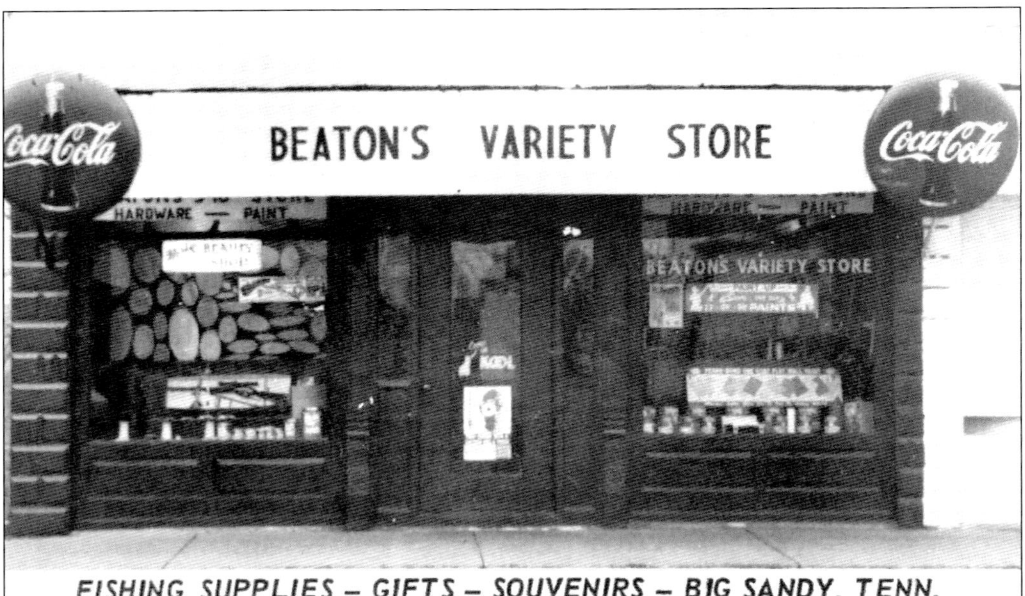

This building was earlier in the location of Mrs. Ed Lindsey's Millinery Shop and then Pafford's Millinery Shop before becoming Beaton's Variety, which had a beauty shop upstairs. Beaton's Variety Store offered gifts, hardware, paint, souvenirs, and fishing supplies in Big Sandy. It was the same building as the original Dowdy building, which was owned by Frank Dowdy. (RD.)

Warren G. Melton owned Melton Service Station in Big Sandy. In 1970, while a storage tank was being refilled, the tank caught fire and burned, causing over $100,000 in damages. The station across the street was closed at the time, so Mr. Melton re-opened there the next day. (BCPL.)

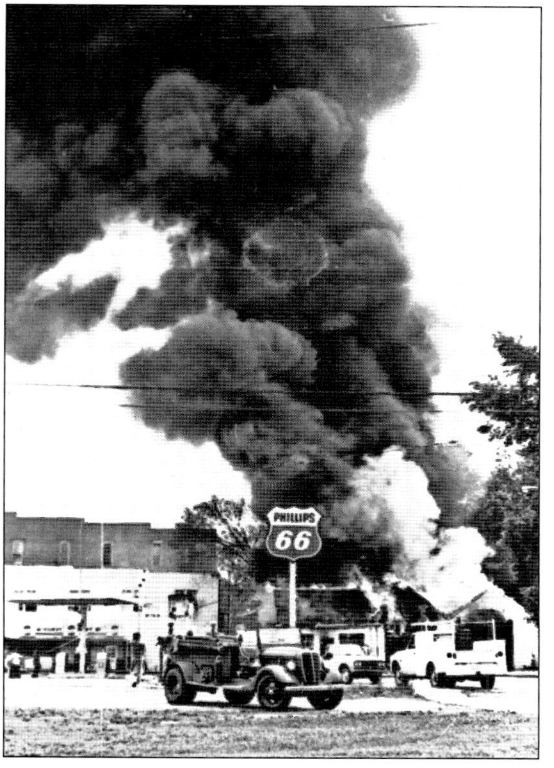

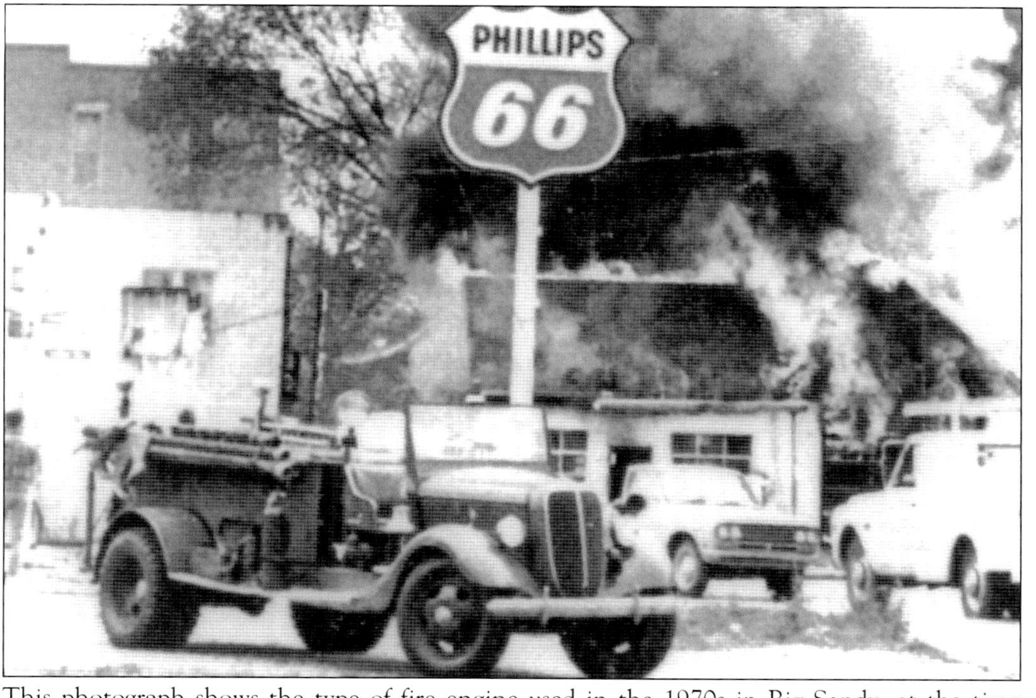

This photograph shows the type of fire engine used in the 1970s in Big Sandy, at the time Melton's Service Station burned. (BCPL.)

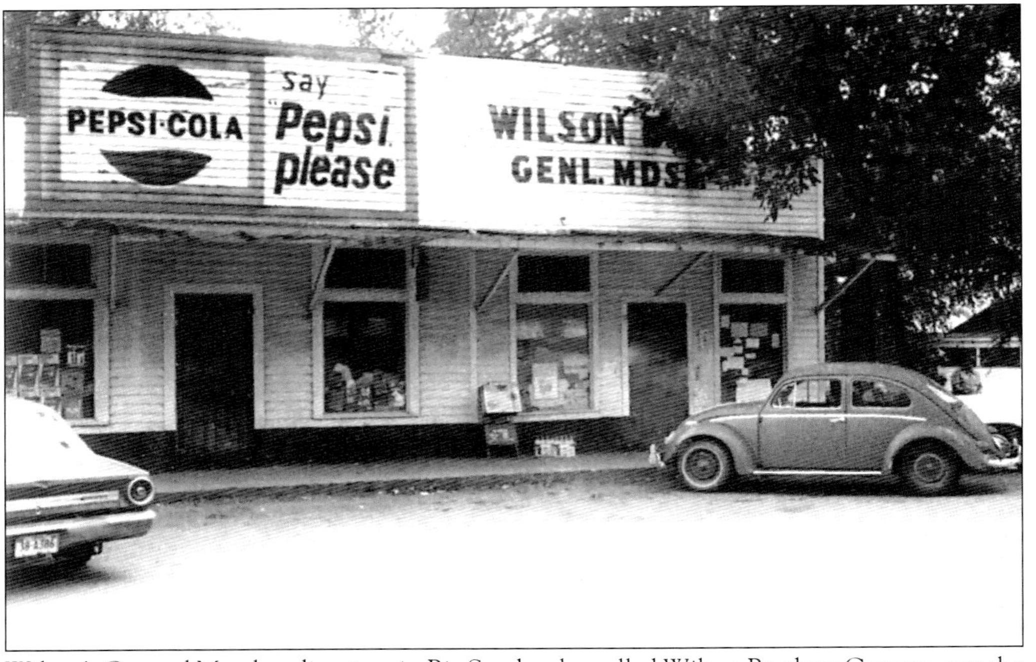

Wilson's General Merchandise store in Big Sandy, also called Wilson Brothers Grocery, was the longest-running establishment in Big Sandy. It was established by John Wilson in 1929 and run by his sons Joe and Quint and daughter Mateusz G., called "Girlie." (BD/TR.)

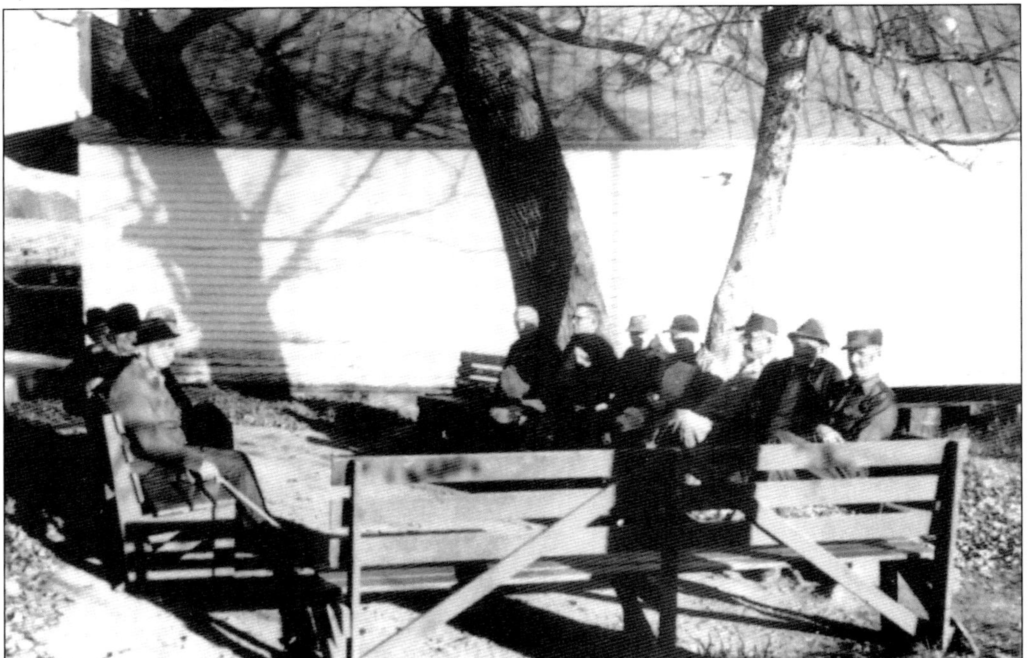

Outside Wilson's store were the benches where the men—usually the older men—brought their pocket knives and whittled and caught up on the latest gossip. These benches became known as the "Liar's Benches." (RD.)

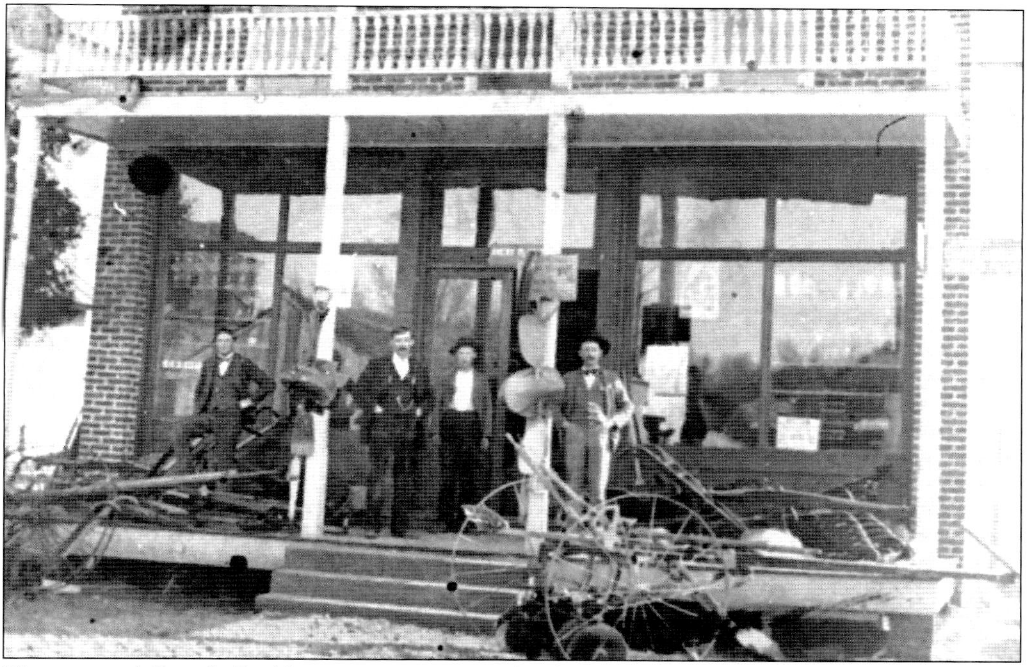

This original Dowdy Building was a two-story brick building on Main Street. In 1912, Frank Dowdy built a new store. The original building was auctioned off on May 3, 1986. (RD.)

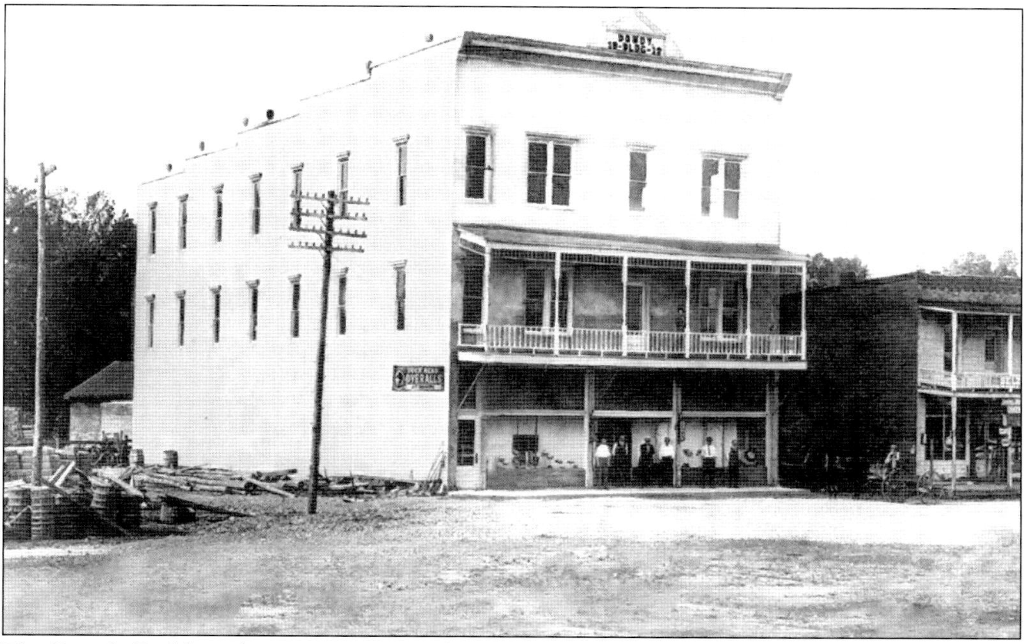

The Dowdy Building that was constructed in 1912 was damaged in an earthquake and destroyed in 1992 by fire in order to accommodate a new post office. The Dowdy Building was a poured concrete structure and had the only freight elevator in Big Sandy. (RD/TR.)

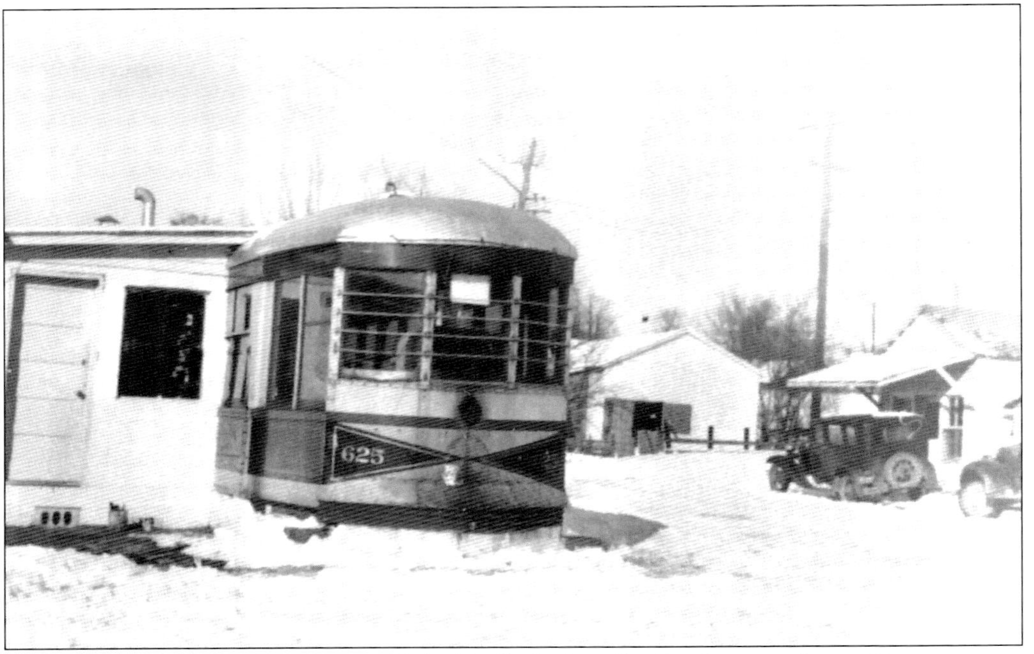

In 1946, Mrs. Ruby DeBruce operated the Trolly Café in Big Sandy; it was located in a streetcar that was moved from Memphis to Big Sandy. As it was being moved, Waldon DeBruce rode on top of it to guide power lines out of the way. He is said to have told people that he was probably the only man ever to ride a streetcar from Memphis to Big Sandy. (BCPL.)

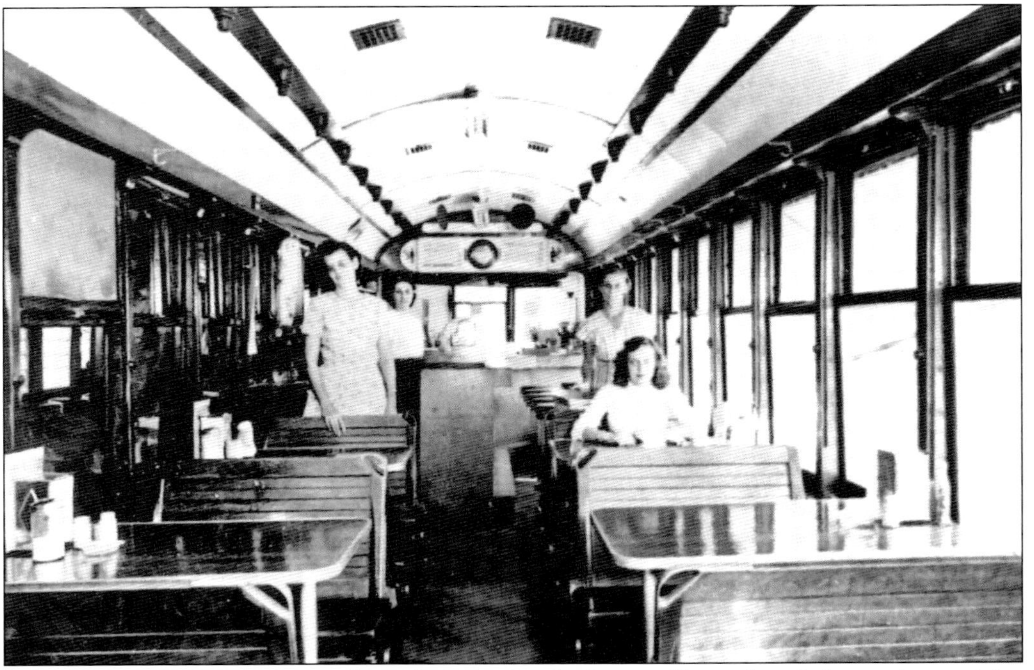

Mrs. Ruby DeBruce ran the Trolly Café in Big Sandy. Pictured here, from left to right, are Mrs. DeBruce, Ruth Brewer Wynn, Sudie Brewer, and Nelda Sue Brewer. (BCPL.)

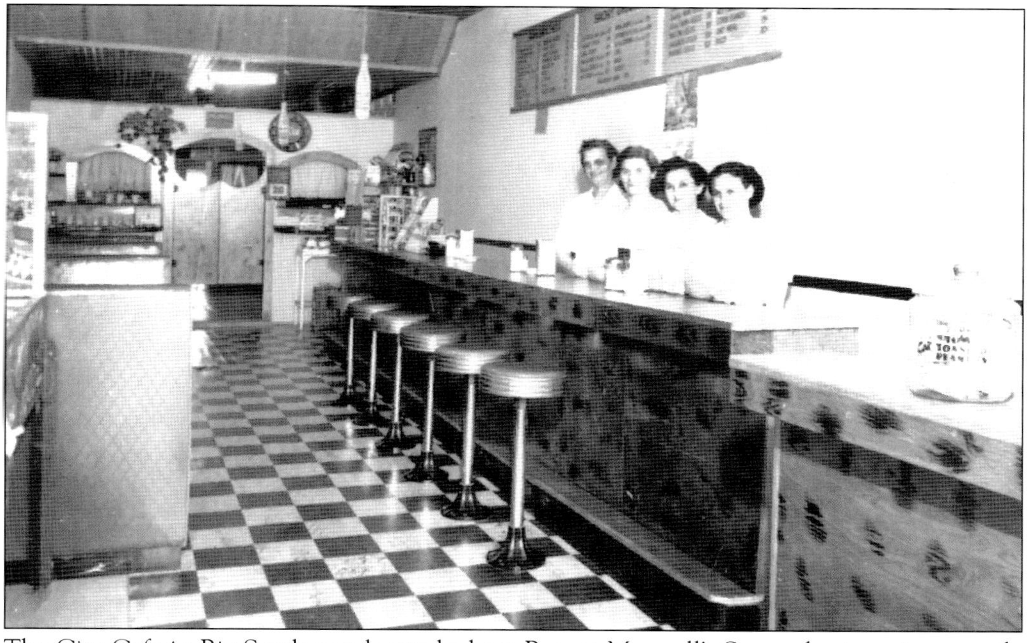

The City Cafe in Big Sandy was located where Barrett Maxwell's Survey business is currently located. Later the café moved to the location where Lillie Dee's Café is now located. From left to right Ruby DeBruce, Martha Stockdale, Maggie Ann Brewer, and O'Dessa McKenzie are ready to serve their customers. (RD.)

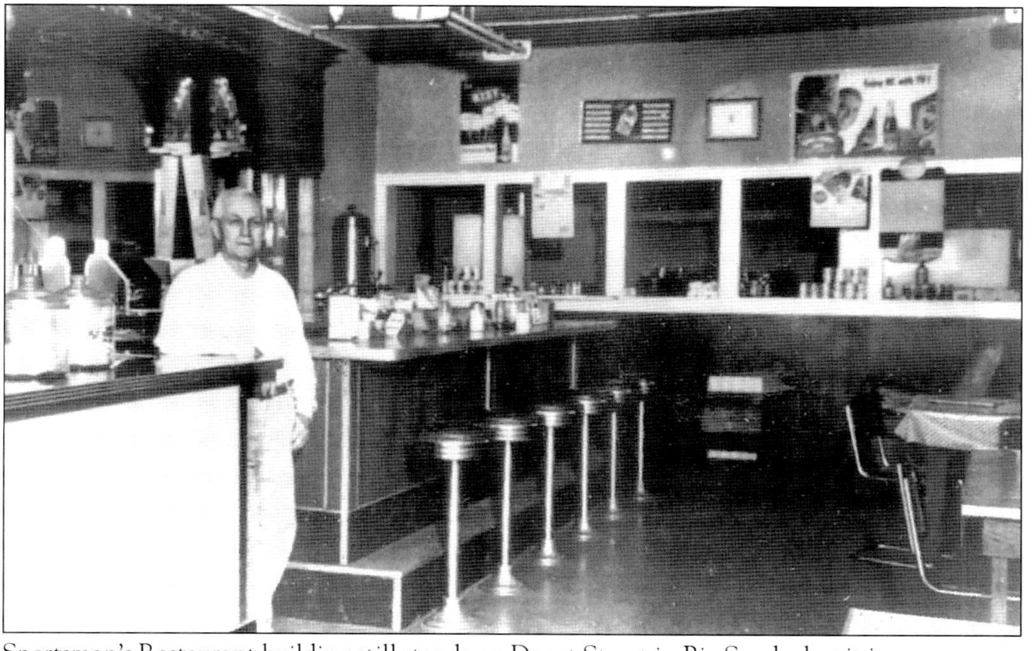

Sportsman's Restaurant building still stands on Depot Street in Big Sandy, but it is now vacant. In years gone by, there was a hotel upstairs. George Christopher, the owner, is pictured here, ready for business. Robert and Gretchen Jackson have recently purchased the building and are repairing it for a future business. (RD.)

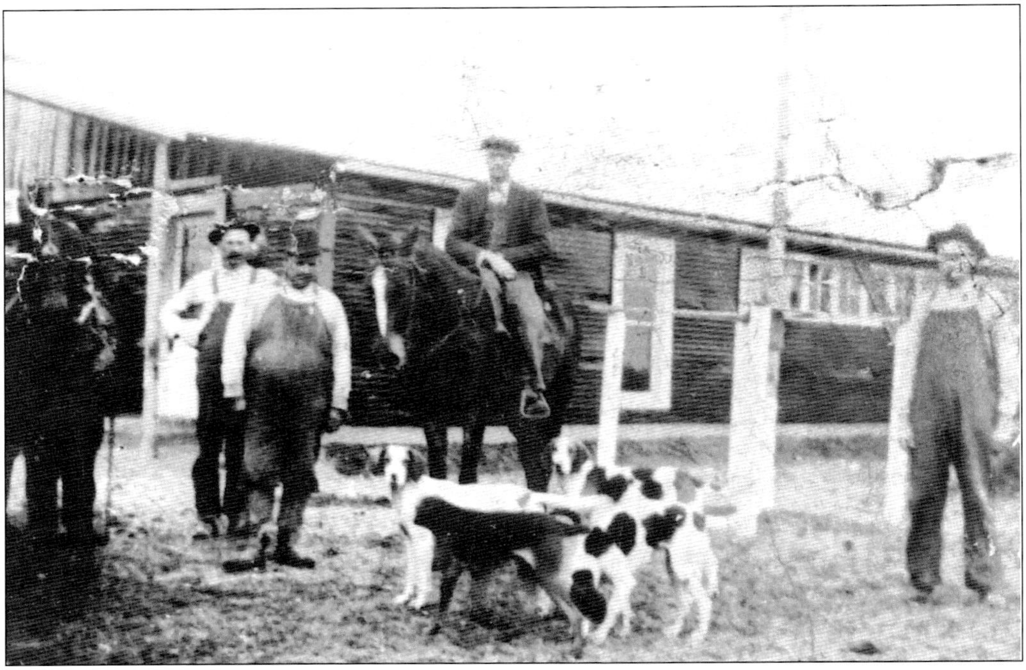

A group is gathered in front of the "Pencil Factory" about 1910 in Big Sandy. The Pencil Factory has a unique history, in that they never manufactured a pencil. People came into town, sold stock, and bought cedar lumber to make pencils, but no machinery was ever moved in and no one was ever hired. There is a Pencil Factory Road today. (BCPL.)

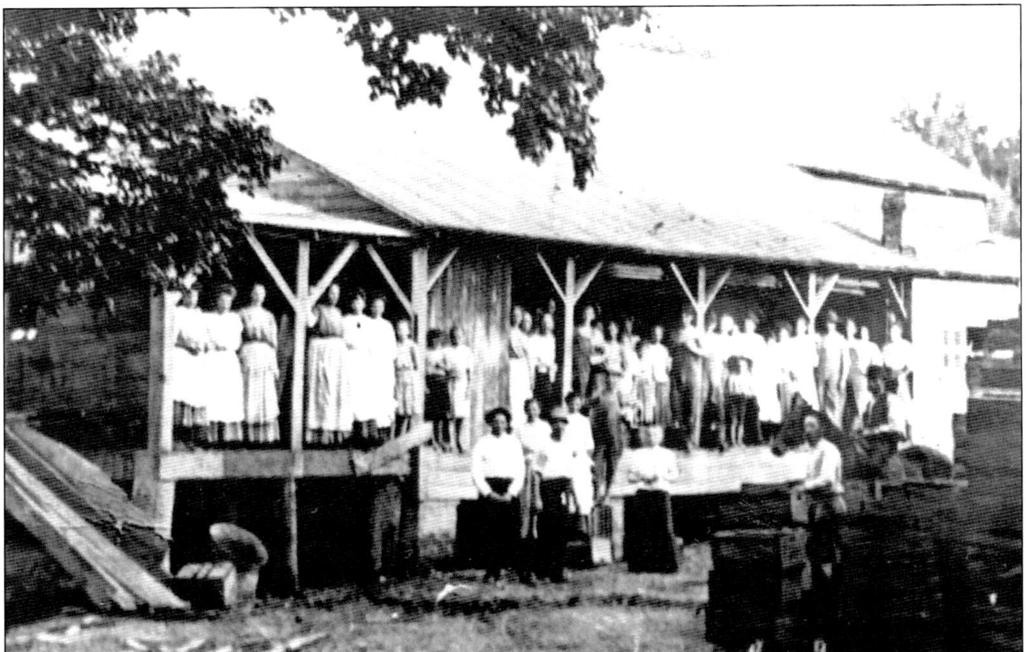

Workers are shown in front of the tomato canning factory at Big Sandy in the early 1900s. It was located west of downtown, near the railroad. (BCPL.)

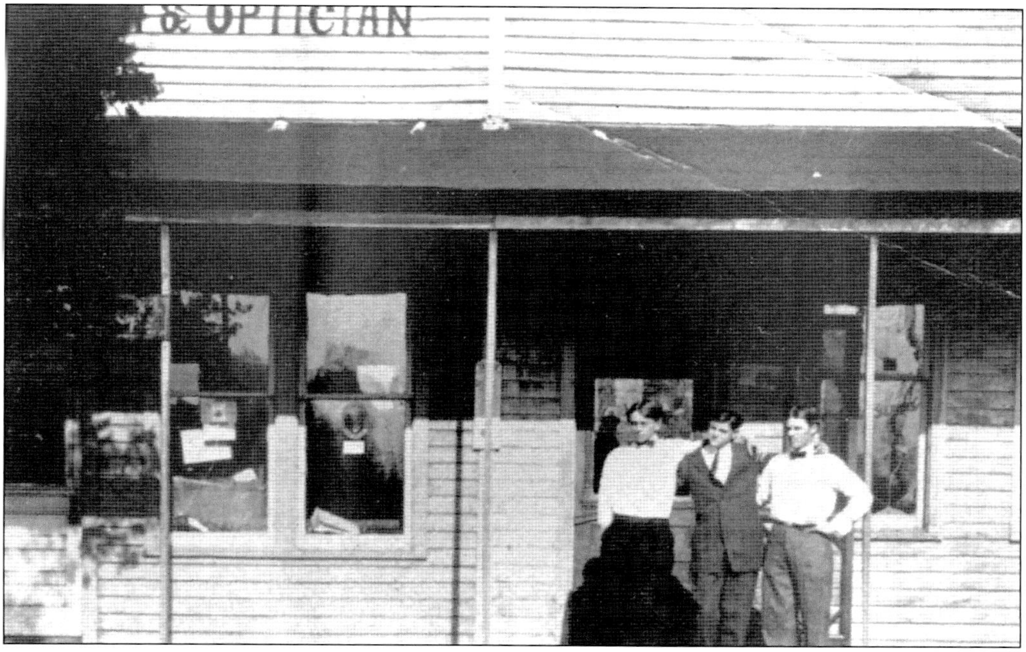

Three dressed-up (unidentified) young men pose in front of Akers Optical in Big Sandy. Akers Optical was just down the street from Caraway & Son's Store. Akers has long been out of business. (RD.)

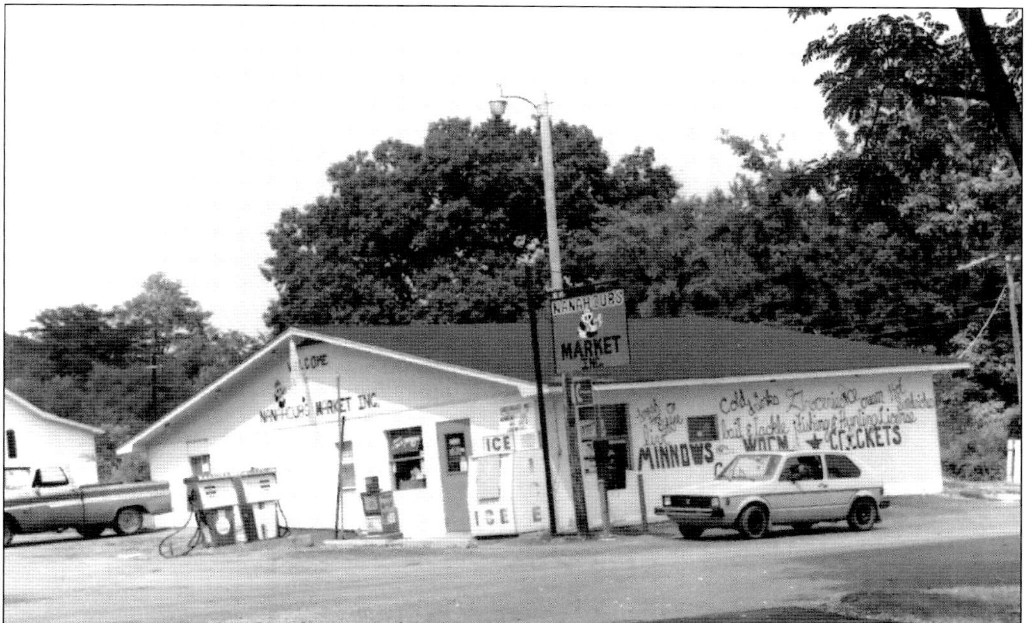

Nanahcub's Market Inc. at Eva started in the early 1960s. It has changed names several times. Darrel and Eurbie Buchanan changed the name from Crossroads Market to Nanahcub's Market, which is Buchanan spelled backwards. They sold it to Mike Jones, and he renamed it Mike's Market. (JD.)

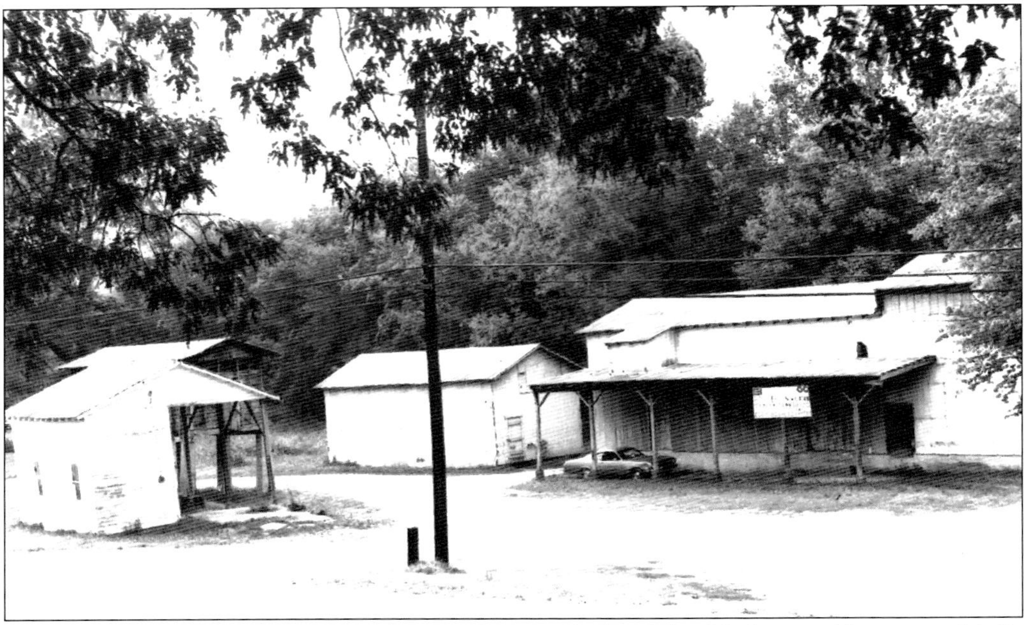

There were several cotton gins in the Camden area before John Hudson and his sisters Molly and Ida started one in what is now the Old Depot area of Camden. John died in 1854 when he fell off a wagon while unloading cotton and broke his neck. Ida married Oscar Merrick, and their daughter Marie Loveall ran the gin for years. The gin closed in 1970. At present, Melton & Sons have rented the building for their insulation business. (JD.)

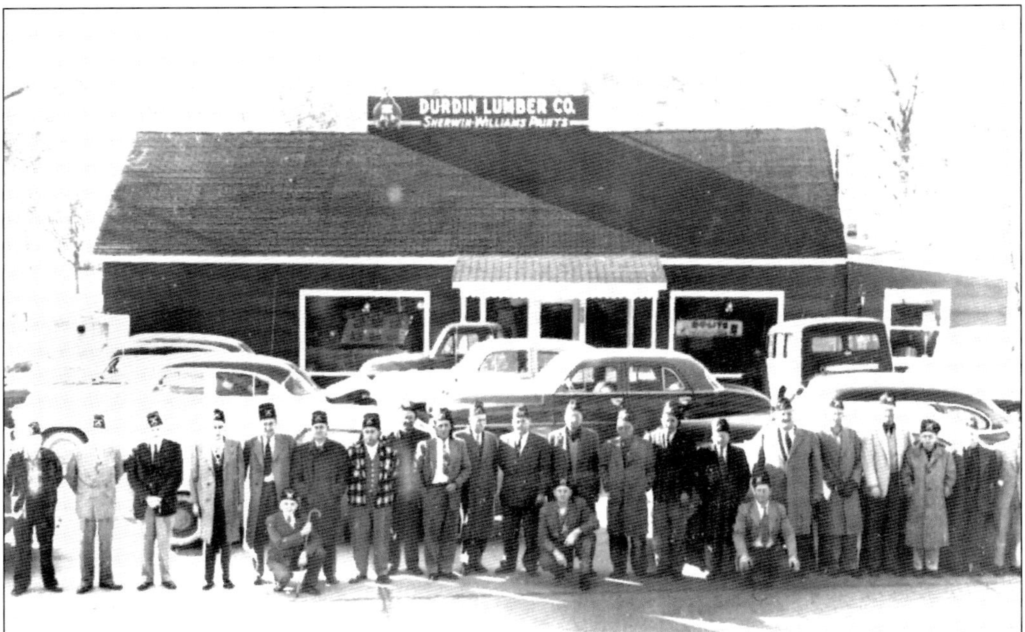

Durdin Lumber Company is pictured in the background as members of the Camden Shriners Club met to deliver Christmas baskets to needy families in December 1956. Durdin's Lumber Company burned in the late 1970s. (BCPL.)

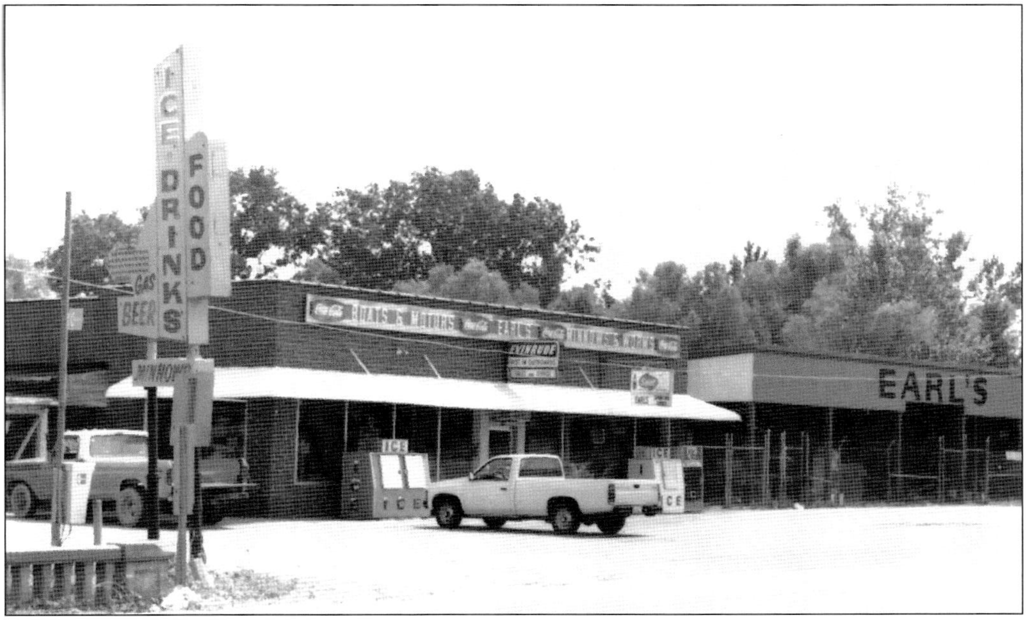

Earl Thompson owned Earl's Sporting Goods Store in Camden from about 1953 to 1970. It was located on West Main Street. He sold everything from Boy Scout uniforms to boats and motors; he also had a repair shop in the back. (JD.)

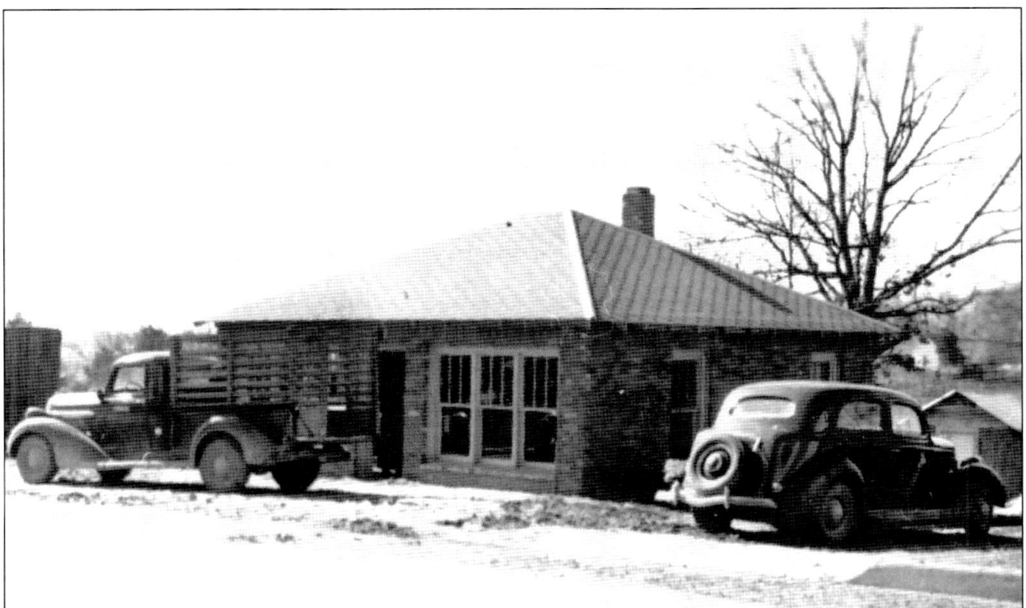

This unidentified bungalow is shown in Camden, Tennessee, during the fall of 1939. (BCPL.)

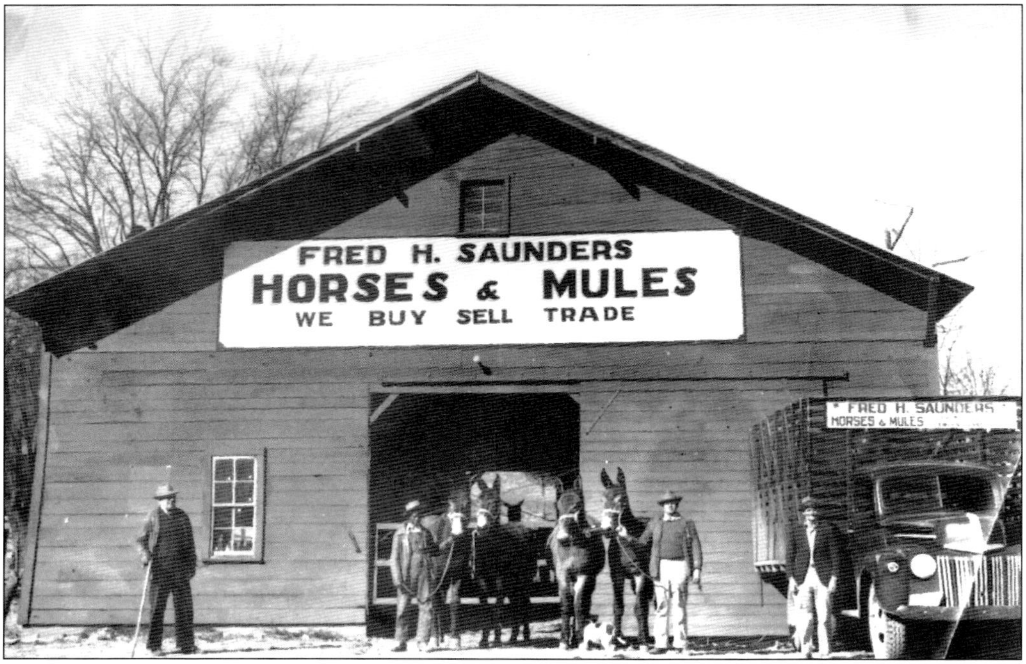

Horses and mules were bought, sold, and traded at Fred H. Saunders's mule barn in Camden. Pictured, from left to right, are Fred Saunders, James Turner, T.L. "Bunk" Floyd, and Willie Walker. This photo was made about 1943. (JD.)

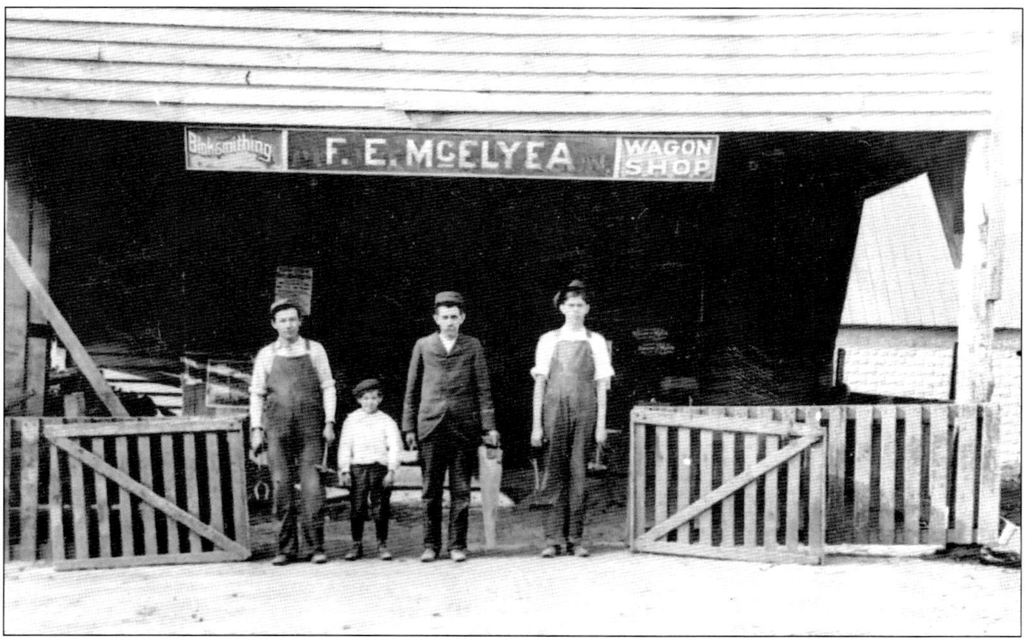

In November 1909, F.E. McElyea operated a blacksmith and wagon shop at 120 Forrest Avenue, where Union Planters Bank (soon to be known as Region's Bank) is now located in Camden. (BCPL.)

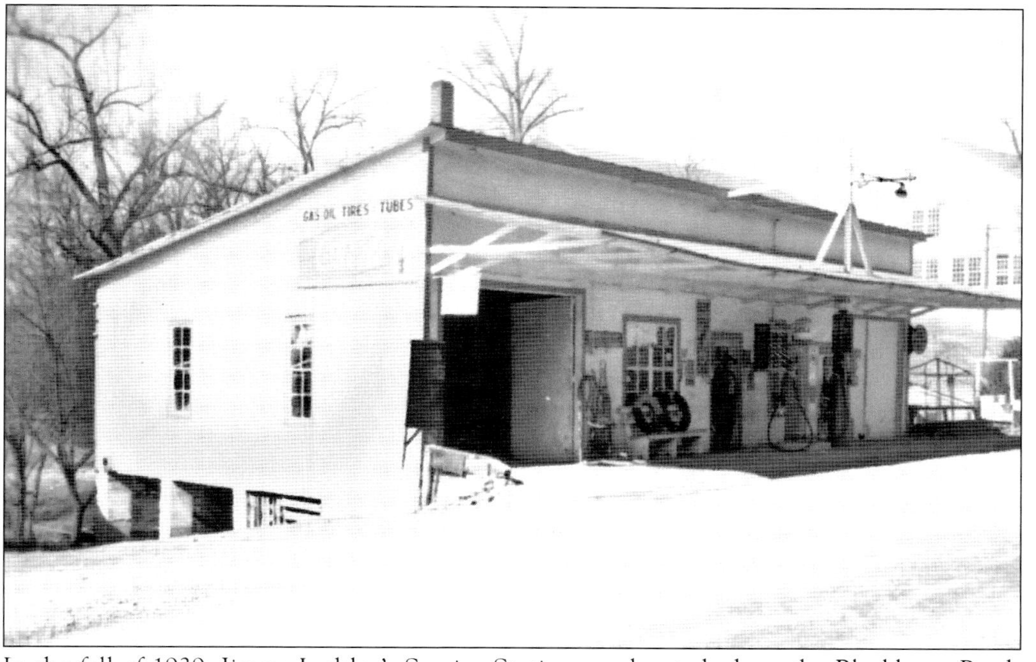

In the fall of 1939, Jimmy Lashlee's Service Station was located where the Blackberry Patch Restaurant is now located on Forrest Avenue in Camden. In the background can be seen the old Camden High School building, which still stands. (BCPL.)

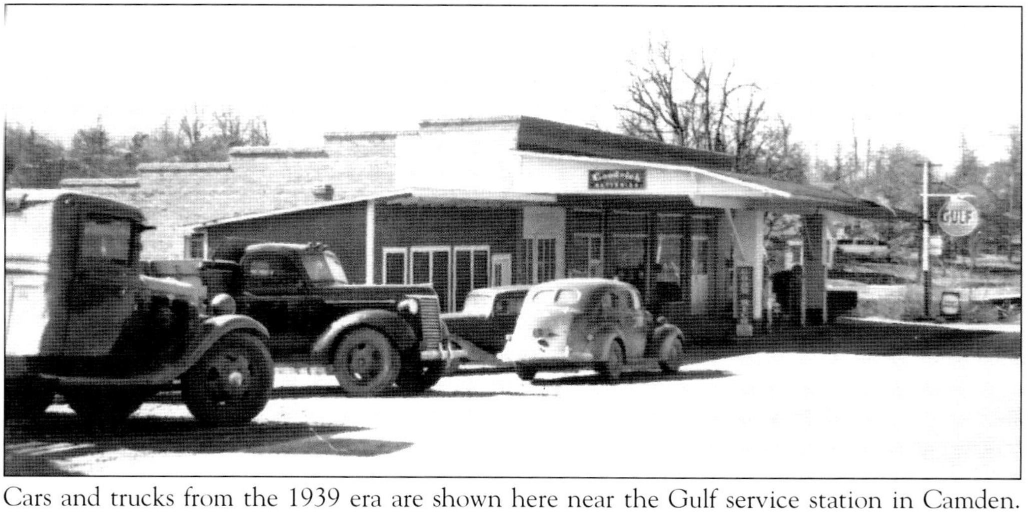

Cars and trucks from the 1939 era are shown here near the Gulf service station in Camden. They sold Goodrich tires. (BCPL.)

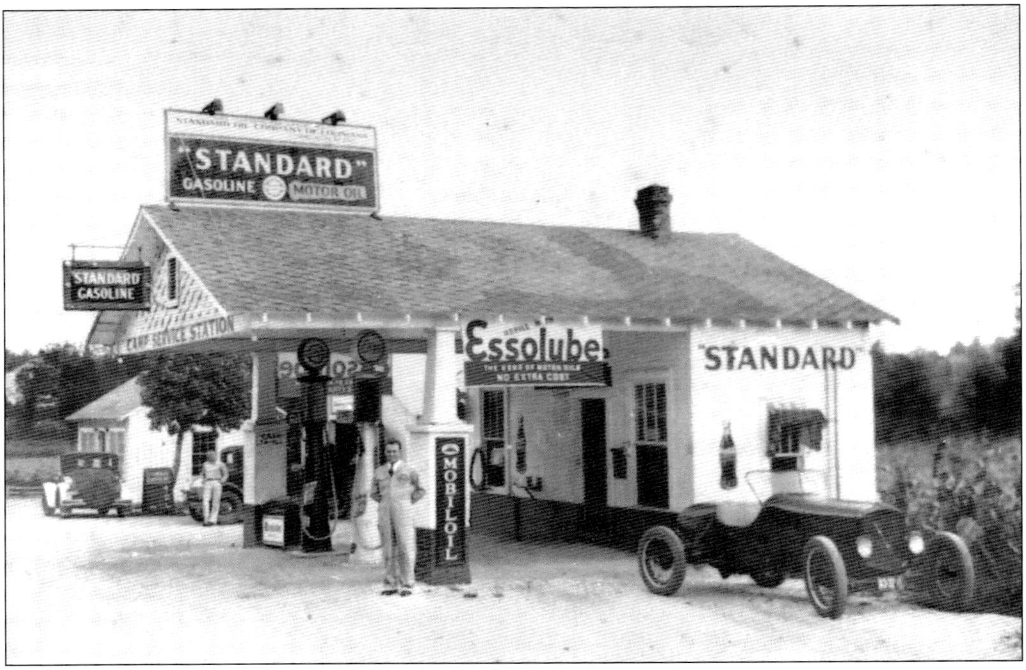

Frazier Brewer is shown in the foreground of Camp Service Station, Garage and Café in the early 1930s. (BCPL.)

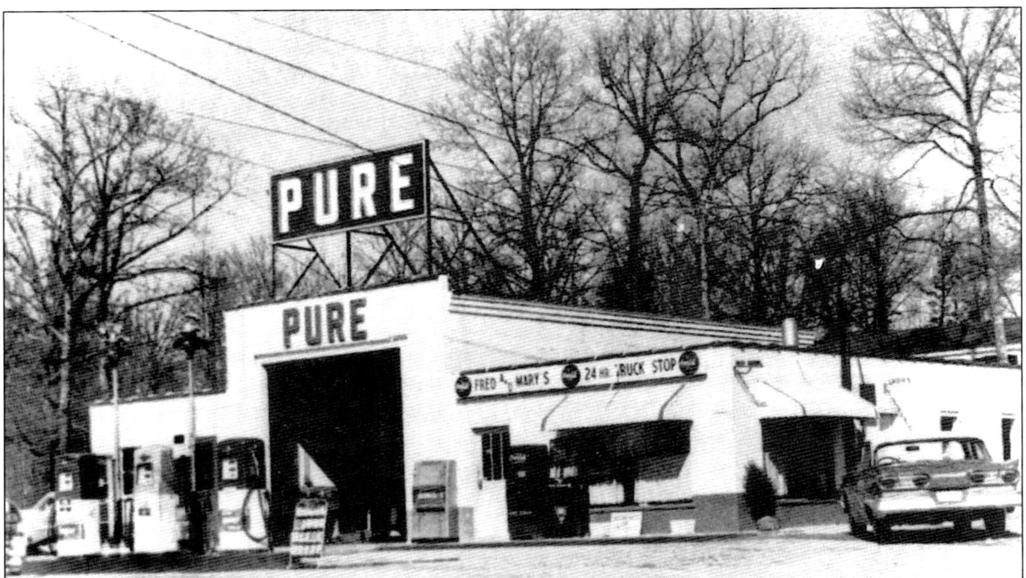

Highway 70 West was the location of Fred and Mary Douglas's Truck Stop in Camden. (BCPL.)

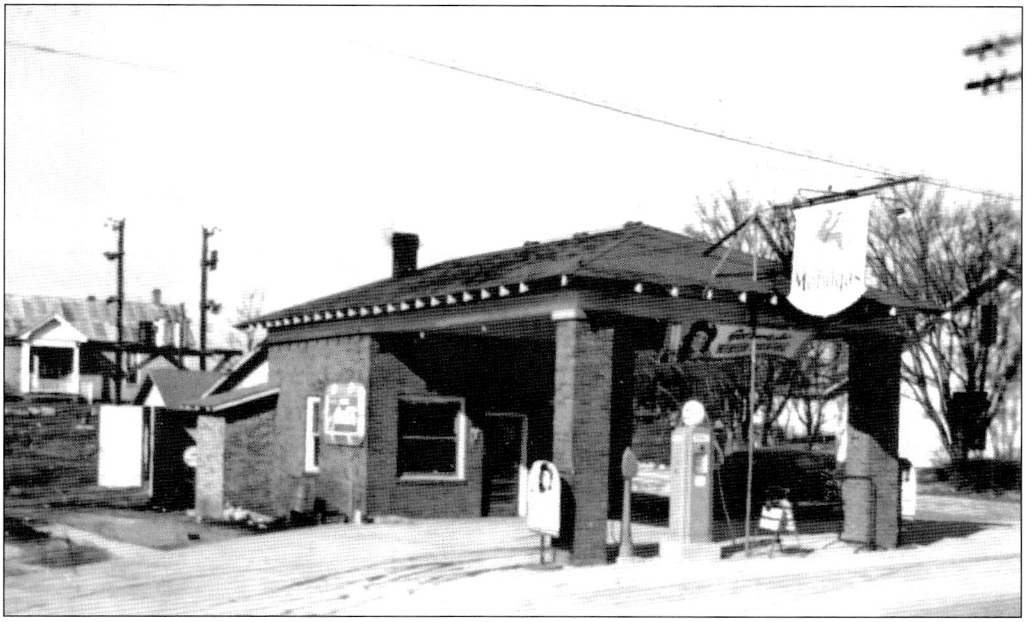

The 81 Service Station and Bus Station was owned by E. Lynn McCullough and Hobert Bradley; Benton Bradley and Kellom Bradley operated it. The photo was made in the fall of 1939. (BCPL.)

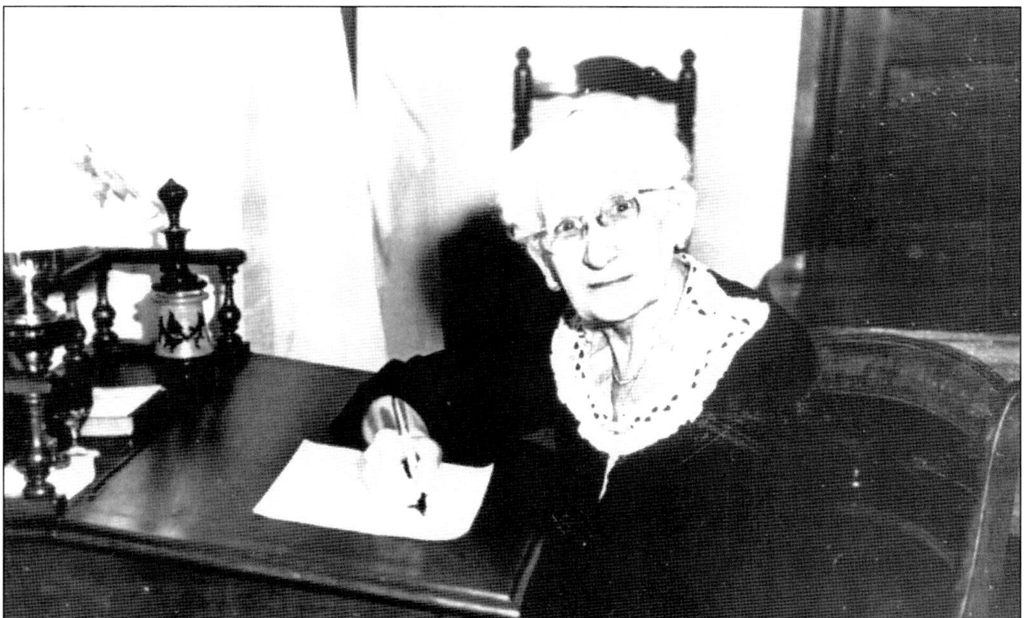

William Priestly Caraway died in 1903 at the age of 32, leaving his wife, Luna (Hawley) Caraway (1873–1962), with two small children and expecting their third child. Her father-in-law, William (Buck) Caraway, helped her start a photography studio in Big Sandy. She later moved her shop next to the Methodist church. She was a lady ahead of her time; she produced high-quality photographs and even wrote poetry. (RD.)

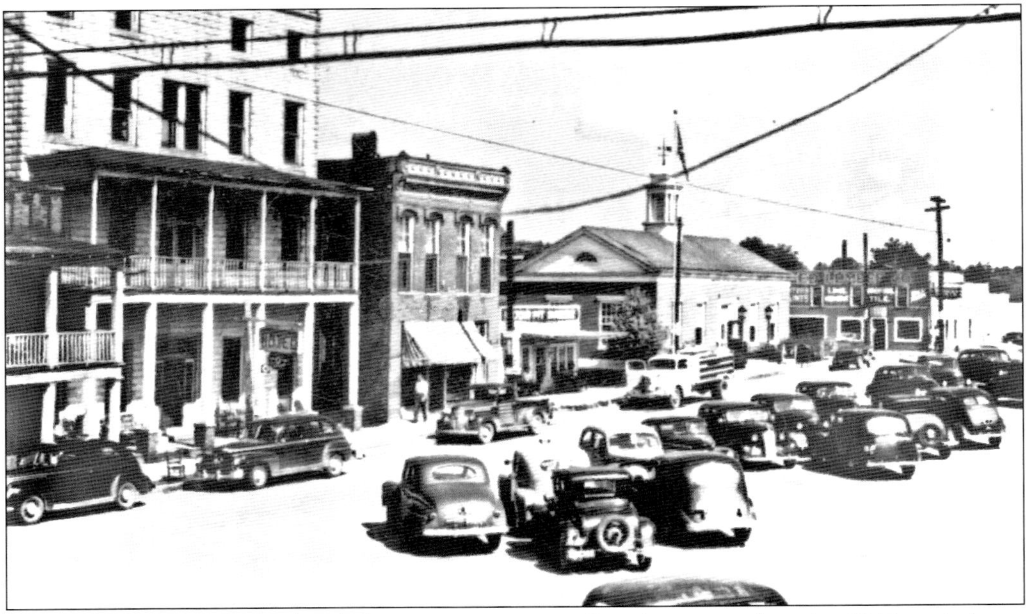

This view of the west side of the court square in Camden was taken in 1946 and shows the Melton Hotel, Melton's Café, and the post office, along with numerous cars of that time. (BCPL.)

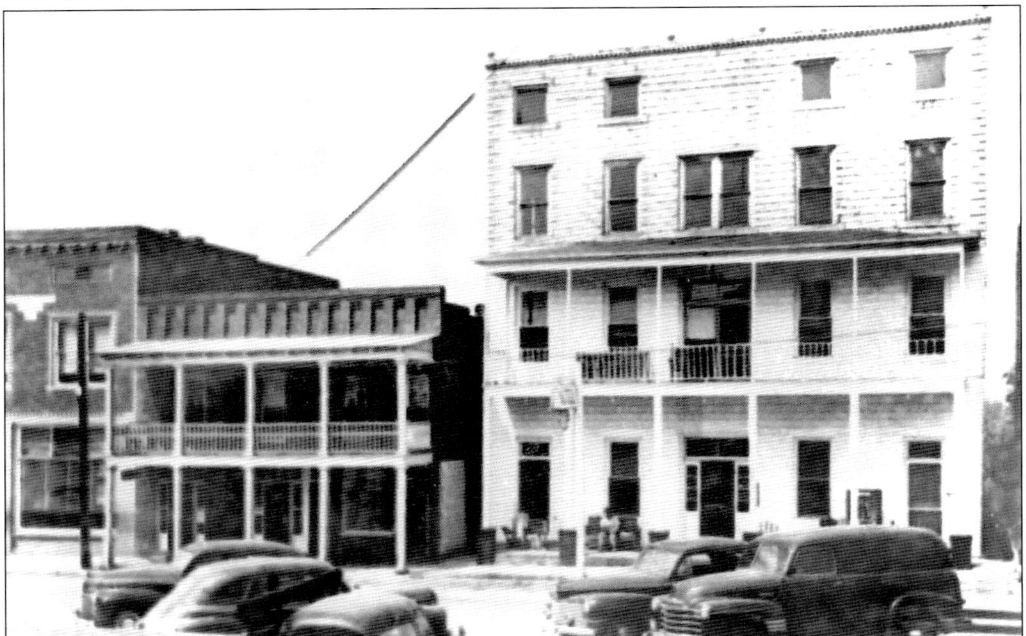

The building on the left was restaurant owned and operated by S.W. "Scaley" Lockhart in the early 1930s. Later David B. and Elsie Pafford ran it and changed the name to Pafford's Café. The hotel was first known as Hotel Theo; it was built by Thomas and Gay Saunders and named after their daughter, Theo Saunders. It was later renamed the Palace Hotel, and in 1946, it was owned by Roy Melton and called the Melton Hotel. It was torn down about 1959. (BCPL.)

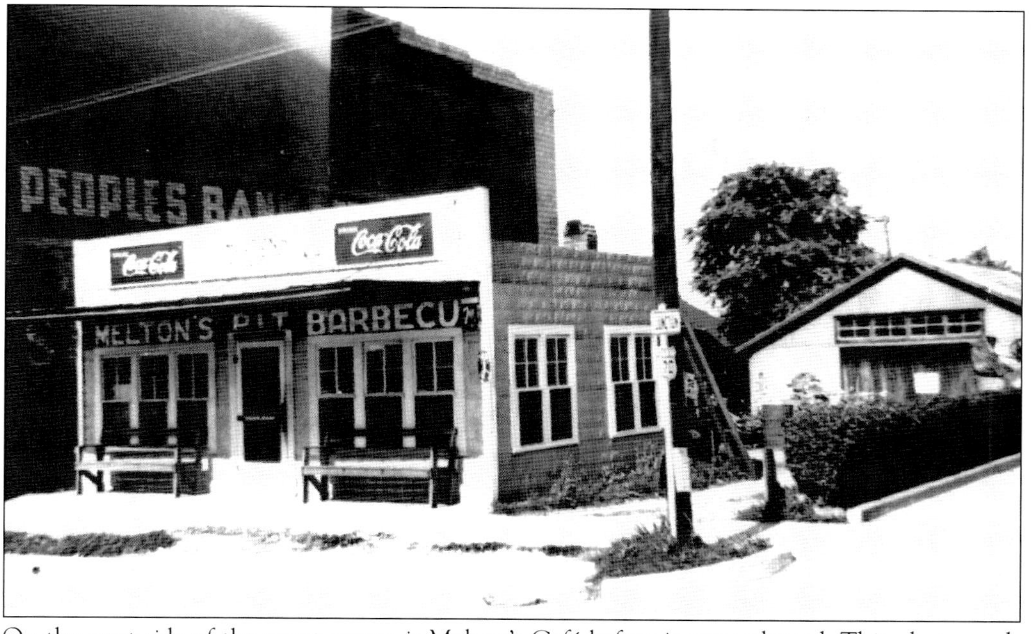

On the west side of the court square is Melton's Café before it was enlarged. This photograph was taken in about 1932, and in the background are a feed store and a grist mill. (BCPL.)

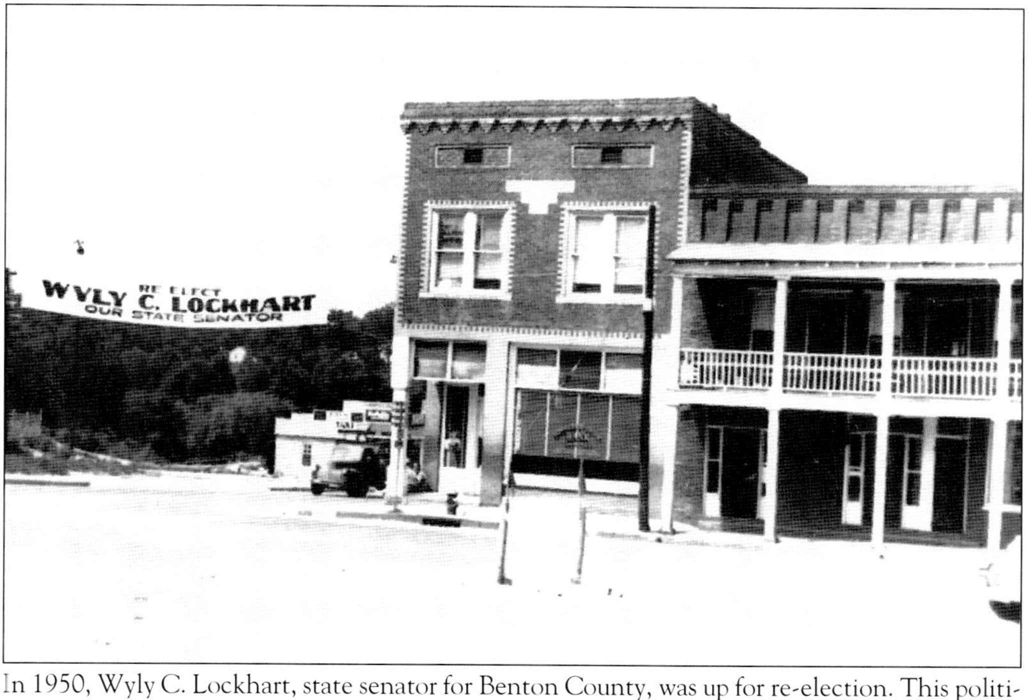

In 1950, Wyly C. Lockhart, state senator for Benton County, was up for re-election. This political banner was displayed on the west side of the court square in Camden. (BCPL.)

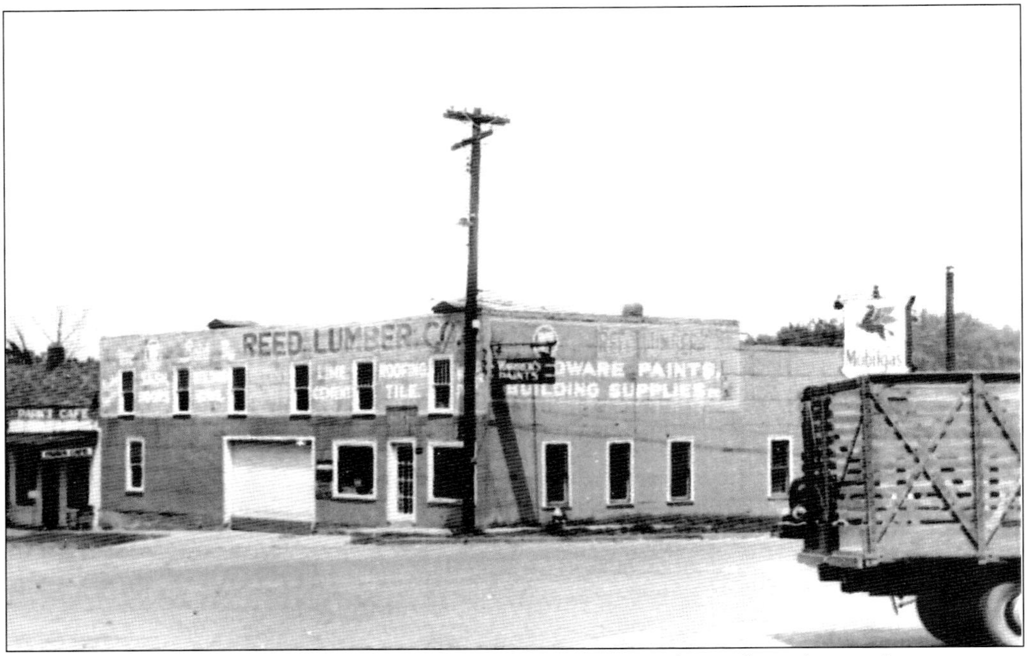

In about 1949–1950, Threadgill Reed Lumber Company was located on the northwest corner of Camden. (BCPL.)

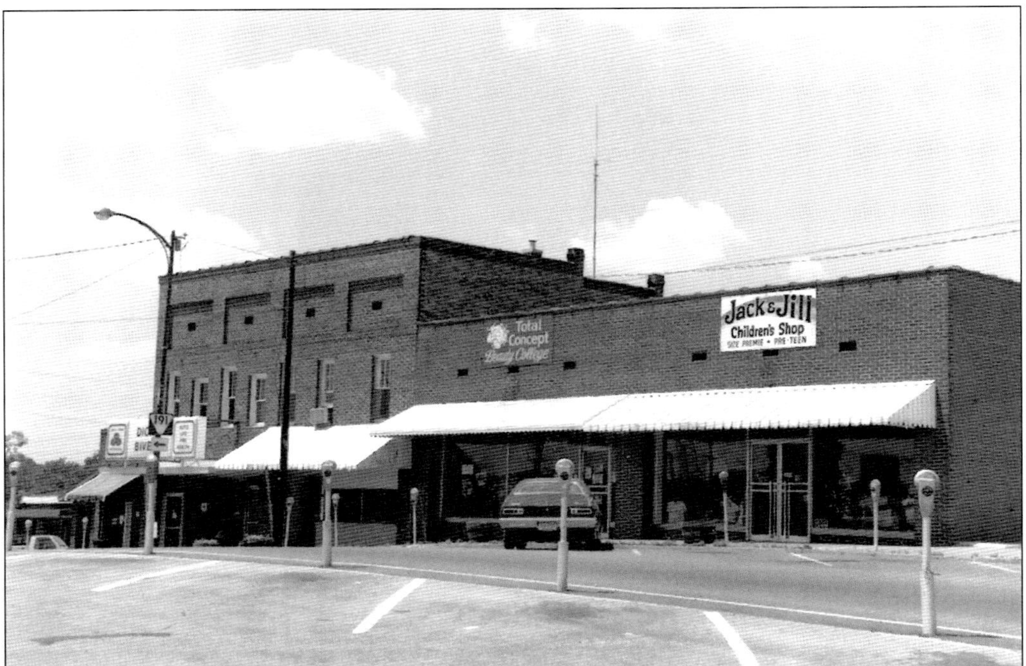

On the north side of the court square was Jack & Jill's Children's Shop, Total Concept Beauty College, and Dickie Bivins State Farm insurance company. (BCPL.)

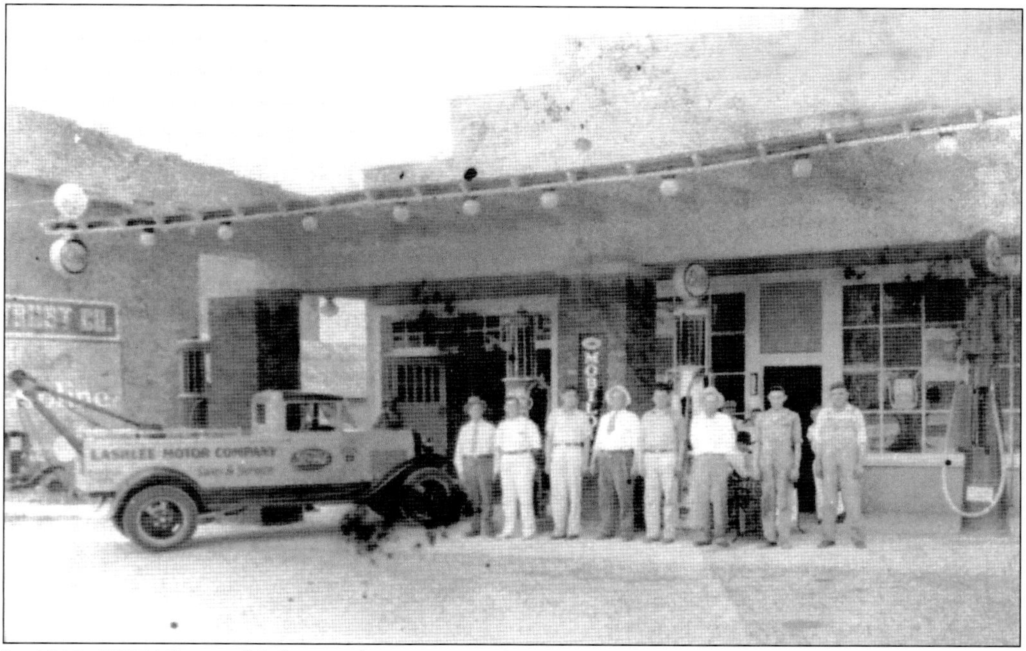

In 1929, W.F. Plant sold the northwest corner lot on the square to O.P. Lashlee. Then Lashlee, J.S. Barnes, and G.B. Holladay purchased the adjacent lot. This business was later leased to S.L. Bawcum, who had a Ford Dealership there. Still later, the Lashlee heirs sold the property to the government, and the current post office was erected there in 1937. O.P. Lashlee is the first man on the left. (BCPL.)

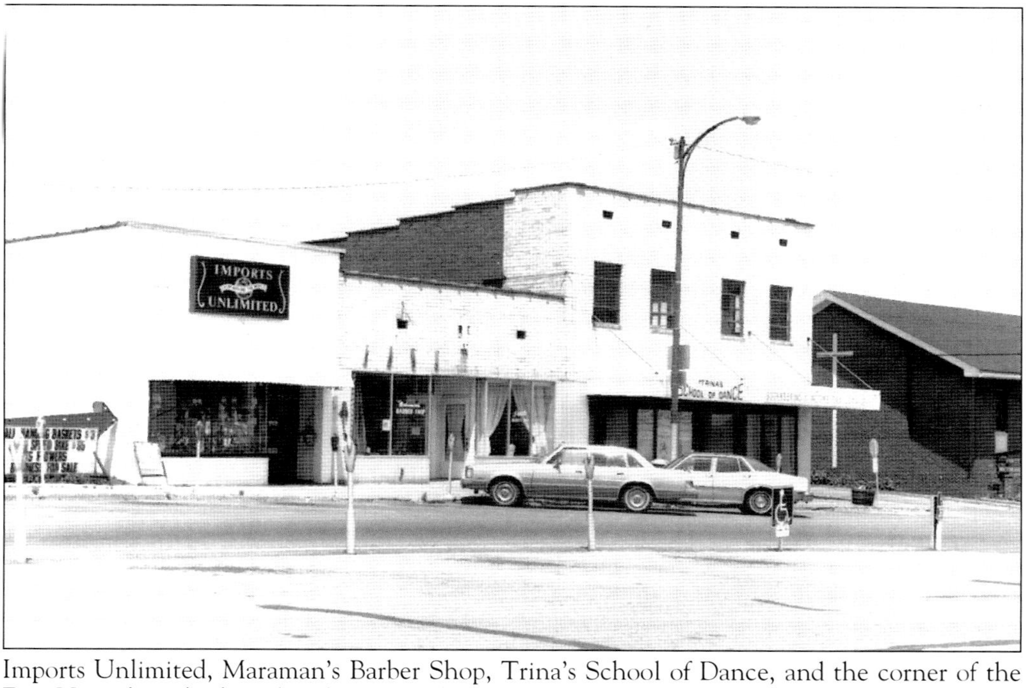

Imports Unlimited, Maraman's Barber Shop, Trina's School of Dance, and the corner of the First United Methodist Church are seen here on the north side of the court square. (BCPL.)

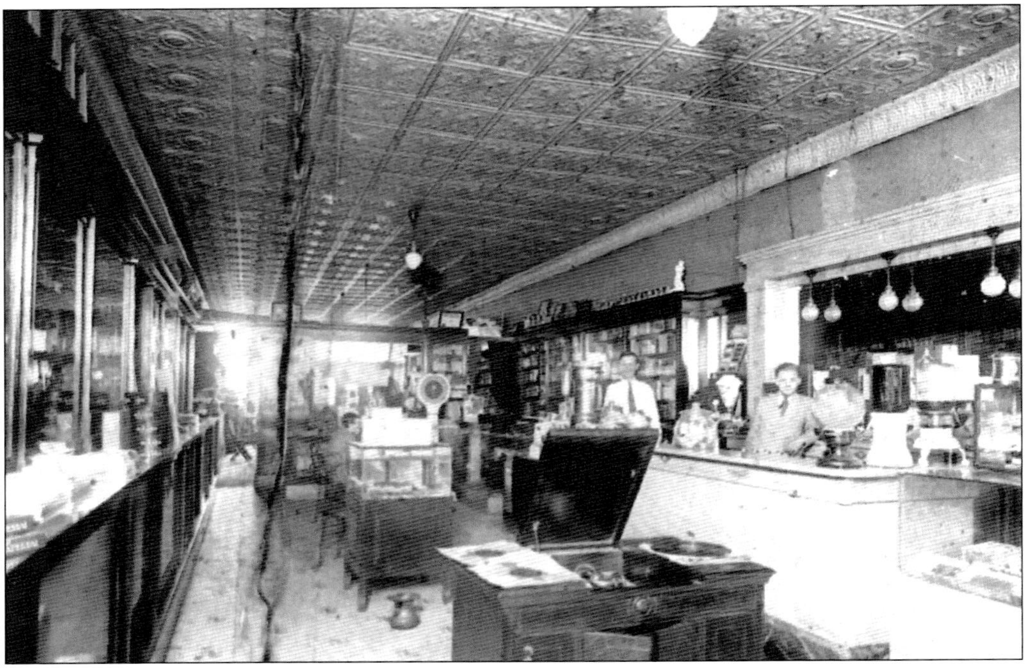

This photograph, taken inside Fry Drug Store on the south side of the court square about 1900, includes Mike Fry and one of his sons. (BCPL.)

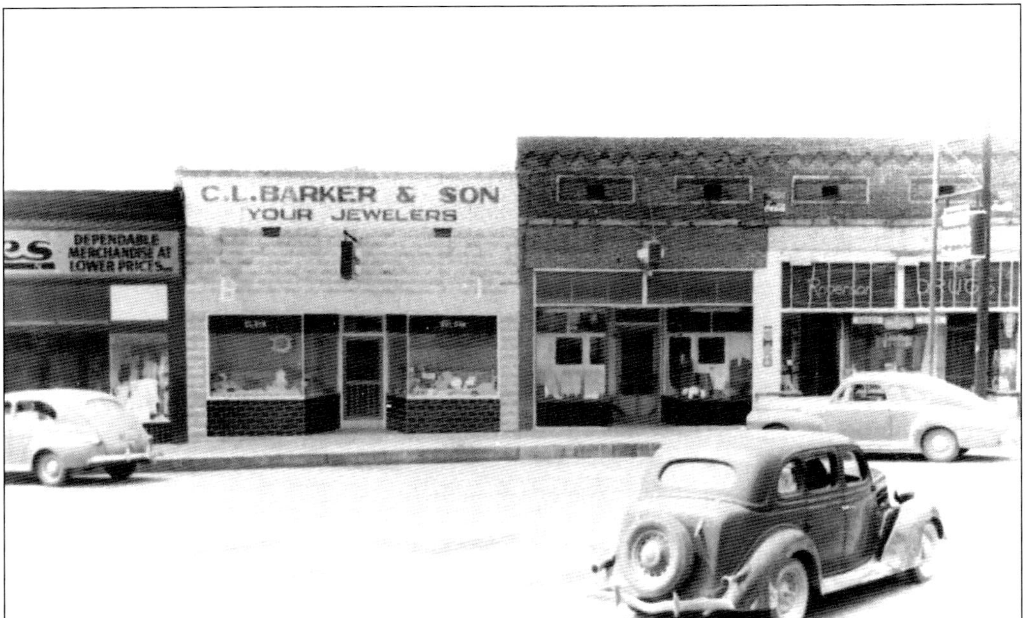

C.L. Barker & Son Jewelers was located on the south side of the court square about 1950. C.L Barker was also a taxidermist. (BCPL.)

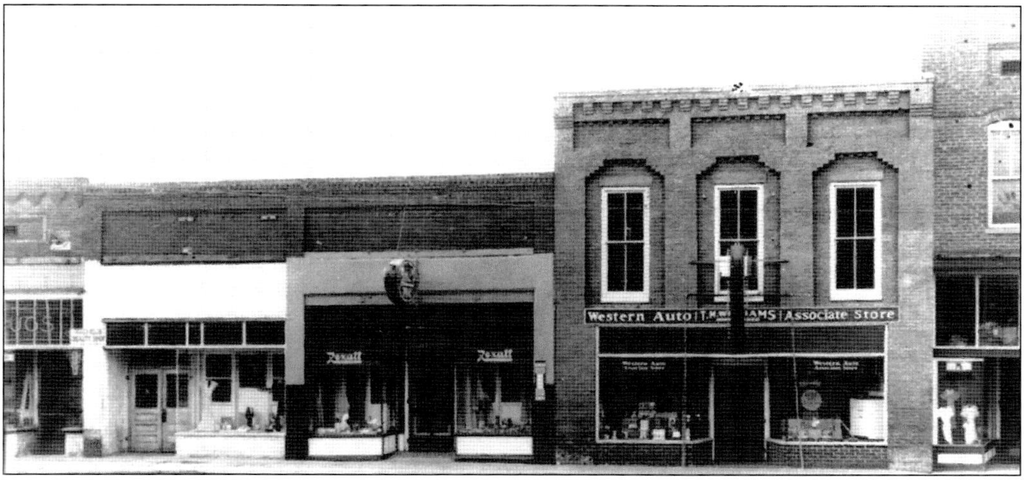

The Rexall Drug Store and Western Auto are shown here on the south side of the court square about 1950. (BCPL.)

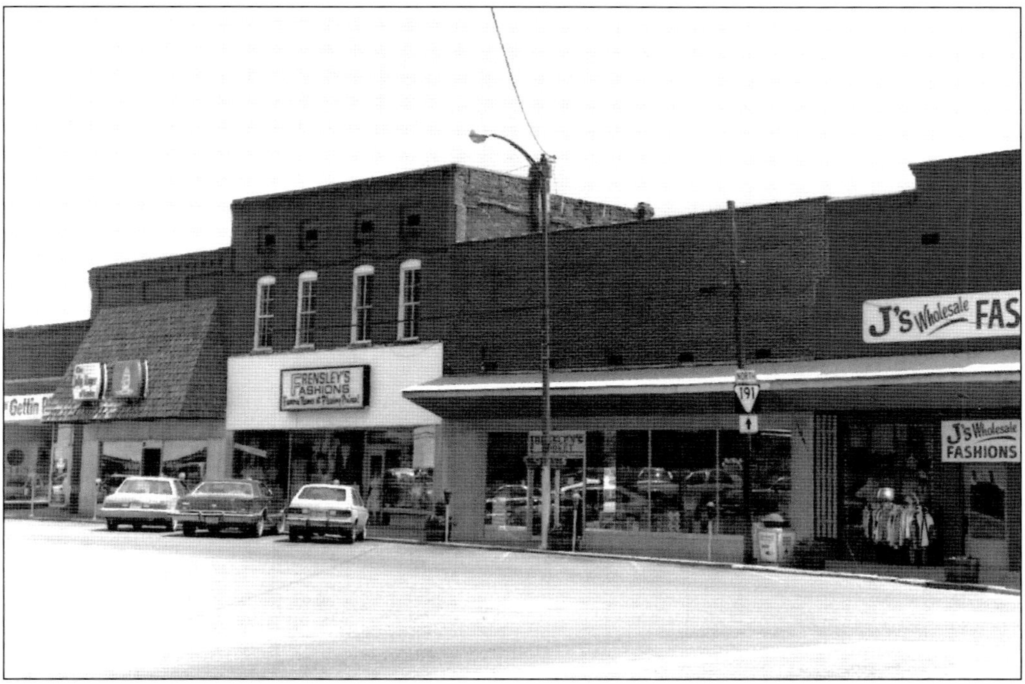

A.C. Frensley operated a women's clothing store on the south side of the court square. Frensley's and J.'s Wholesale Fashions are shown here. (JD.)

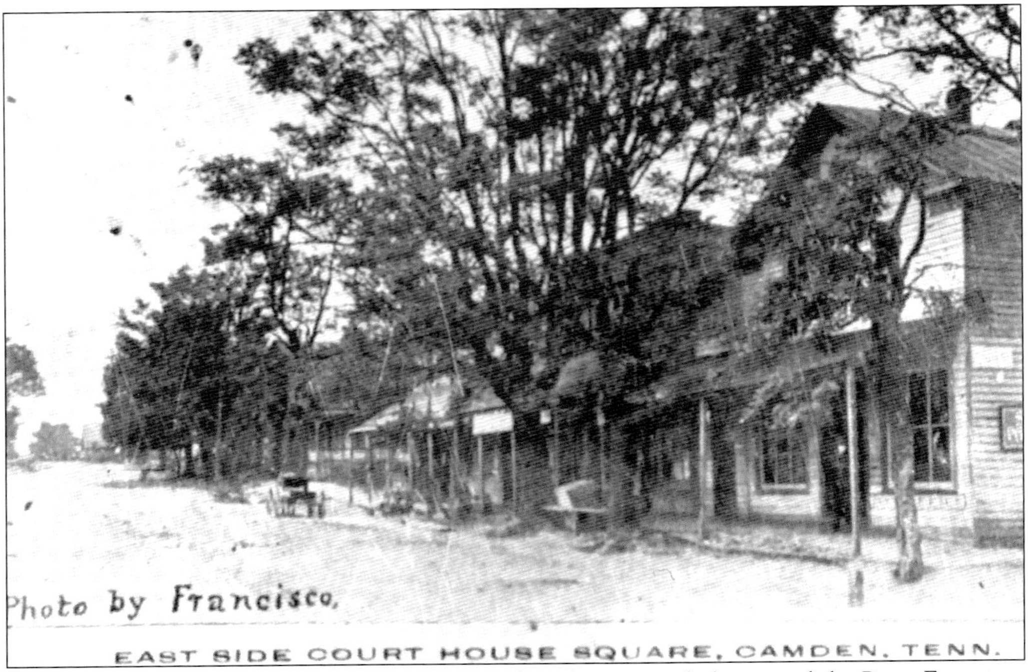

This is the east side of the court square in Camden; this original photograph by Peter Francisco is believed to have been taken prior to 1900. (BCPL.)

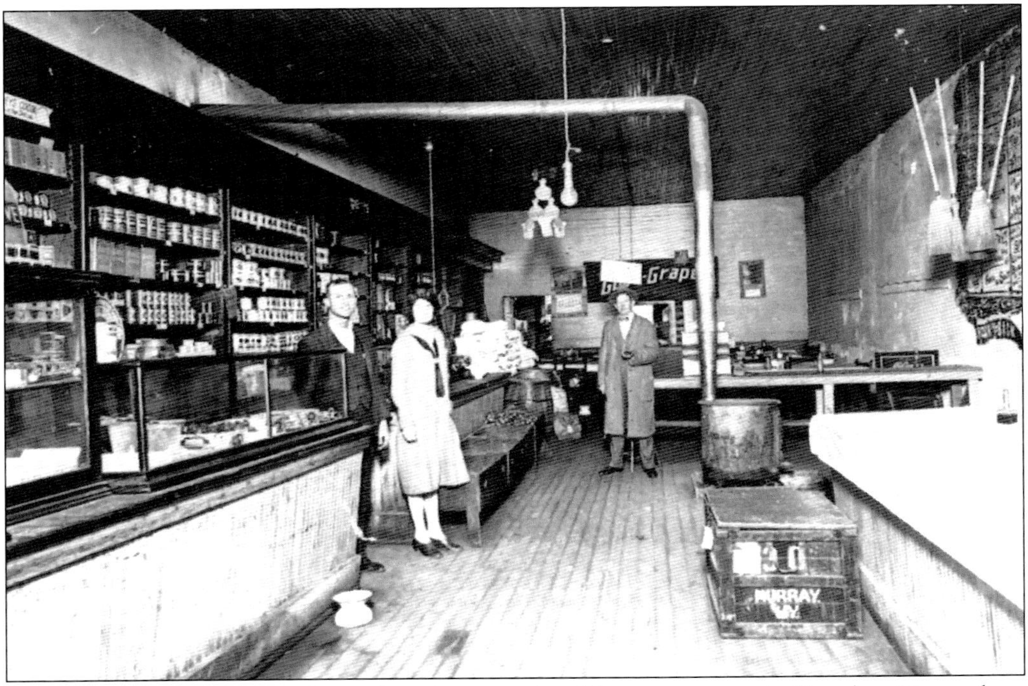

In 1926, Watson's Cafe was located on the east side of the court square in Camden. Pictured are Charlie Watson, his daughter Grey Watson Travis, and a salesman. Sandwiches were made on the white covered counter. Chandler's Furniture was later opened in this location. (BCPL.)

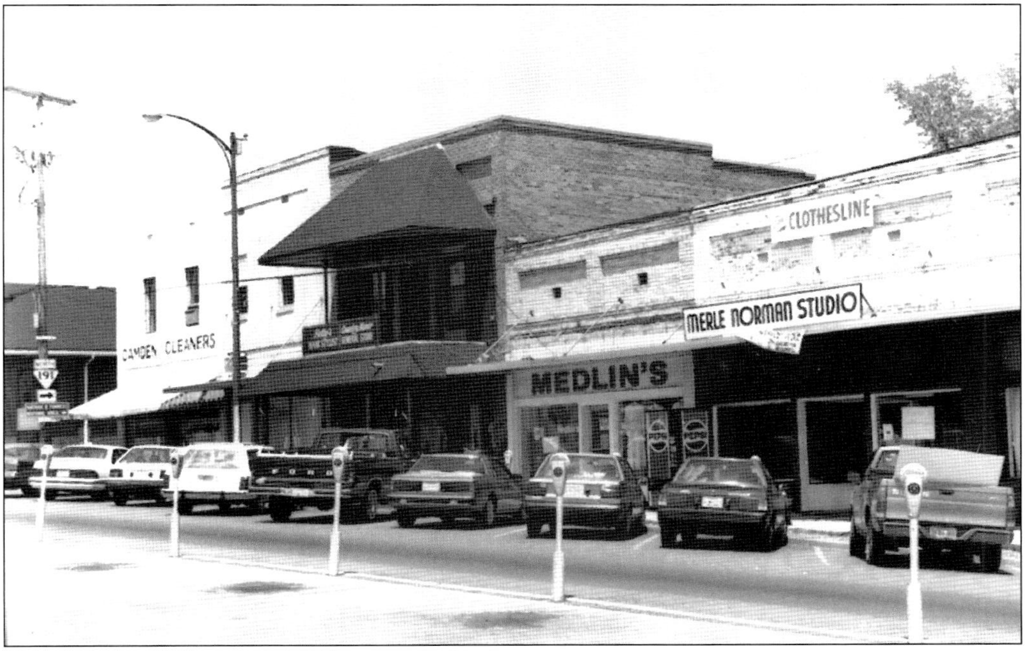

The Camden Cleaners, Medlins, and Merle Norman Studio were located on the east side of the court square. (JD.)

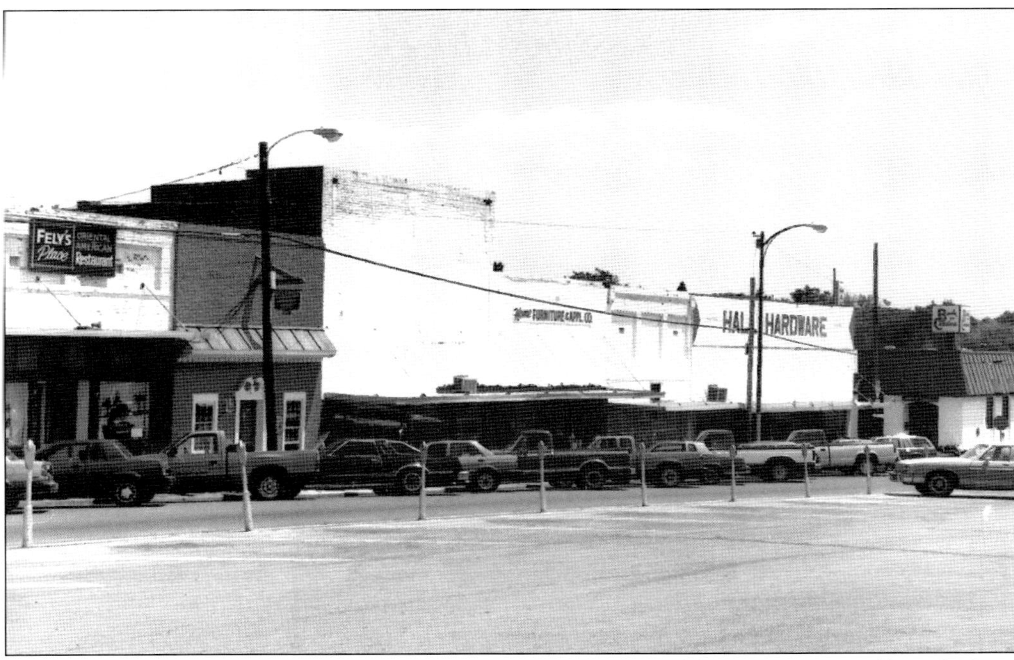

On the east side of the courthouse is Hall's Hardware, owned by Wayne L. Hall, and Home Furniture and Appliance. Next door was Fely's Place, featuring Oriental and American foods. It was owned by Felicita Hatley and located here from 1983 to 1990. Fely's is still in operation but at a different location.(BCPL.)

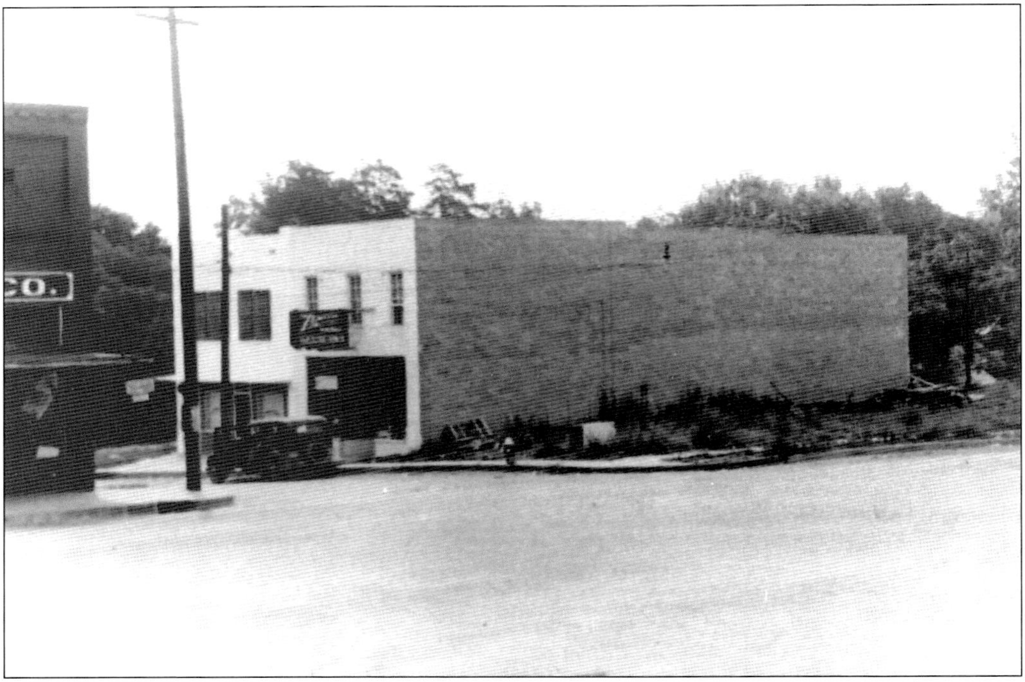

In the 1950s, this building stood on the southeast corner of the court square, where the present Bank of Camden is located. (BCPL.)

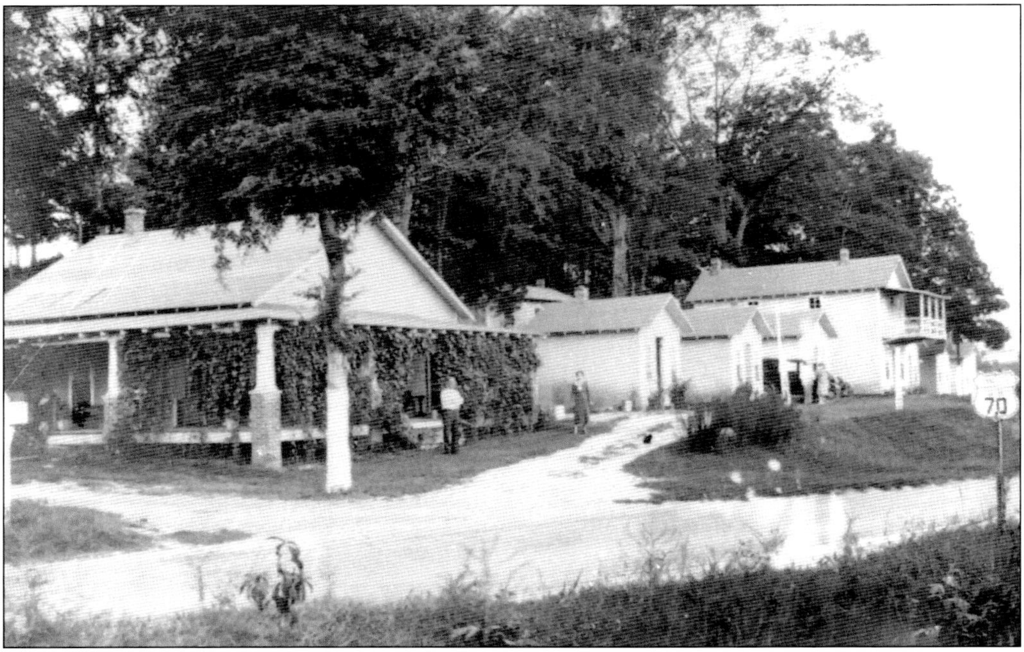

In the early 1930s, the Lockhart Cabins were a place of lodging in Camden. Several of the cabins are still in use today. At one time, Mr. and Mrs. Otis Brewer managed the cabins. In 1948, they were advertised as Lockhart's Motor Court. (BCPL.)

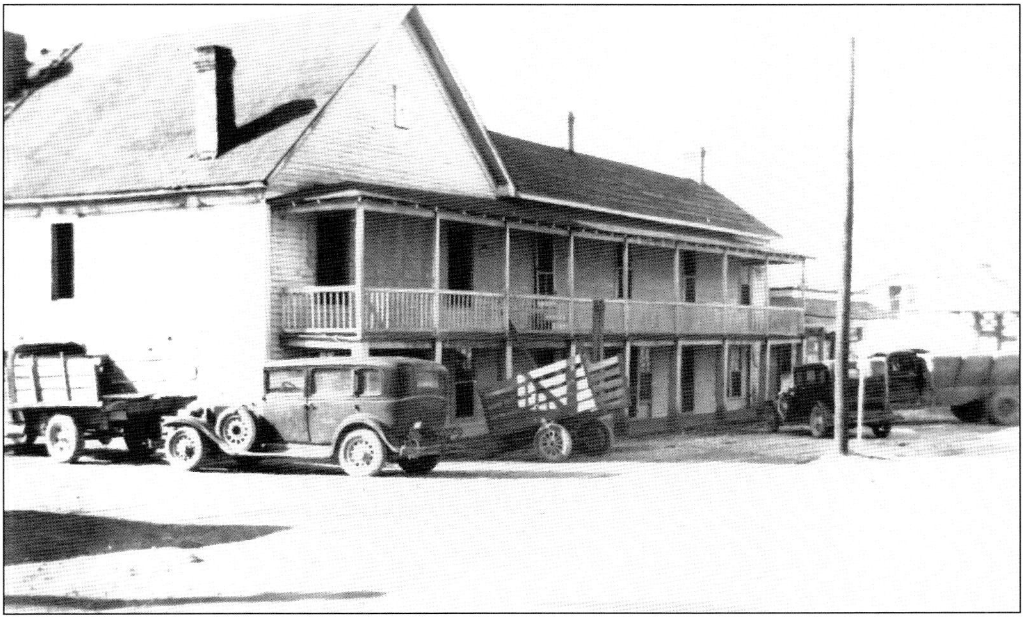

The Cain Hotel was probably run by Marcellus Cain earlier, as his daughter Ozie Lee Cain ran it for a while. Later it was bought by John and Mary Pafford, where they lived and ran a boarding house. (BCPL.)

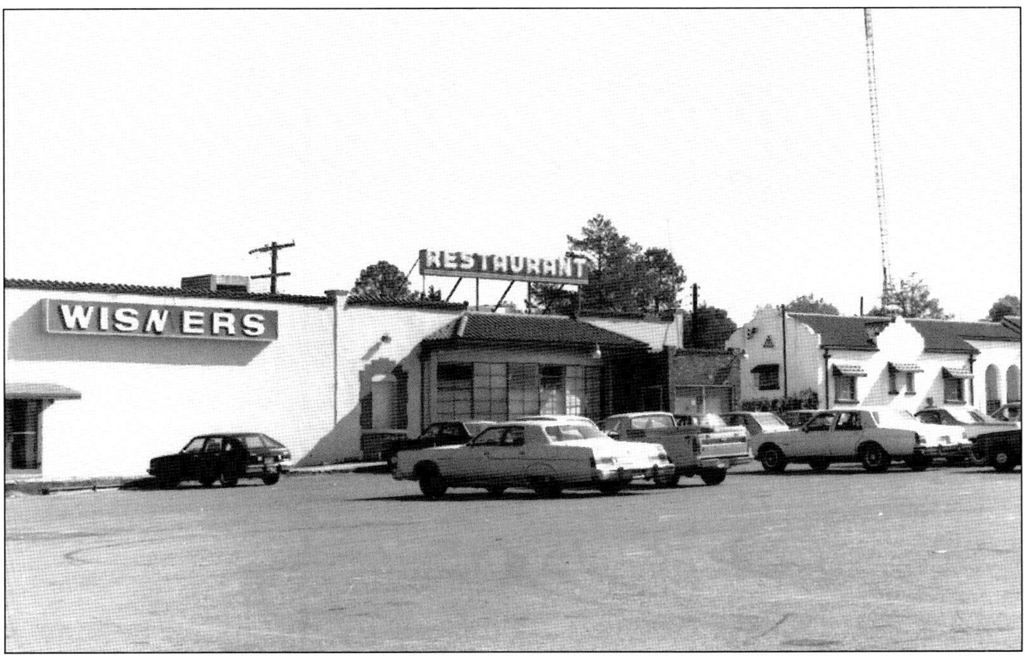

Wismer's Restaurant and Cabins was a place of lodging in Camden. The cabins are still in use as Budget Inn. (JD.)

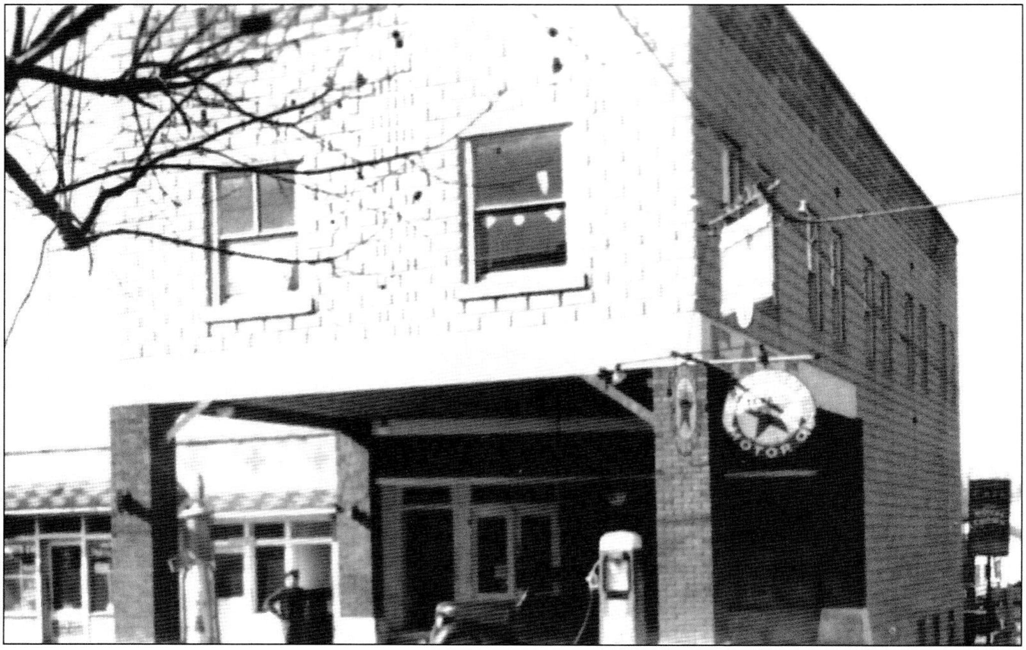

Blue Goose Cafe was a popular place in 1939. The Cain family ran it, and at one time, it was owned by Wyly C. Lockhart. (BCPL.)

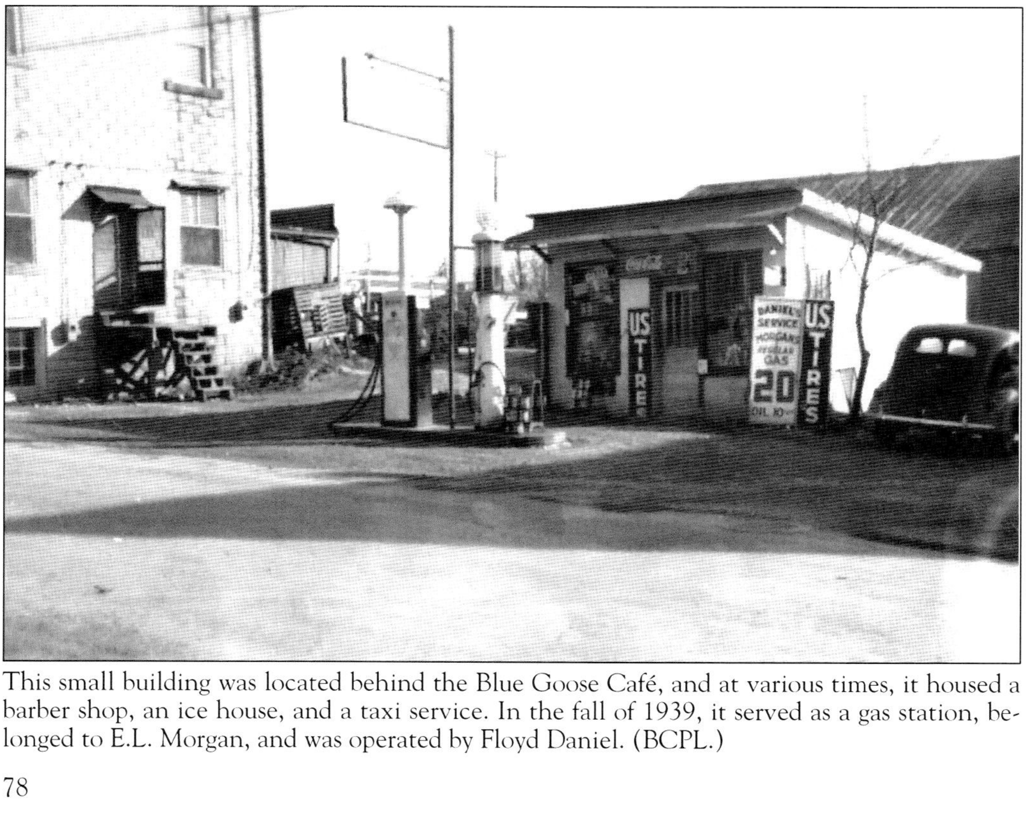

This small building was located behind the Blue Goose Café, and at various times, it housed a barber shop, an ice house, and a taxi service. In the fall of 1939, it served as a gas station, belonged to E.L. Morgan, and was operated by Floyd Daniel. (BCPL.)

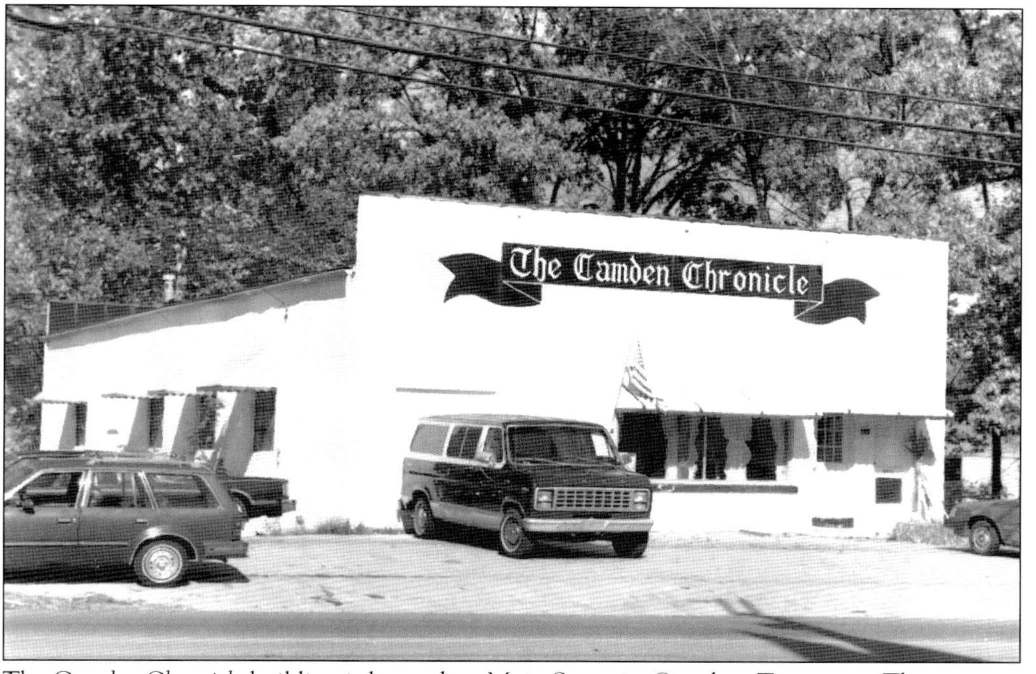

The *Camden Chronicle* building is located on Main Street in Camden, Tennessee. The newspaper was started by Charles Newton Travis with the first issue printed April 25, 1890. It was then known as *The Old Reliable*. It is now owned by Dennis and Lisa Richardson. (JD.)

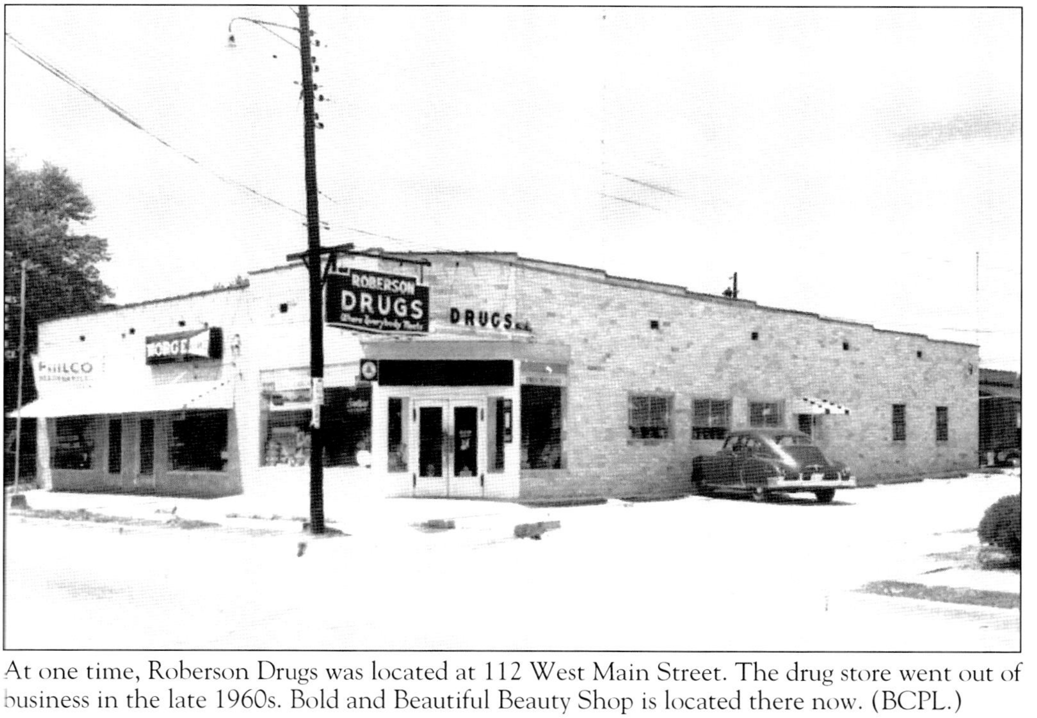

At one time, Roberson Drugs was located at 112 West Main Street. The drug store went out of business in the late 1960s. Bold and Beautiful Beauty Shop is located there now. (BCPL.)

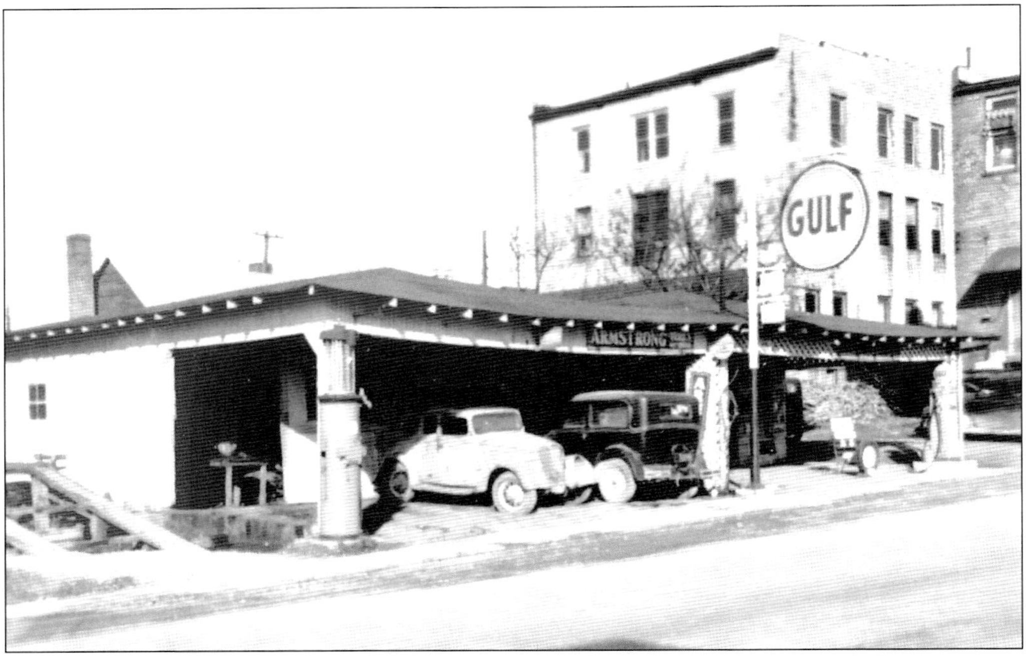

In 1946, Herbert Wiseman owned this Gulf Service Station. It was located on West Main Street between the Masonic Lodge and the bank. (BCPL.)

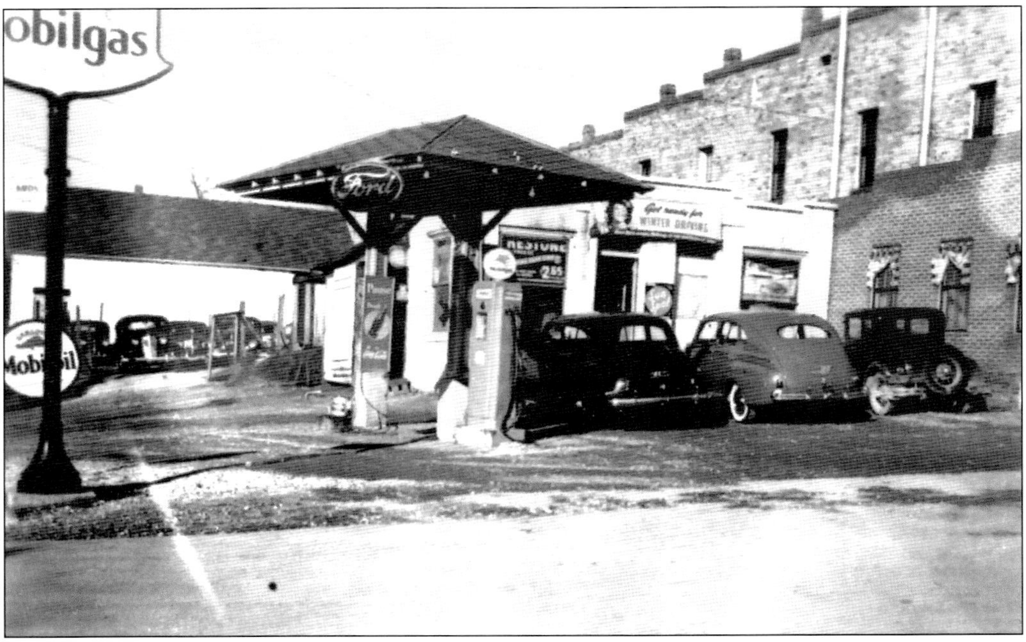

This taxi stand and service station, photographed in the fall of 1939, was located on the northwest corner of the court square. The station was run by Walter Marchbanks, and the taxi was driven by Andy Harris. (BCPL.)

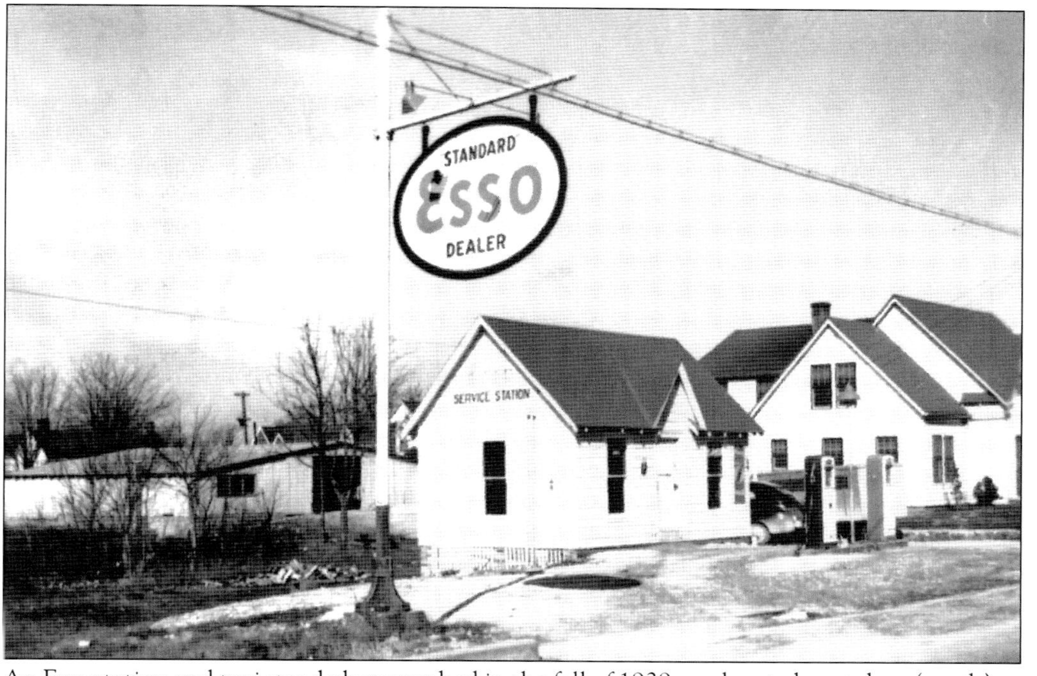

An Esso station and taxi stand photographed in the fall of 1939 was located next door (south) to the site of the present American Legion building, now the public defenders' office. (BCPL.)

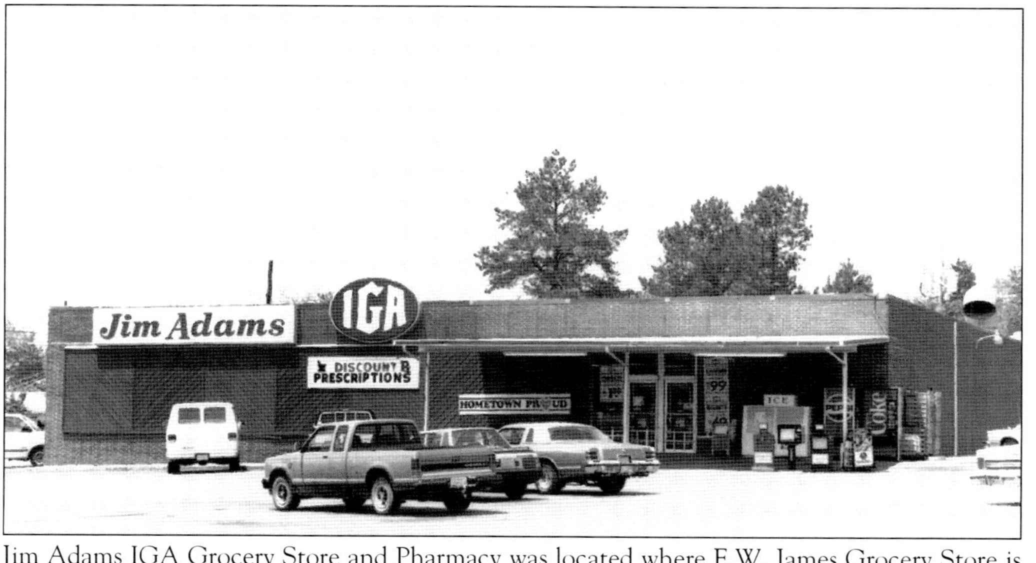

Jim Adams IGA Grocery Store and Pharmacy was located where E.W. James Grocery Store is now located on Main Street in Camden. (JD.)

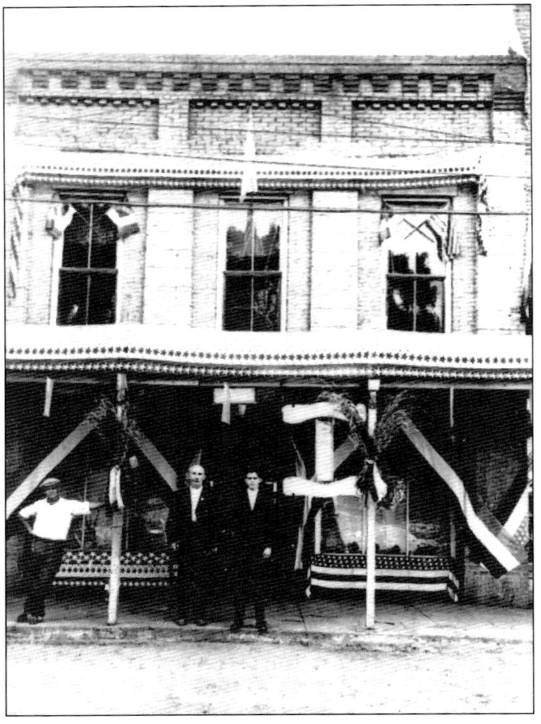

Democrat Thomas C. Rye was a great favorite for governor of Tennessee and was given a rousing reception on November 4, 1914, when his train coming from Paris to Nashville stopped in South Camden. Shown here is O.W. Lashlee's General Store decorated with bunting for Rye's visit. This was where Rye announced his candidacy. (BCPL.)

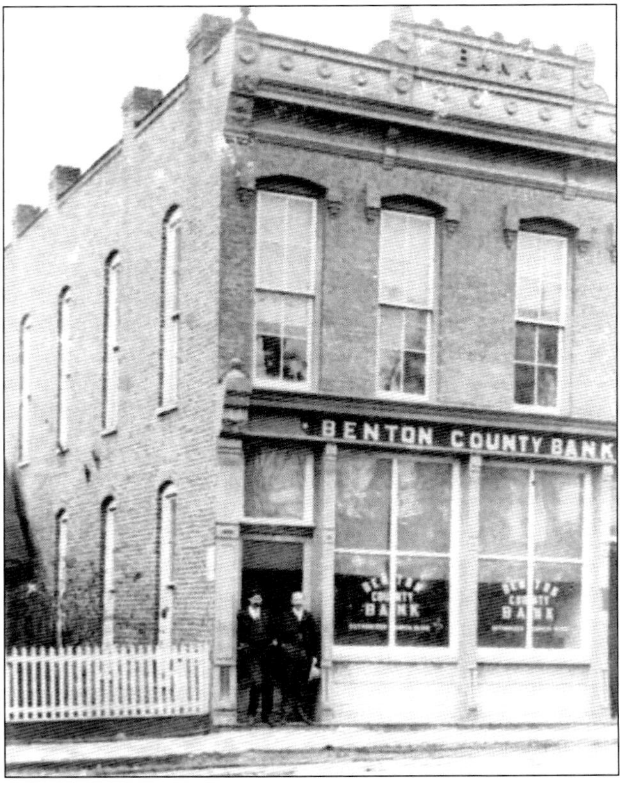

Benton County Bank was located on Forrest Avenue North, on the court square in Camden. This photograph was taken about 1900. (BCPL.)

Four

Government, Military, and Organizations

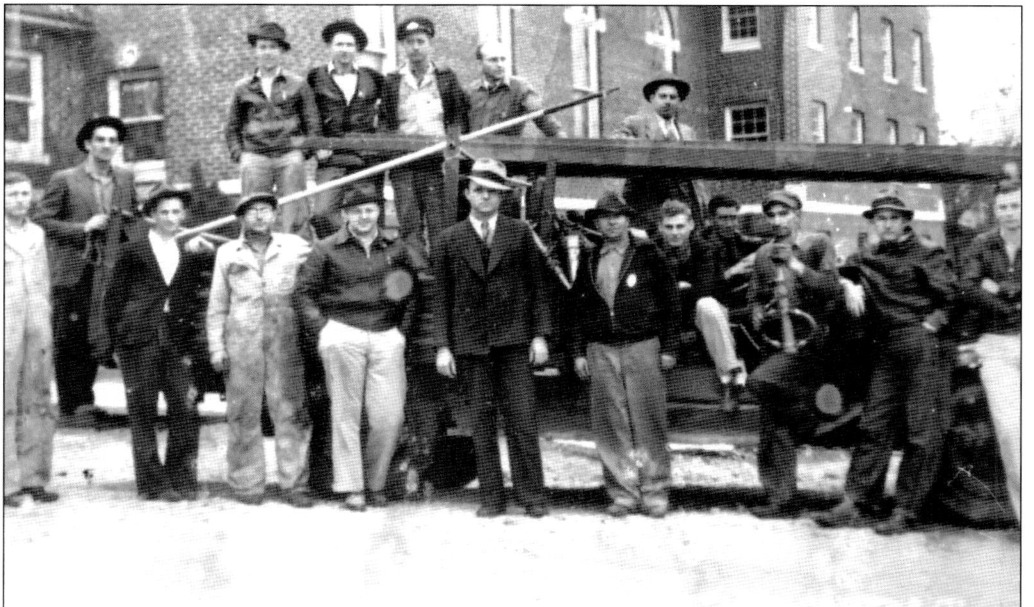

Morgan Sims built the fire truck used by the Camden Volunteer Fire Department in the 1940s. Standing in front of the truck, from left to right, are Hoyt Furr, Terry Hale, Remah Hamer, Fred Smith, Harry Griggs, Henry "Hank" Hale, Chief C.S. "Chick" Wyatt, Nelson "Red" Herndon, Harold M. Stigall, Morgan Sims, Kellom Bradley, and Kenneth Odle. Those standing on the truck are Hoyl Marchbanks, "Bussy" Stigall, Leburn Jones, Clyde Allen, and J.G. "Tommy" Thomas. (BCPL.)

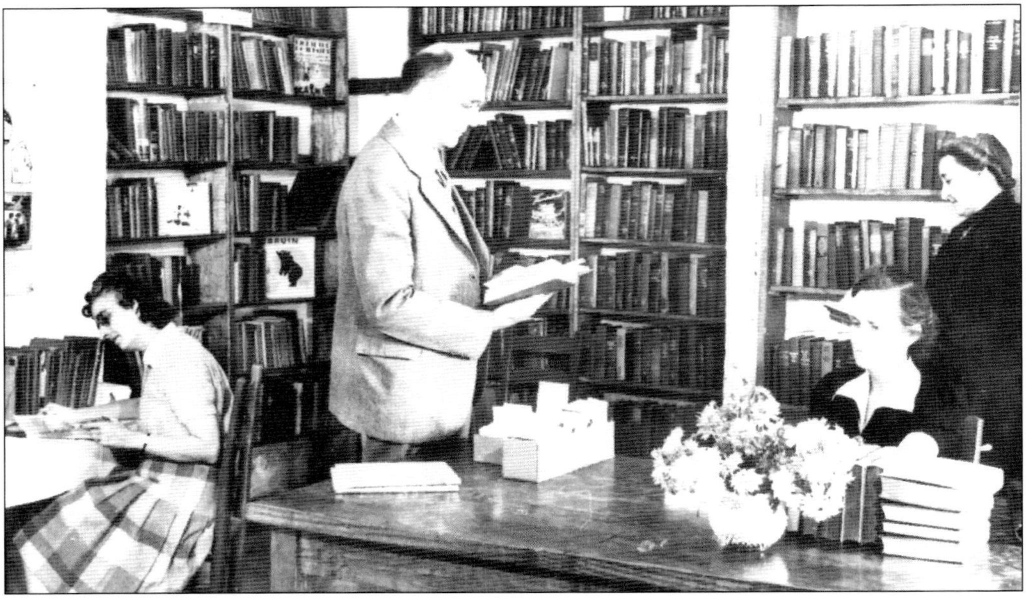

Before the county court established the Benton County Library in 1942, a local ladies reading club along with the Girl Scouts gathered books and began a small library in Camden. From left to right, Velma Bryan, supervising teacher; W.C. Johnson, superintendent of schools; Mrs. Finley Lindsey, librarian; and Mrs. E. Lynn McCollough, chairwoman of the library board, are shown in the basement of the courthouse, where it was located until June 1951. (BCPL.)

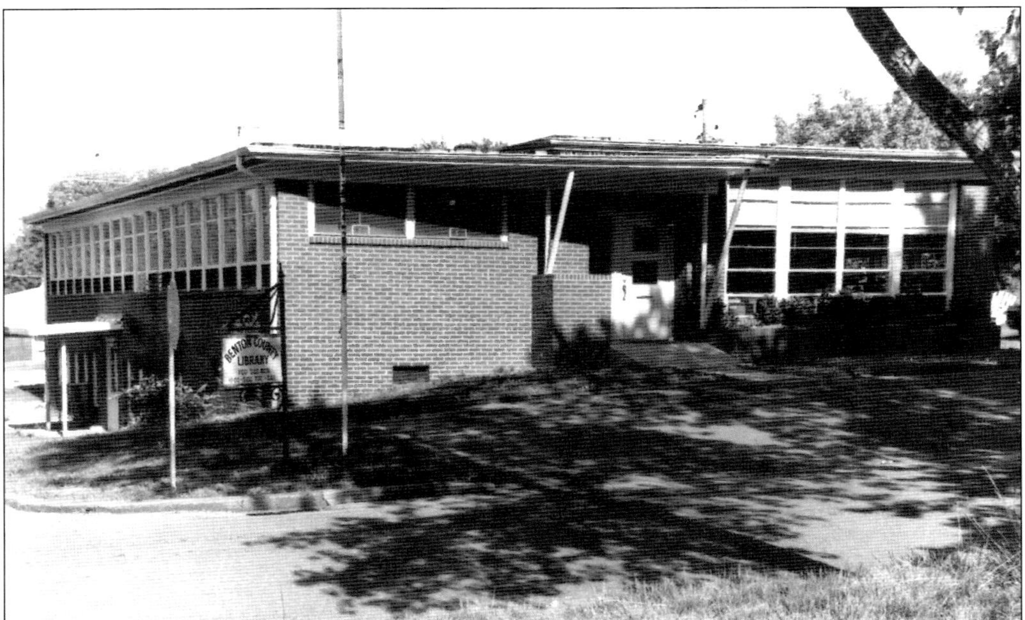

From June 1951 until March 1957, the library occupied the basement of the Bank of Camden. The library then moved to the basement of the Benton County Health Department and remained there for 22 years. In April 1979, the library moved upstairs when the health department moved out. It is shown here in 1987. (JD.)

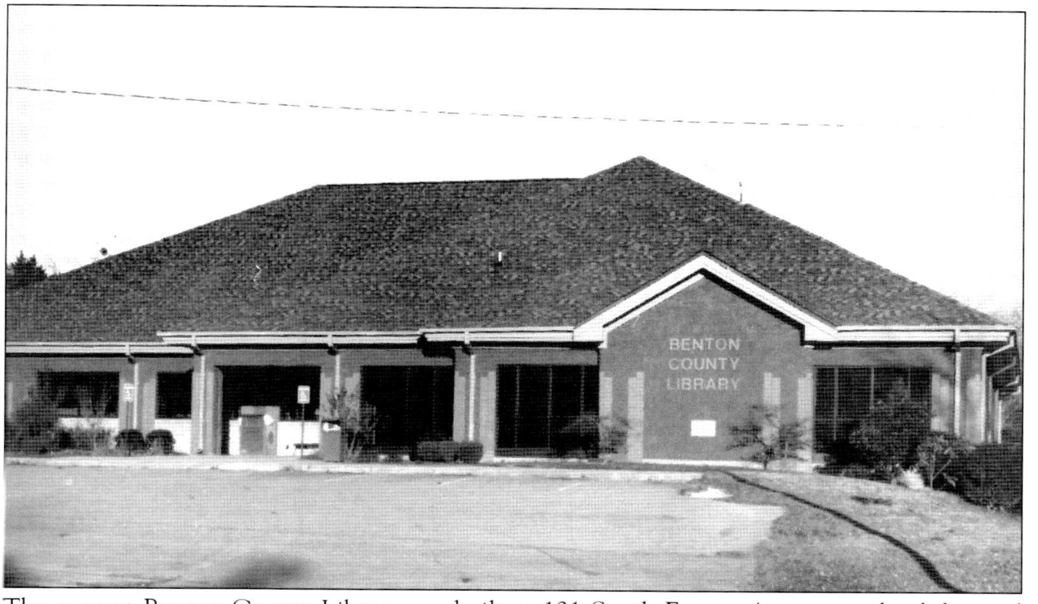

The current Benton County Library was built at 121 South Forrest Avenue on land donated by heirs of Ruth and Wyly Lockhart, including Virginia Lockhart Whitworth, who served the library for nearly 39 years as its director, and her sister Jean Lockhart Fry. The library opened to the public on September 10, 1999, with a dedication and open house on November 14, 1999. (JG.)

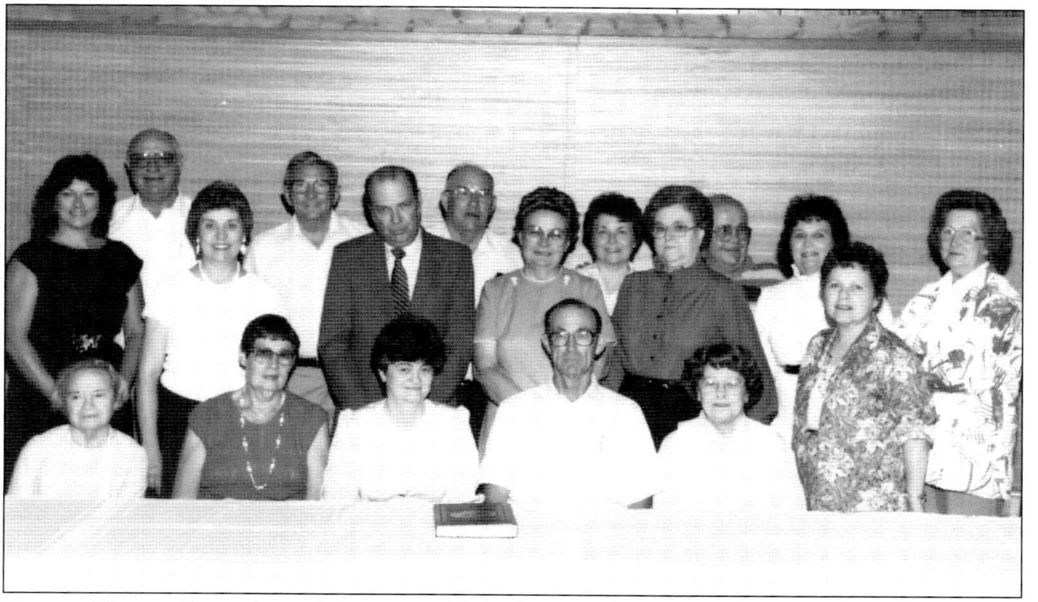

Benton County Genealogical Society published two volumes of *Families and Histories* to raise funds to help build the current library. The organization works to preserve local history. Shown here in 1987 are (seated) Robbie Hartley, Frances Sims, Joan Hatley, F.B. Cain, and Mavis Jones; (standing) Darlene Heathcott, W.C. McDaniel, Virginia Whitworth, E.J. Sims, Elton Hatley, Floyd and Peggy Robins, Sue Kee, Marie Phifer, Raymond Lindsey, Elizabeth Brewer, Virginia Pafford, and Dona Taylor. (JD.)

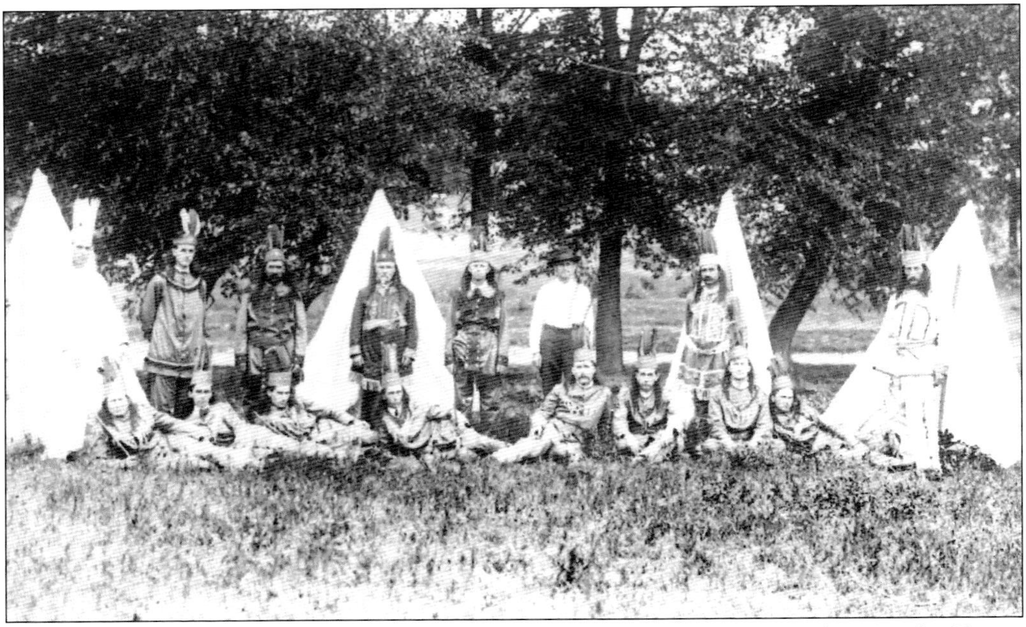

The Imperial Order of Redmen was an active fraternal organization. In March 1909, the Tippecanoe Tribe No. 85 met each week in Camden. C.H. Sullivan was sachem (chief), and P.H. Lowry was chief of records. Included here are Jeb Anderson, R.G. Hudson, W. H. Jingles, L.A. Wyatt, T. J. Lowry, A.J. Utley, Paleface Royal R. Melton, S.A. Clement, J.A. Cole, George H. Cowell, Percy Lowry, Nolie Wilson, and Tom Tucker. (BCPL.)

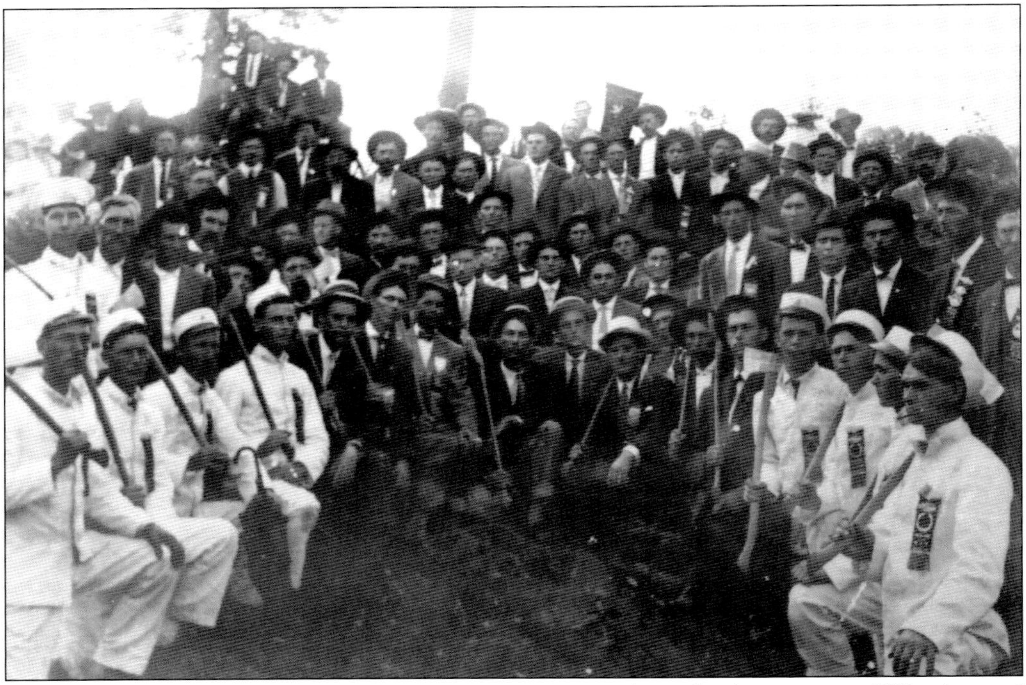

This unidentified event must have been an important one for such a large group of Woodmen of the World to be in attendance; most are dressed in their Sunday best or in uniforms. (BCPL.)

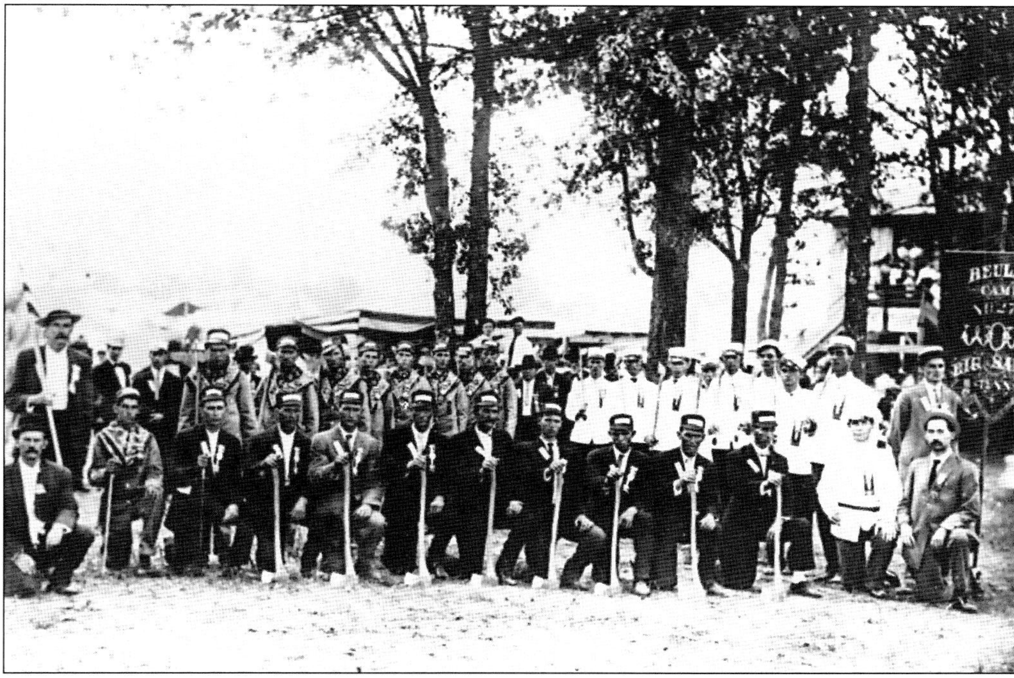

Beulah Camp No. 276 of Woodmen of the World, as well as the Masons, held meetings upstairs at the Big Sandy United Methodist Church, downtown in Big Sandy, Tennessee. (RD.)

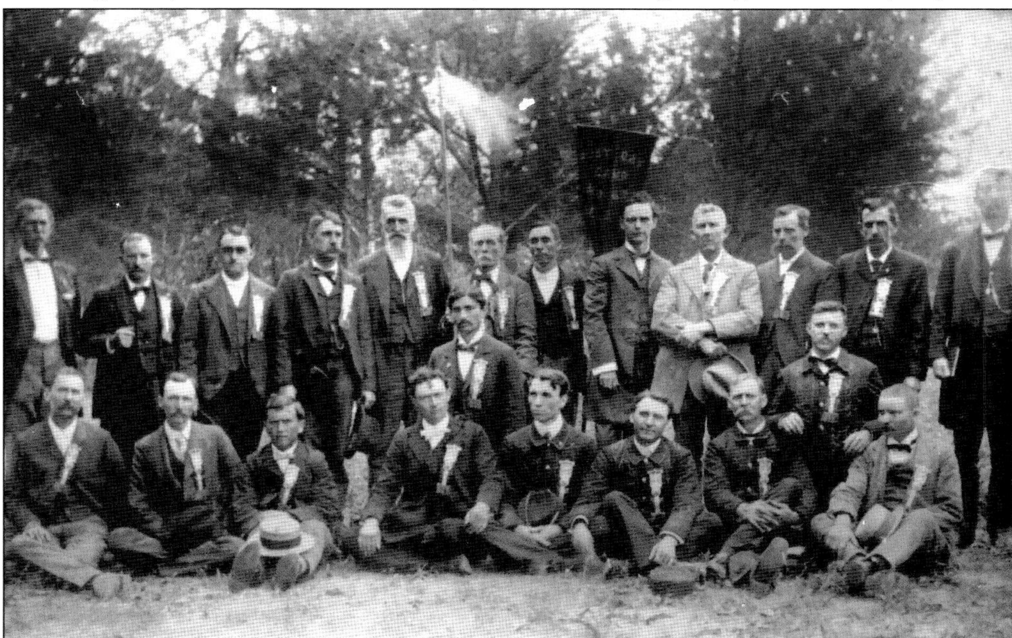

The original charter was issued to Post Oak Camp No. 47 of Woodmen of the World on December 28, 1896. In 1900, the officers were F.E. McElyea, J.B. Vickery, T.H. Bateman, J.G. Robbins, W.L. McElyea, A.G. Hudson, W.P McGill, W.G. Corbett, O.C. Hudson, E.M. McAuby, C.V. Hawley, and E.L. Hudson. (BCPL.)

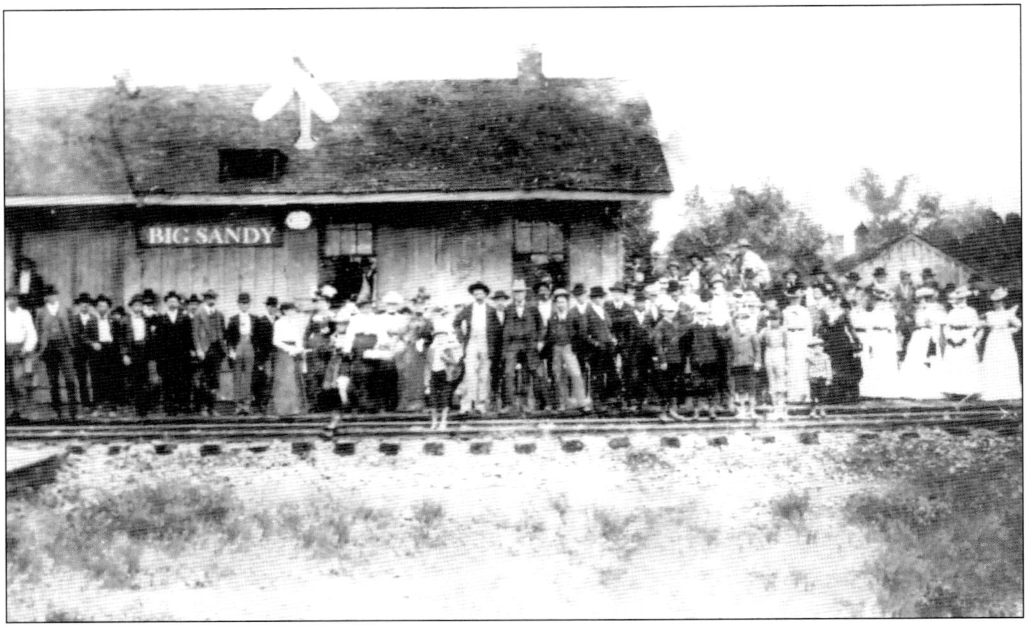

A large group of people gather at the first depot in Big Sandy, Tennessee, before 1912. (RD.)

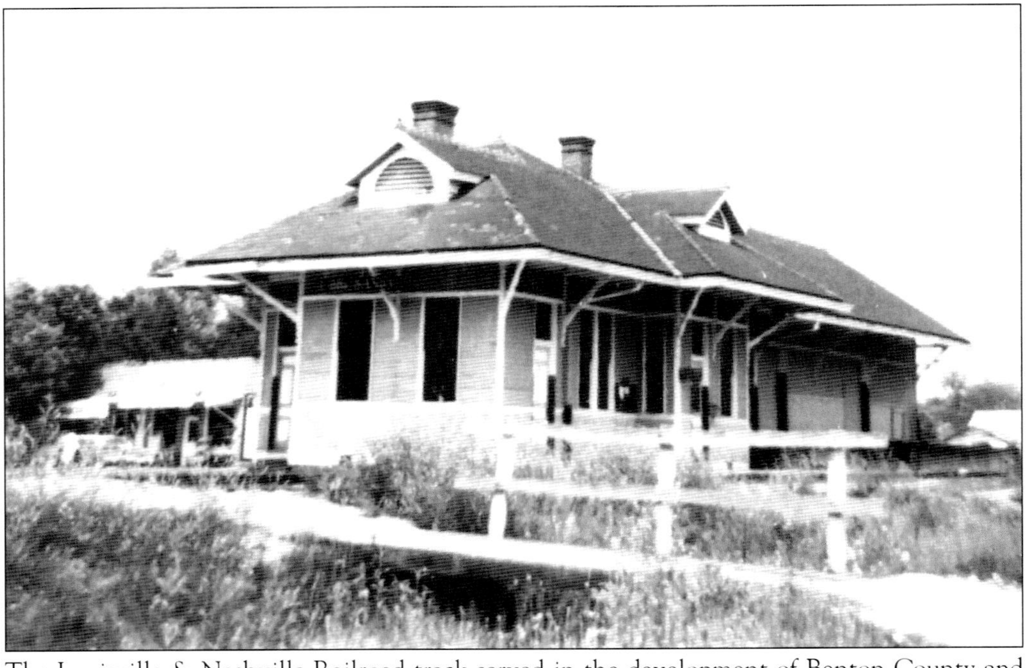

The Louisville & Nashville Railroad track served in the development of Benton County and was only one of two railroad bridges spanning the Tennessee River. This is the L&N Railroad Depot in Big Sandy about 1930. The depot has been demolished, and the tracks have been taken up. (BCPL.)

The building on the far left is the Caraway & Sons Store in Big Sandy. They had wagons, farm equipment, and other merchandise in front. In the back was a bank, and the *Benton County Star* newspaper was on the right inside also. Upstairs was a millinery shop that had hats, gloves, and women's wear. This photograph, made in about 1925, shows the public well and windmill. (BCPL.)

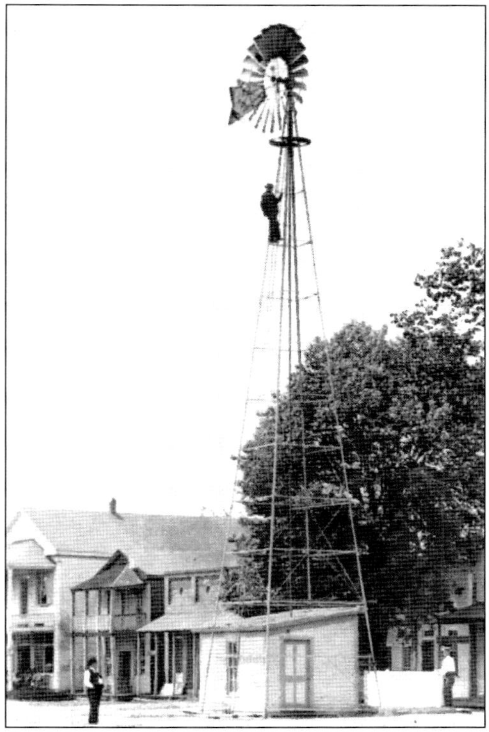

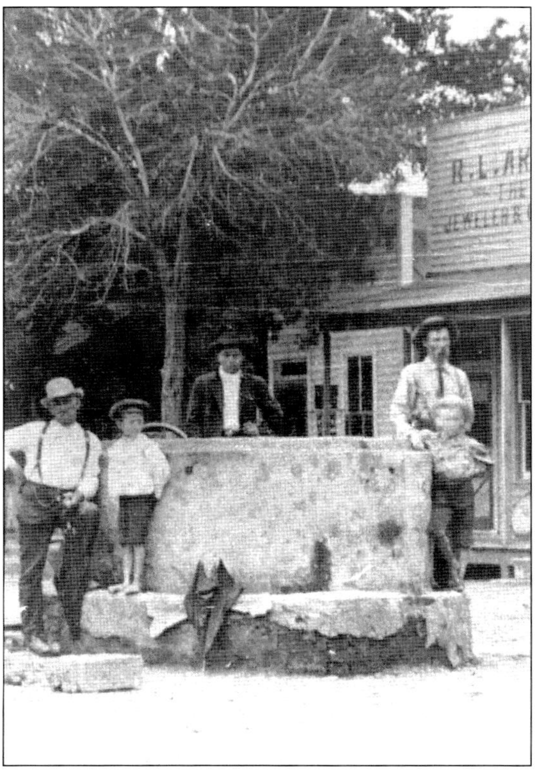

The Big Sandy public water well was built prior to 1900. It was located in front of R.L. Akers Dry Goods and Jewelry store, which is no longer in existence. The man on the left is Jake Davis, and the boy beside him is Joseph Davis. (BCPL.)

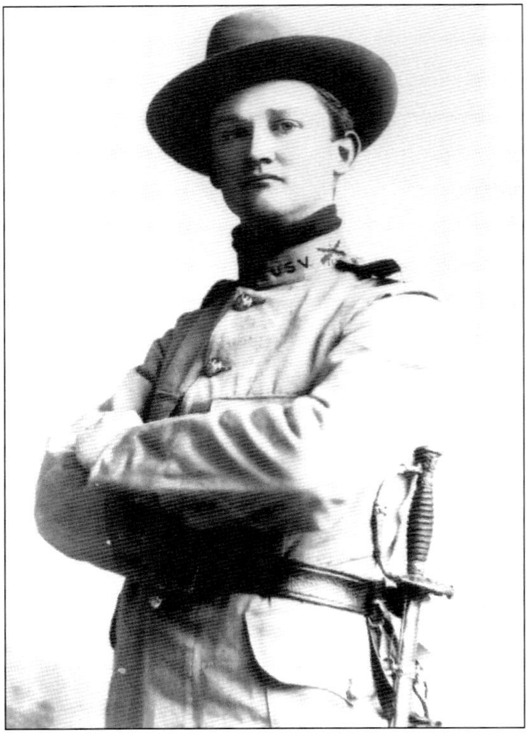

Leon Caraway (1874–1939) graduated from Vanderbilt and was practicing law when he was mustered into the First Regiment Tennessee Infantry as a first lieutenant. He was promoted to captain in the Spanish-American War. He resigned as postmaster at Big Sandy and went to Paris, Tennessee, to organize Battery D, when America entered World War I. When Caraway faced difficulties serving due to his age and health problems, his unit was taken over by Lt. Gordon Browning, who later became governor of Tennessee. Captain Caraway is buried in Arlington National Cemetery. (RD.)

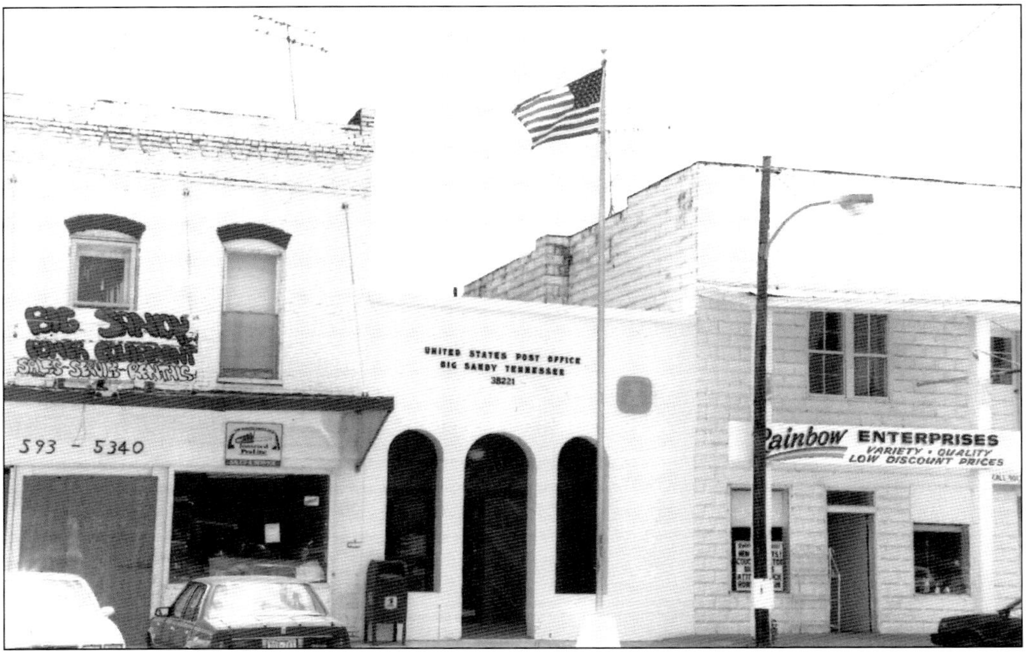

The first post office around Big Sandy was established as Sand (or Sandy) Springs, with William Caraway as postmaster. The name was changed to Onward, and on November 23, 1866, it changed to Big Sandy Post Office. This building now houses Shear Designs Beauty Shop. A new post office office was built in 1992. (JD.)

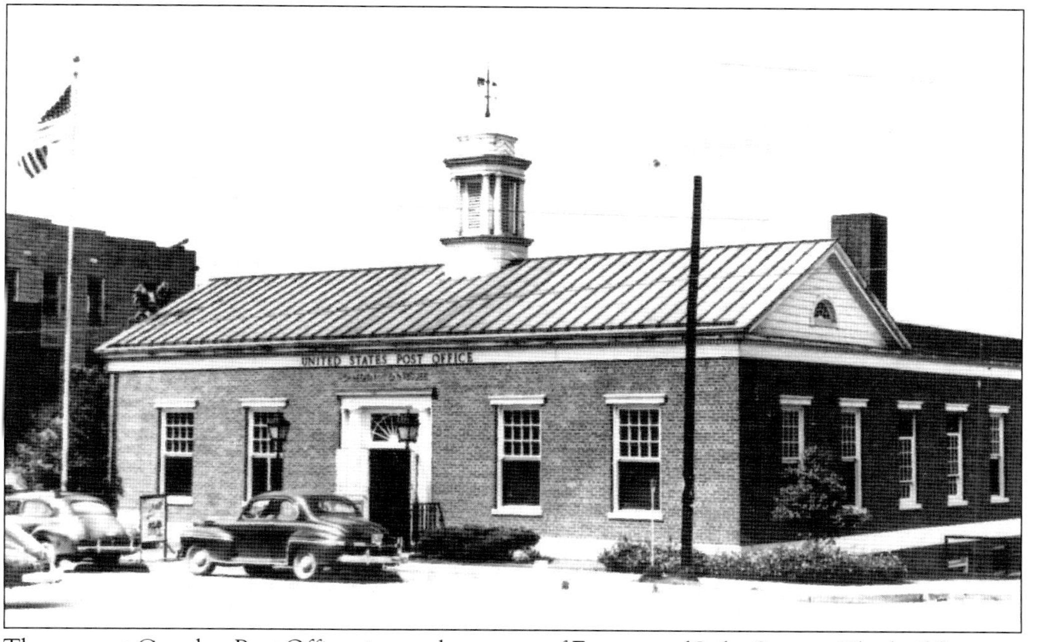

The present Camden Post Office sits on the corner of Forrest and Lake Streets. The building was constructed in 1936 and occupied in early 1937; this photograph was made in the 1950s. Since that time, additions have been made to the building. (JD.)

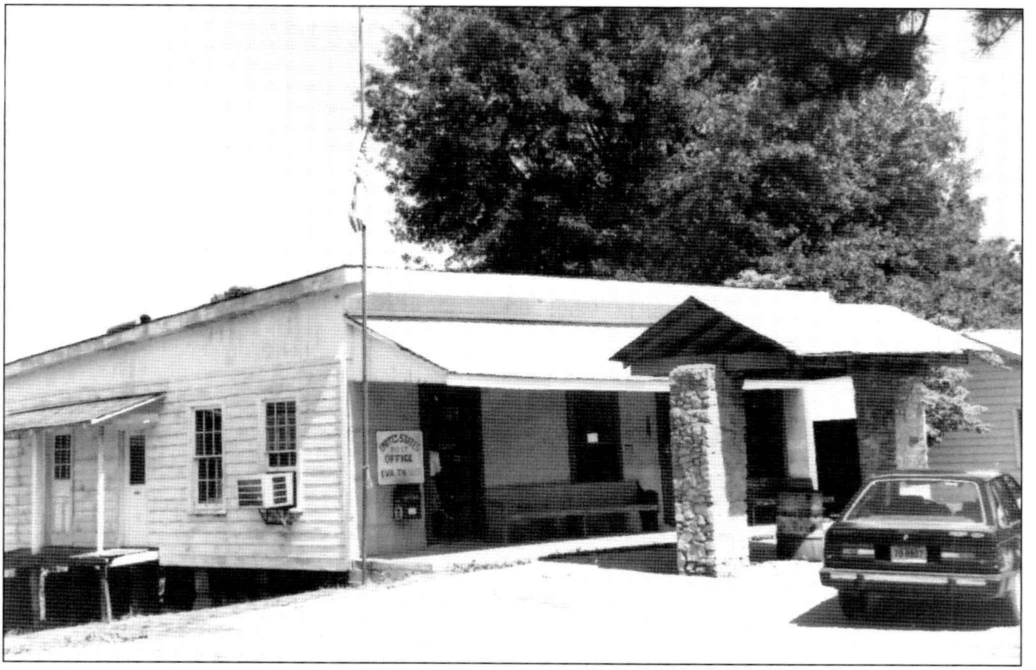

The Eva Post Office was established on January 26, 1881. Thomas J. Lowry was postmaster. Other postmasters have been Arthur E. Justice, Andrew J. Sykes, Lindsey Melton, Green D. Dillon, Linas L. Melton, Dorsey B. Holland, Laymon Cuff, Marshall Holland, and Bessie Phifer. A new post office replaced this one in 1998. (JD.)

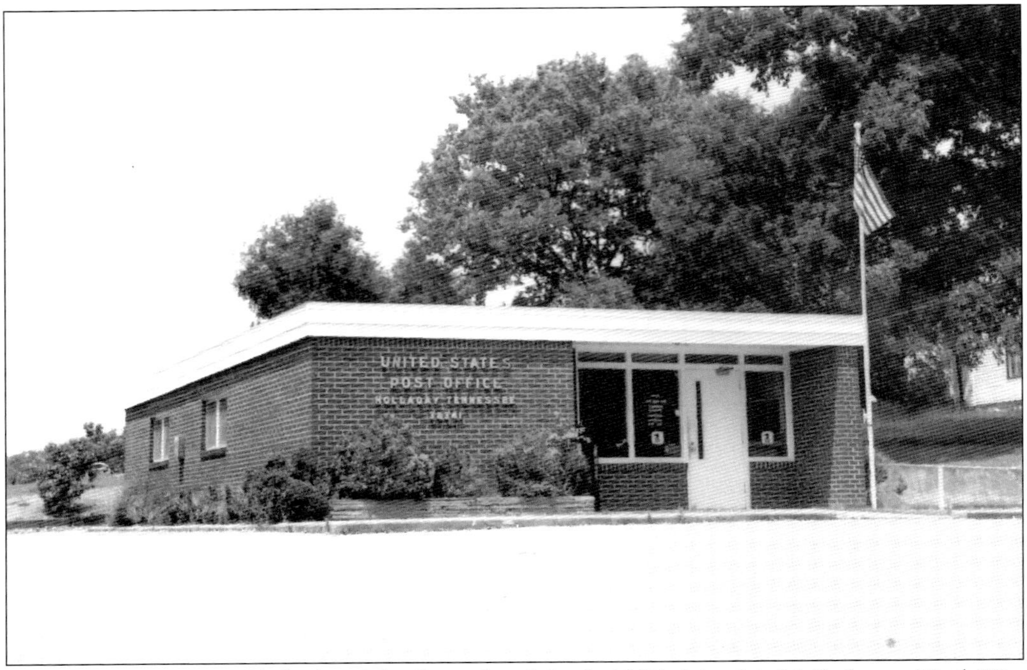

A post office was established at Mt. Carmel in March 1887. John M. Holladay, a Civil War veteran, was its first postmaster, and it was named for him. Thereafter, the little community of Mt. Carmel was known as Holladay. Three rural routes ran out of this office, serving a large portion of south Benton County, North Decatur County, and a portion of Carroll and Henderson Counties. (JD.)

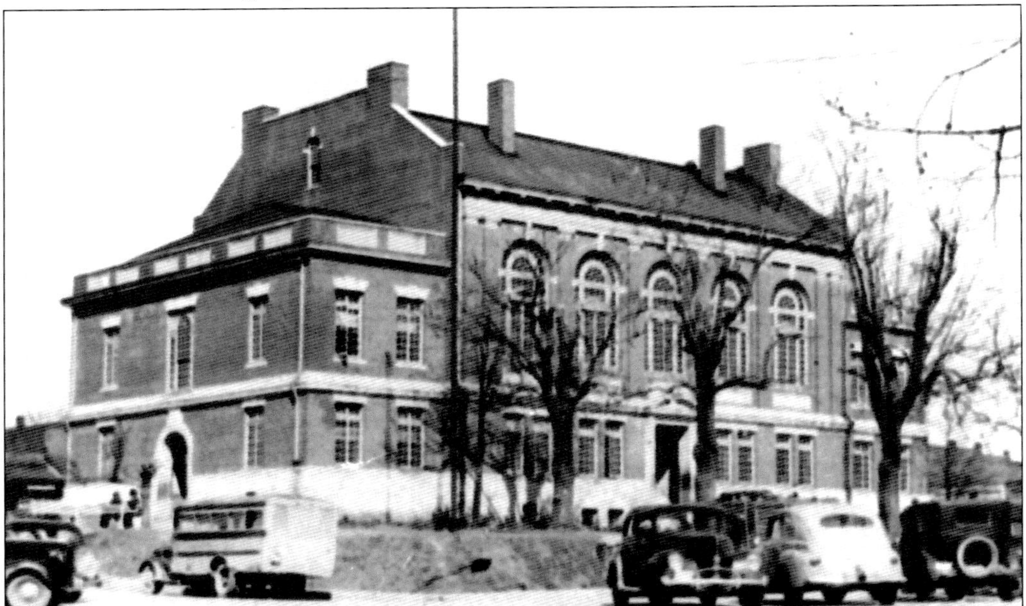

The Benton County Courthouse, seen here c. 1943, was built in August 1915 and torn down in 1972. (BCPL.)

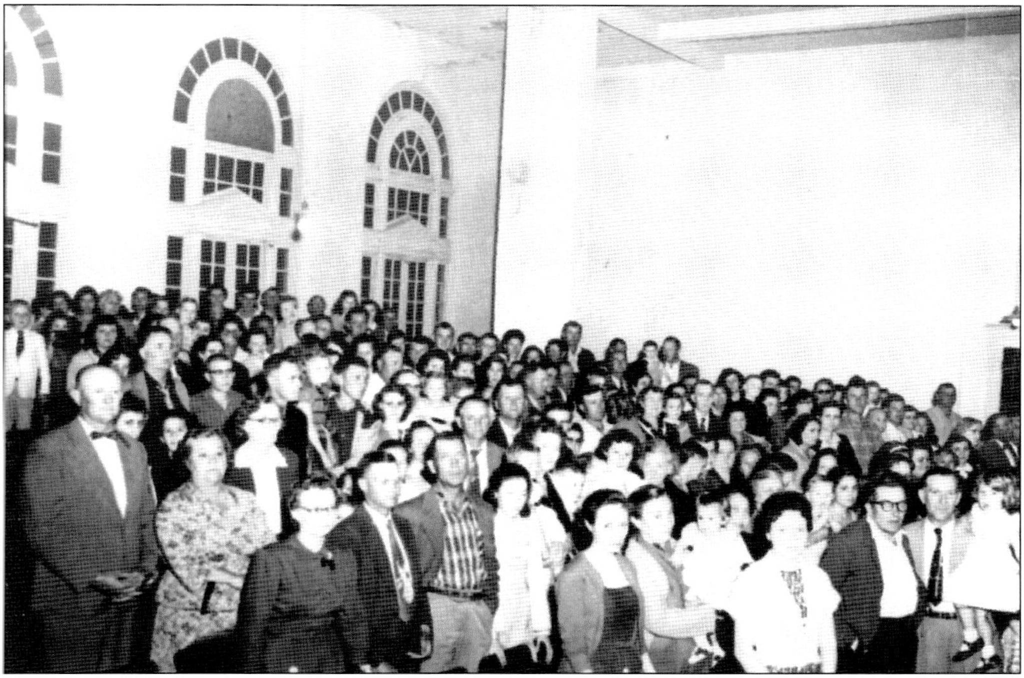

Religious services were held in the courtroom of the old courthouse on April 25, 1958, when a traveling revival with Bro. James Burkett met there. (BCPL.)

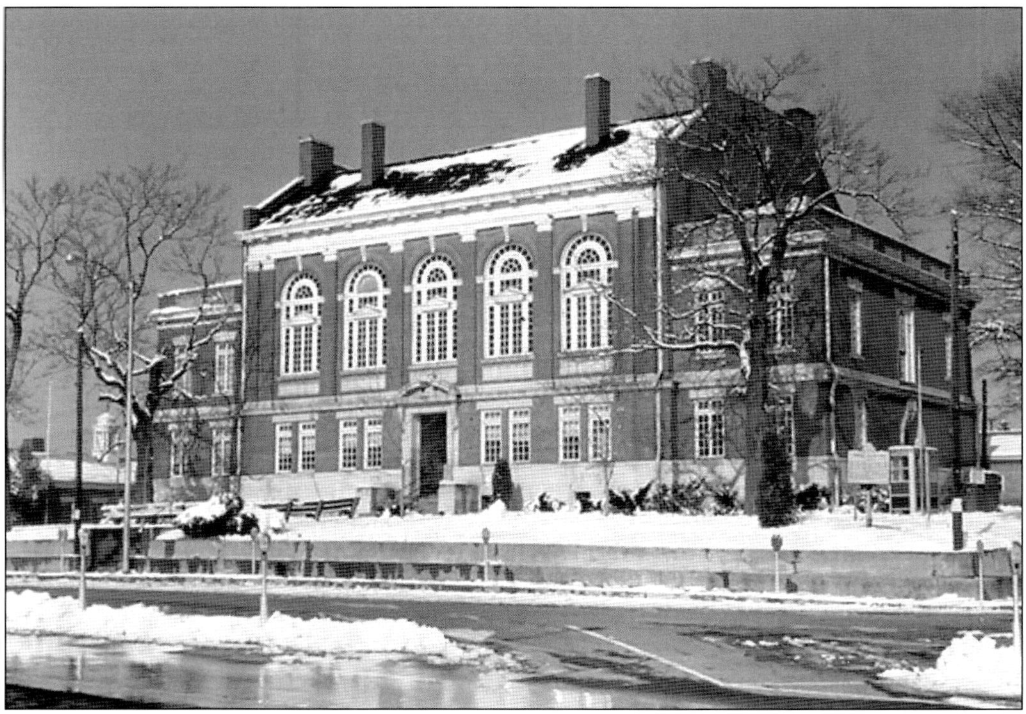

This photograph, made after a snow in 1966, shows the architectural beauty of the old courthouse not many years before it was demolished to build the new courthouse in 1974. (JD.)

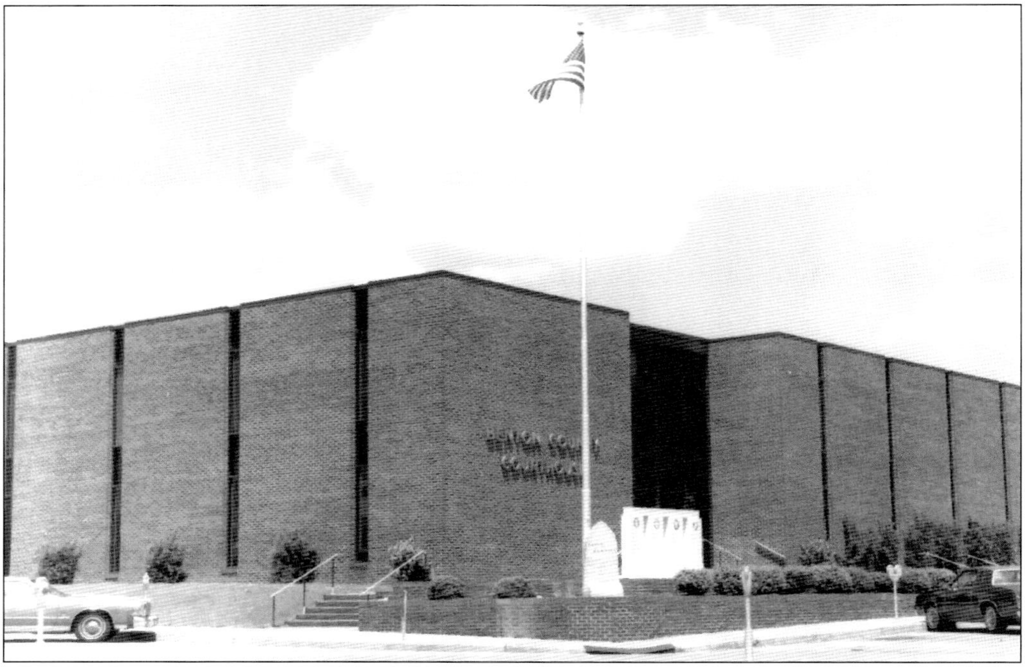

The current courthouse was first occupied on November 13, 1974, and was dedicated on December 12, 1974. (JD.)

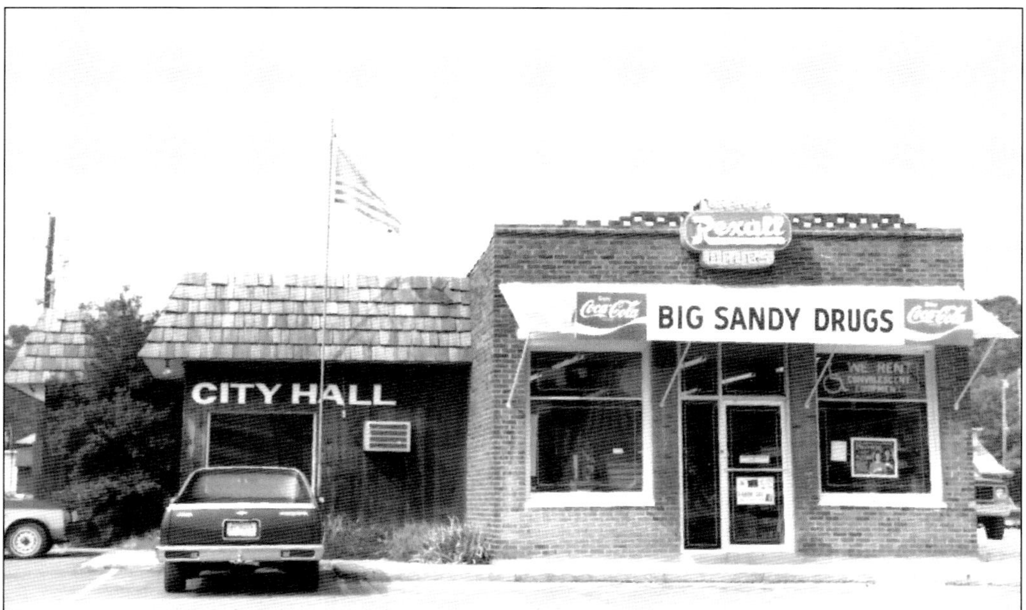

Big Sandy City Hall was located next door to the Big Sandy Drugs on Front Street. The building that was Big Sandy Drugs is now the Big Sandy library. This City Hall building is now vacant, and a new city hall was built in 2003. (JD.)

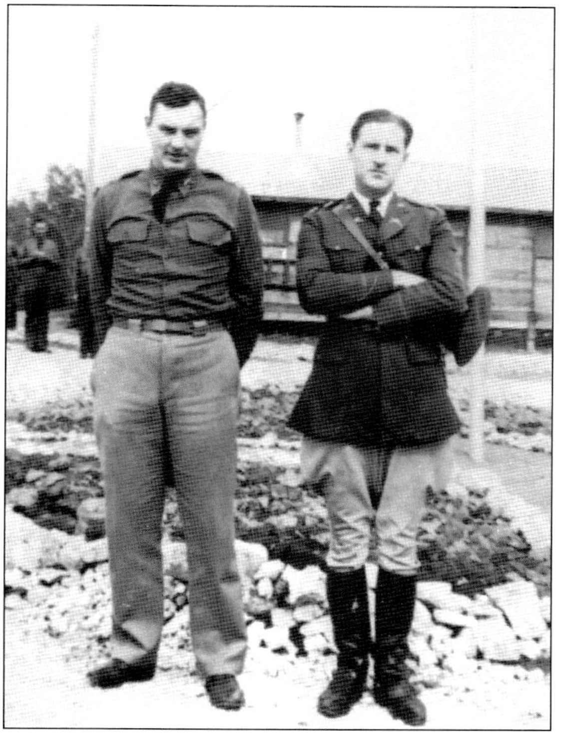

Capt. William A. Cathy and Lieutenant Taylor of the Civilian Conservation Corp are shown here. (BCPL.)

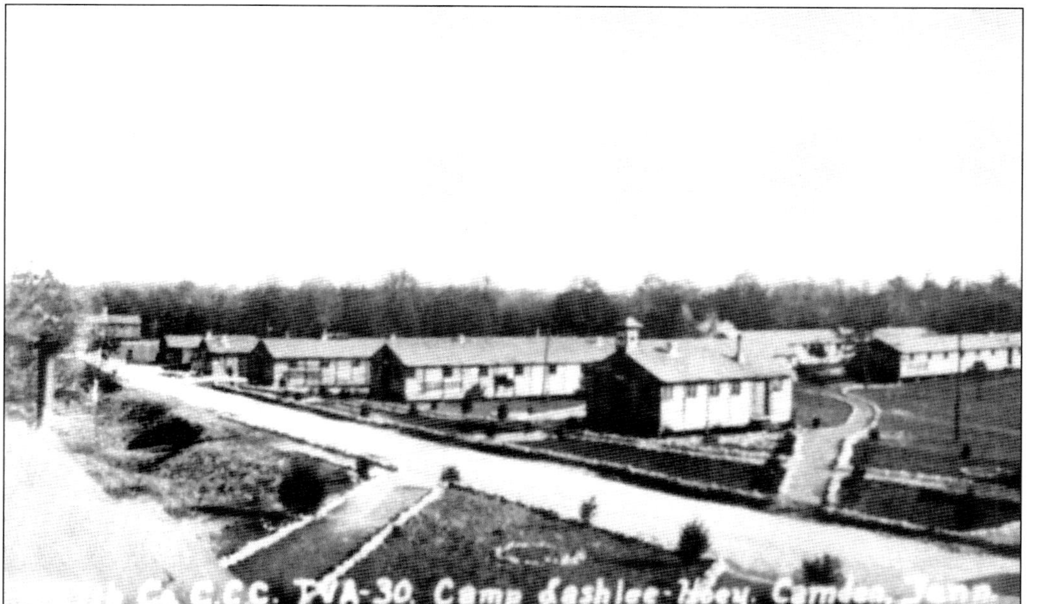

Camp Lashlee-Hoey, 497th Company, Civilian Conservation Corp, TVA 30, Camden is clearly shown on the photograph. TVA 30 was the number given by the state to the project and this camp; 497 was a number given by the federal government to each company. The 497th company occupied this spot as of June 29, 1935, and was located one mile north of the closest railroad stop at Camden. (BCPL.)

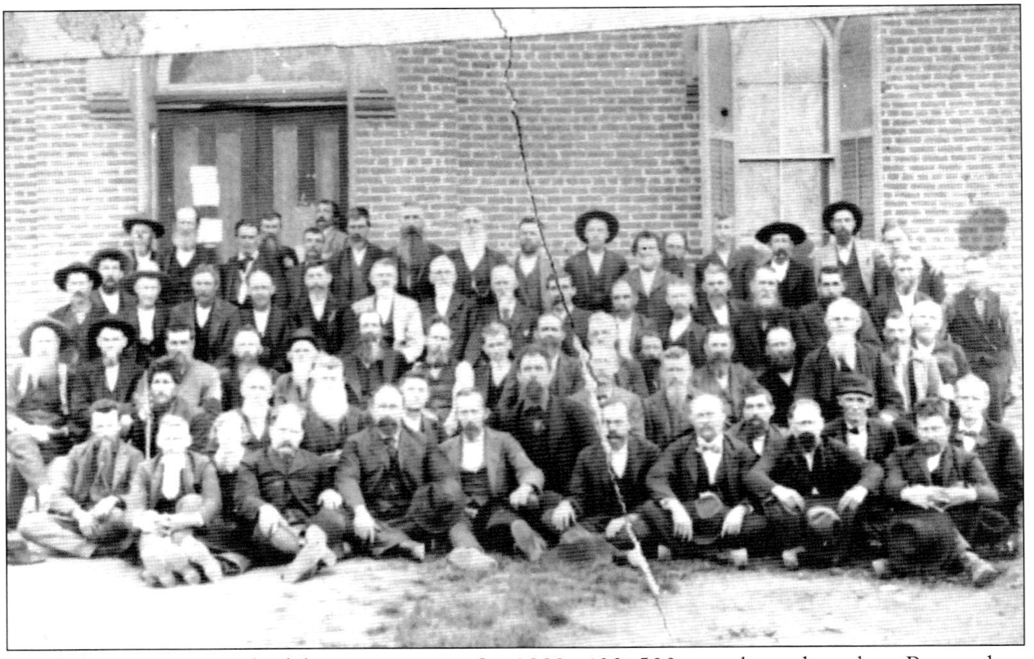

Confederate veterans had large meetings. In 1889, 400–500 people gathered at Beaverdam camp. In 1891, they gathered in August at Cowells Chapel and in 1898 at Holland's Spring. On October 11, 1901, they gathered at Sulphur Springs, and on August 8, 1907, they gathered at Eva. They are pictured here gathered in front of the Benton County Courthouse, but the year is unidentified. (BCPL.)

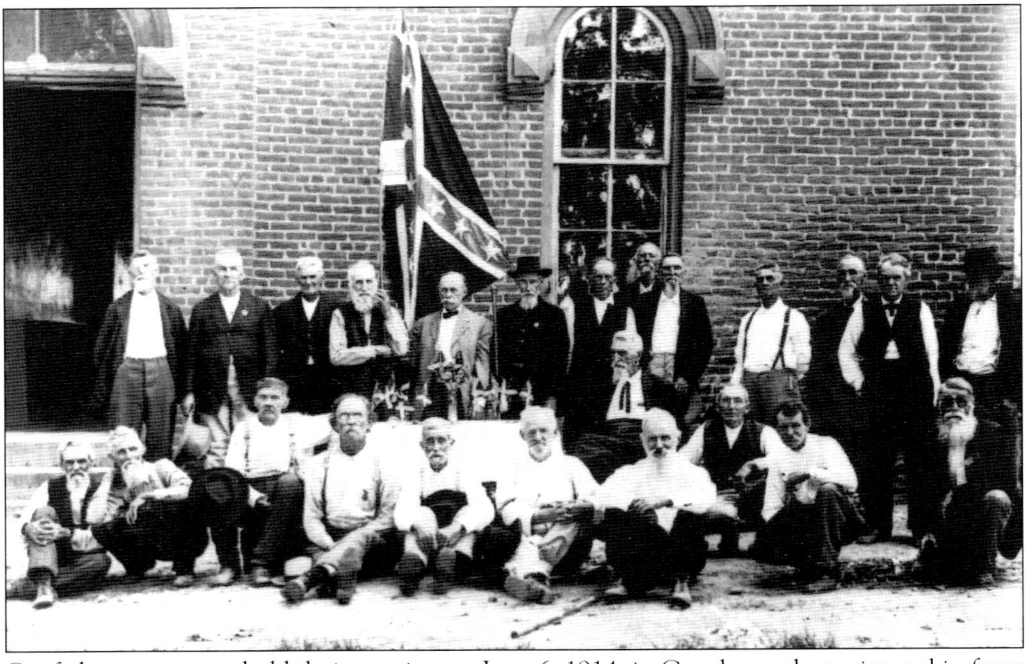

Confederate veterans held their reunion on June 6, 1914, in Camden and are pictured in front of the Benton County Courthouse. (BCPL.)

James William "Willie" Melton was inducted into the U.S. Army on September 6, 1918, and served in World War I. On the ship going to France, he almost died and was unconscious most of the trip. The doctor sent men three times to throw him overboard as dead, but the nurse wouldn't let them. He was discharged in 1919, married, raised a family, and died on April 10, 1976. (BCPL.)

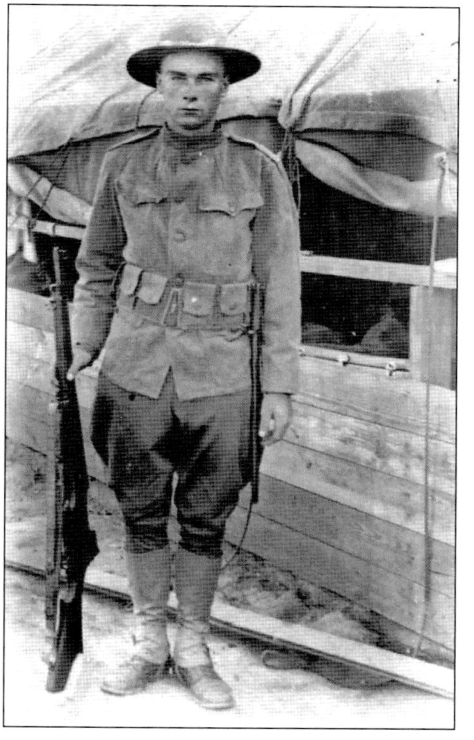

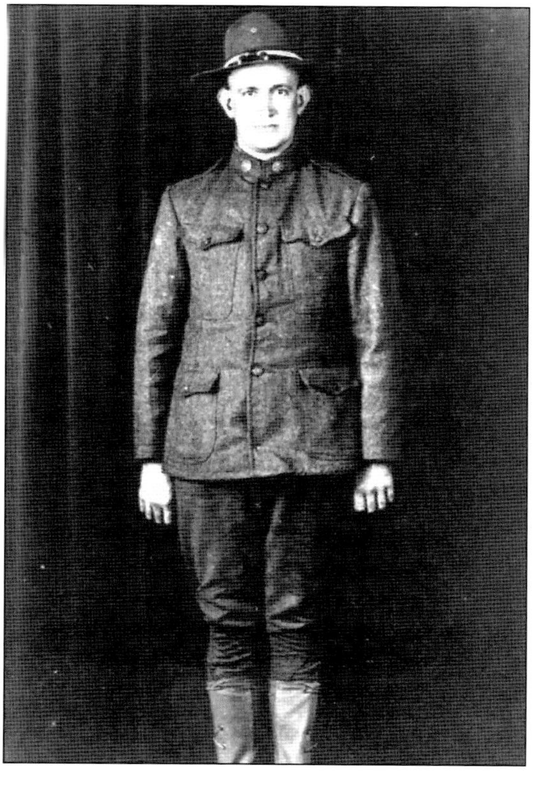

Clarence Gilbert "Gibby" McKenzie is shown here in his World War I uniform on April 29, 1923. He is buried at McRae's Chapel Cemetery. (BCPL.)

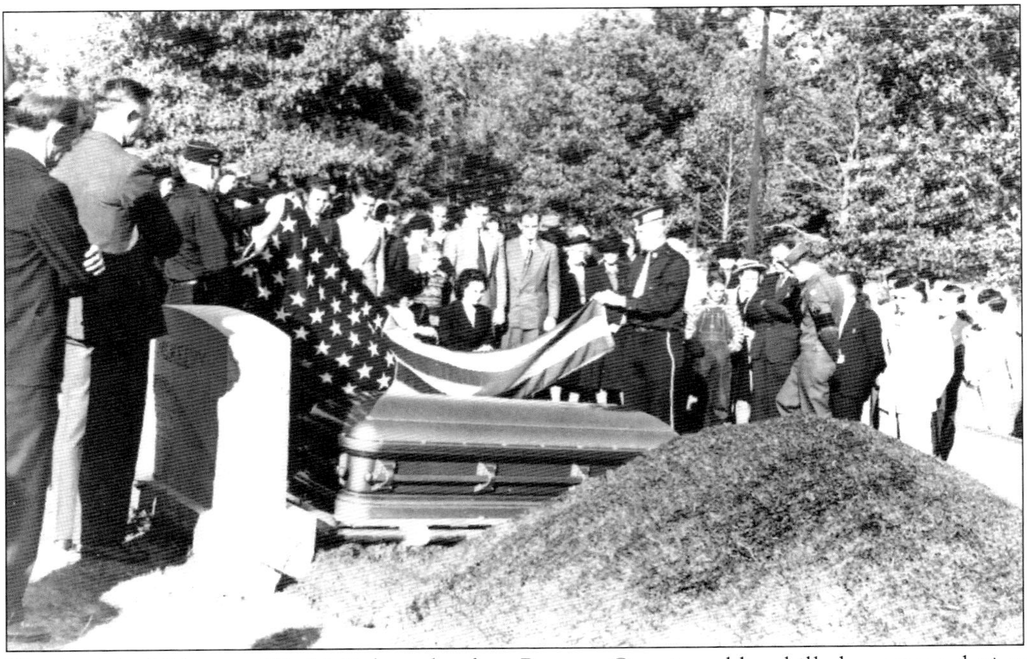

The burial of Thomas W. McKelvy, the first Benton County soldier killed overseas during World War II, was conducted by the Burial Squad of the American Legion Post 102, at Liberty Cemetery. He was killed on August 1, 1942. (BCPL.)

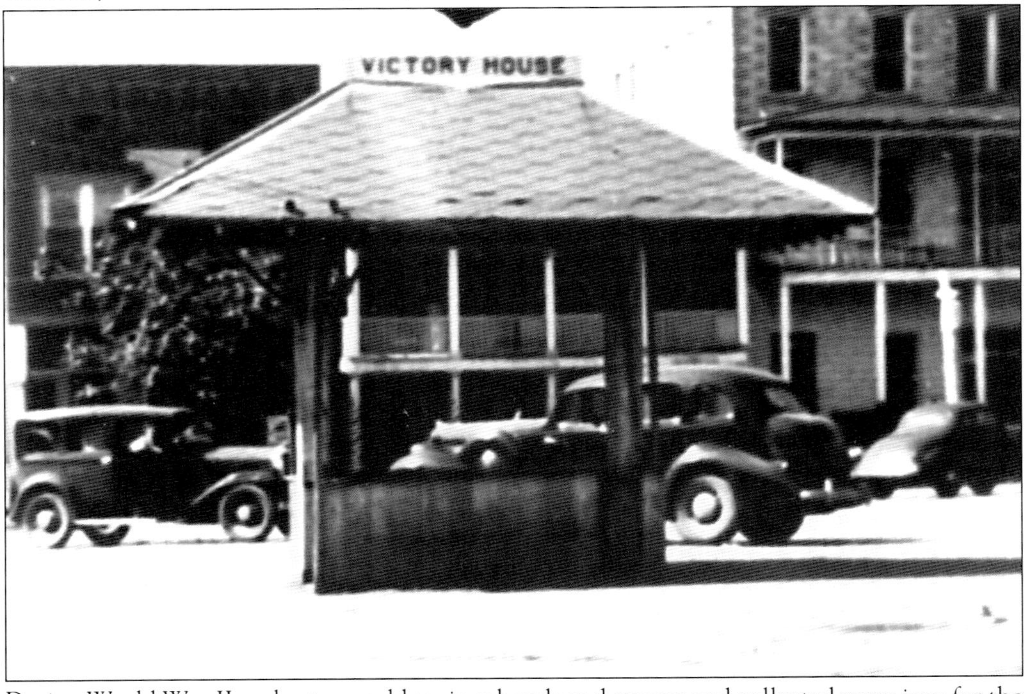

During World War II, volunteers sold savings bonds and stamps and collected scrap iron for the war effort. The Victory House was built on Main Street on the court square in Camden for this purpose. (BCPL.)

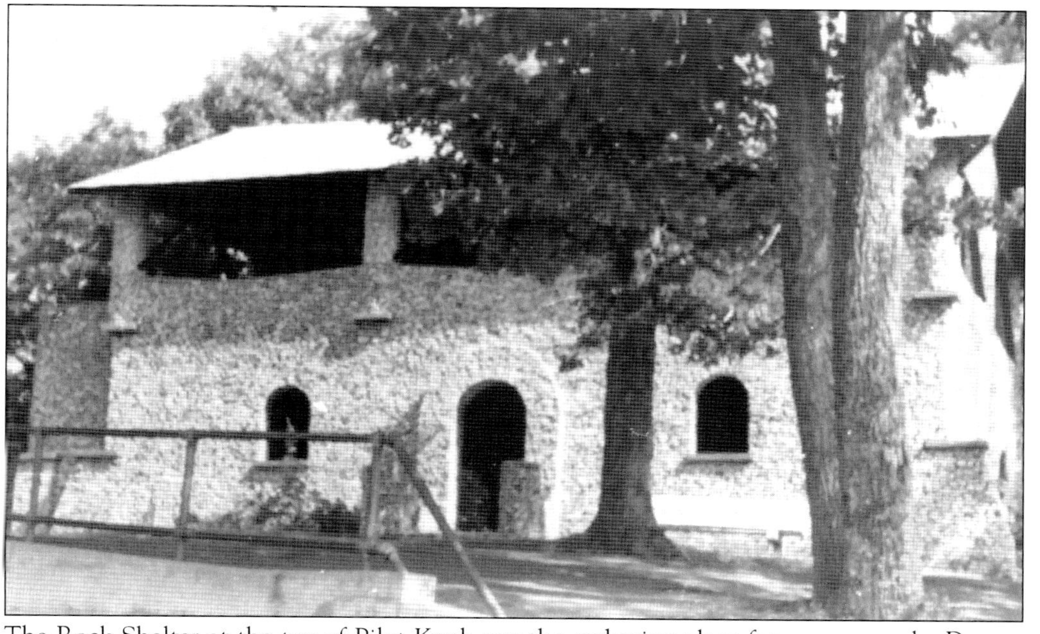

The Rock Shelter at the top of Pilot Knob was the gathering place for young people. Dances were held there and many proposals of marriage occurred here, in what is now Nathan Bedford Forrest State Park. The old rock shelter was torn down and a new folk museum replaced it. (CW.)

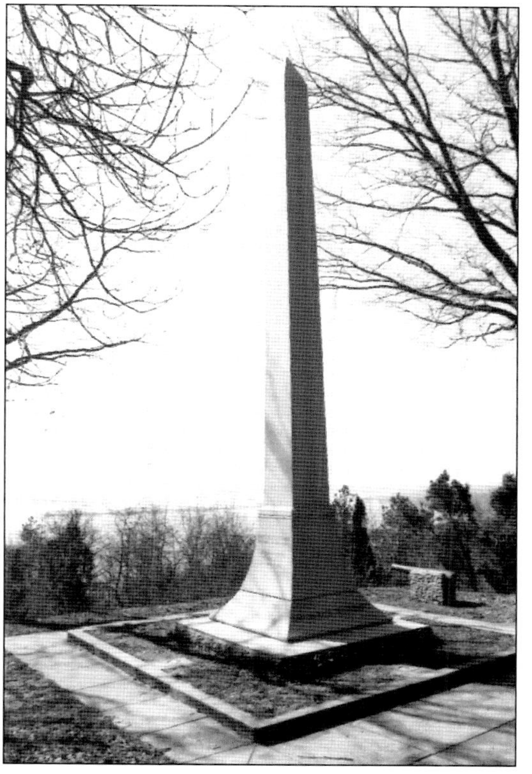

This monument in honor of Gen. Nathan Bedford Forrest is located at the top of Pilot Knob in Nathan Bedford Forrest State Park. It arrived at Eva Depot in three sections from Calhoun, Georgia, in the fall of 1931. Albert Cherry and Oscar Pafford were paid $500 to take it to the park and erect it. It proved to be a very big job to get it up the hill. (JD.)

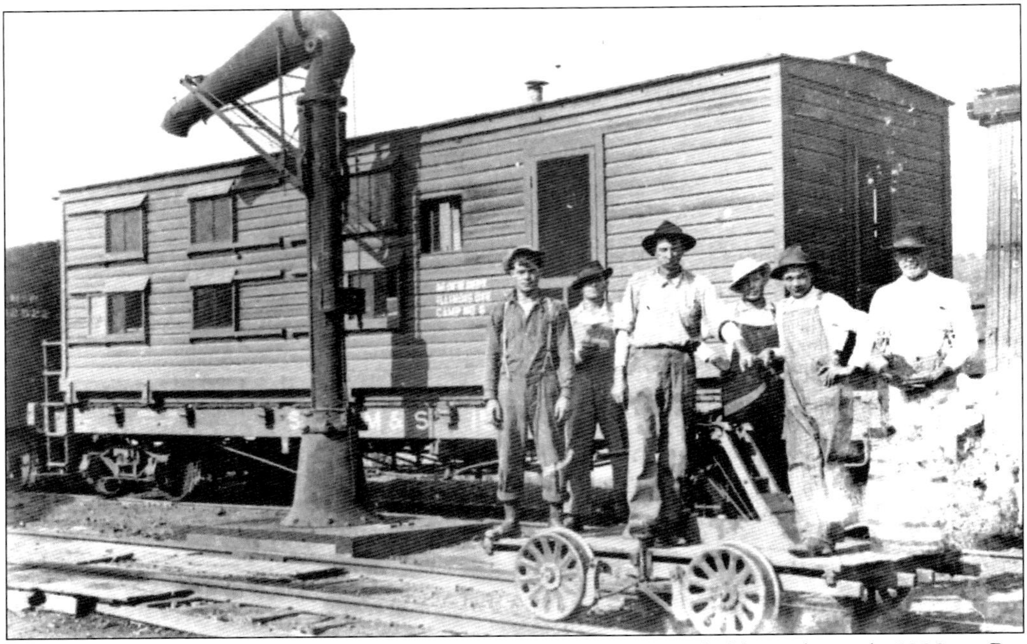

Handcars and the section hands are shown in the foreground, probably in the early 1900s in Big Sandy, when the railroad was in its heyday. (BCPL.)

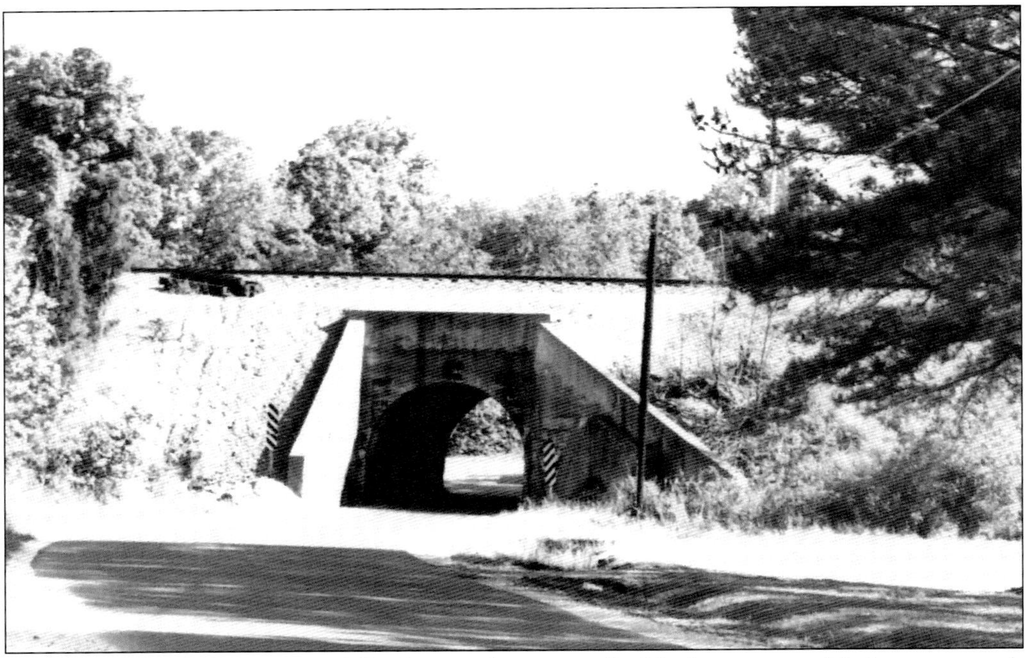

Many small towns experience difficulties with train traffic blocking streets. Underpasses, such as this one on Natchez Trace Road, help traffic flow smoothly in Camden. However, it has its downside as many cars failed to negotiate the curve, and it became known as "Dead Man's Curve." (JD.)

Five

HOMES AND PEOPLE

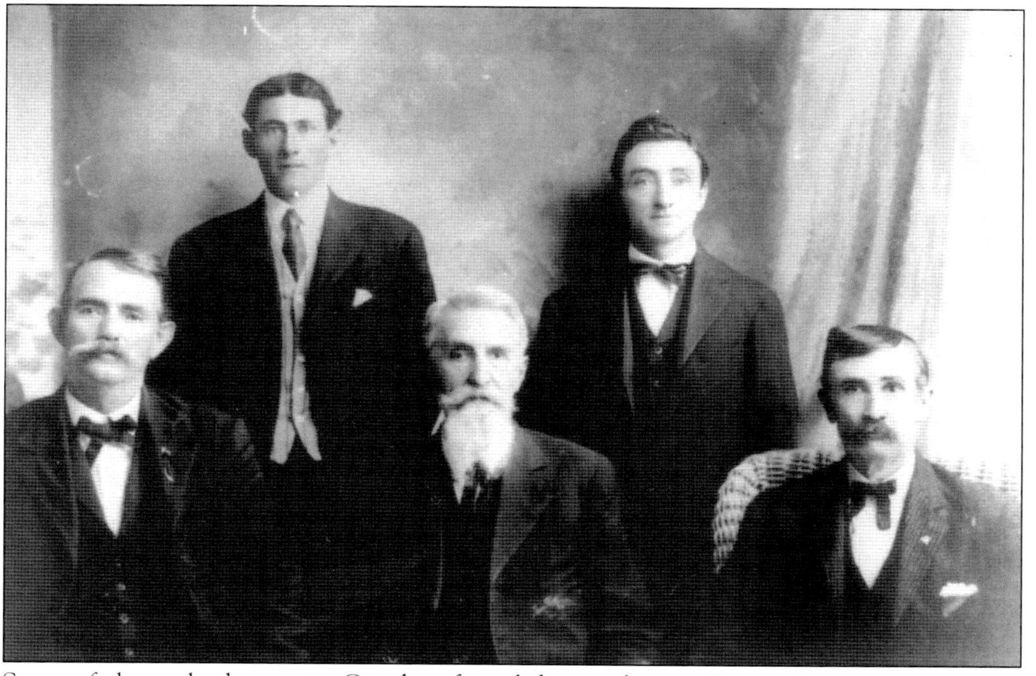

Some of the early doctors in Camden, from left to right, are Dr. William P. McGill, Dr. Felix Grundy Hudson, Dr. John I. Bradley, Dr. G.P. Hicks (standing), and Dr. Robert Lewis Barker. (BCPL.)

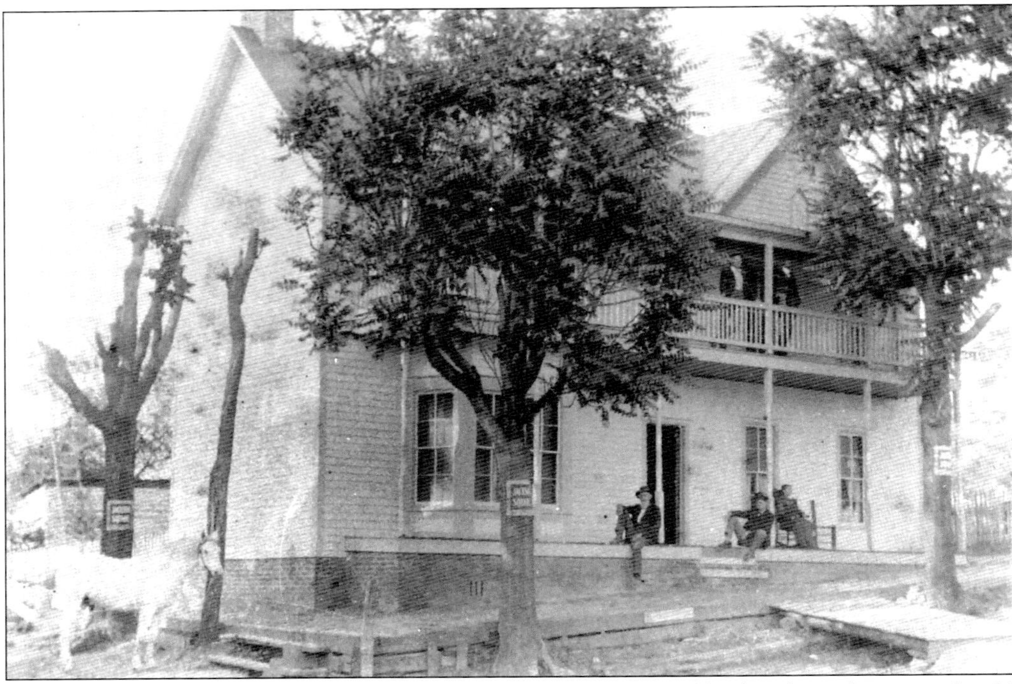

Dr. Felix Hudson bought lot numbers 15 and 16 in Camden and built a frame house on lot 16. On the east corner of lot 15, he built a block building, which served as his office. This was on the northwest corner of the court square. (BCPL.)

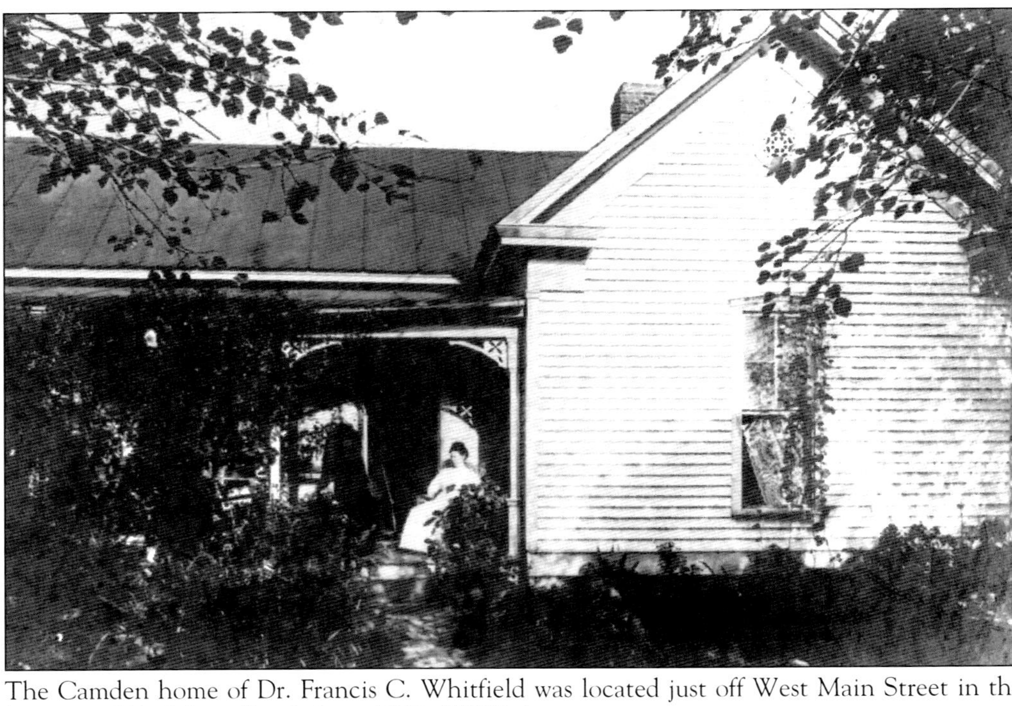

The Camden home of Dr. Francis C. Whitfield was located just off West Main Street in the location of Vicksburg Road about 1900. (BCPL.)

Noah Melton is pictured in front of the Camden Clinic, the first block building in Camden. Dr. Robert L Horton Sr. performed minor surgery at his Camden Clinic; it was located here from the mid-1940s until 1951. (BCPL.)

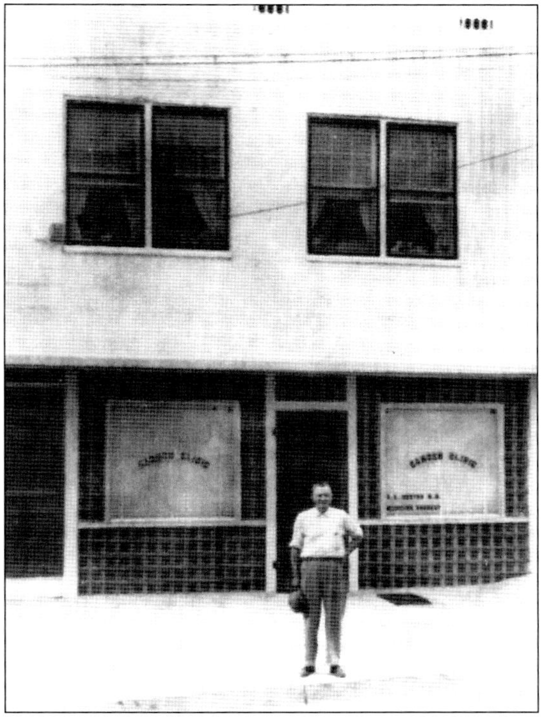

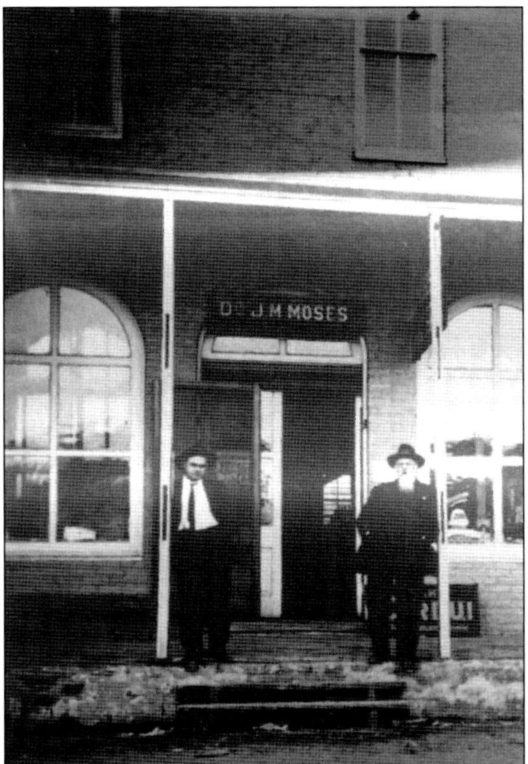

In the 19th century, Dr. James M. Moses was one of Camden's physicians; he later moved to Big Sandy and practiced there. He died at the age of 77 in Big Sandy and had been a physician for at least 35 years. (RD.)

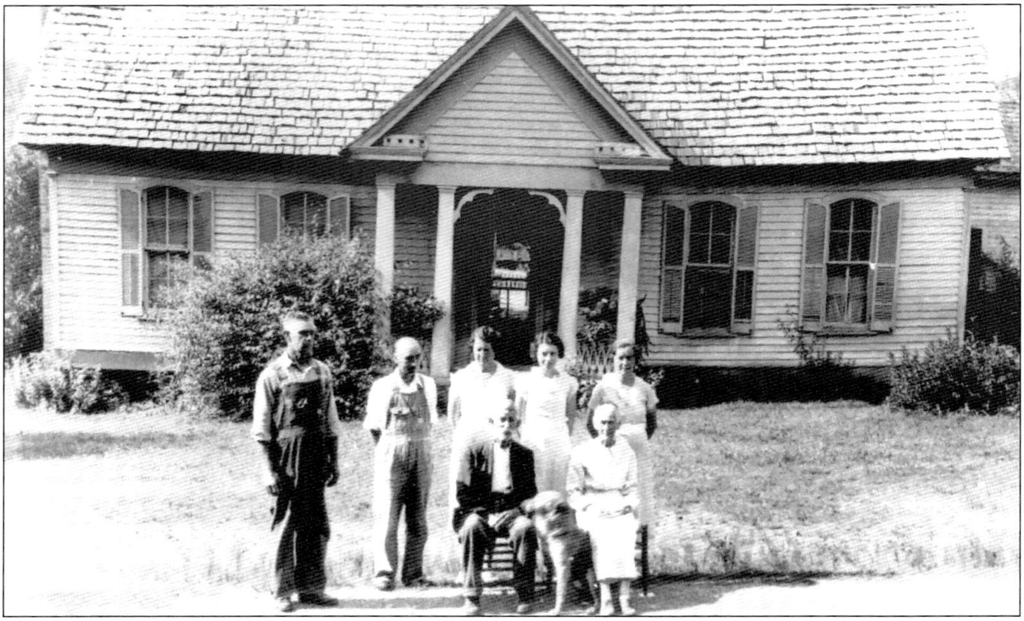

This house, pictured here in 1937, was built by Etheldred Melton in 1880 in Harmon's Creek Community. After Melton's death in 1885, the house went to his youngest son, Andrew Jackson Melton. Identified from left to right are (seated) Andrew J. Melton and his wife, Martha Beatrice Lowry Melton; (standing) Augustus Elnoe Melton (son), Robert W. Jones (son-in-law), Nodle Melton Jones (daughter), Mavis Madlin Jones (granddaughter), Lula Brunettie Cagle (daughter), and Jargo, the family dog. (BCPL.)

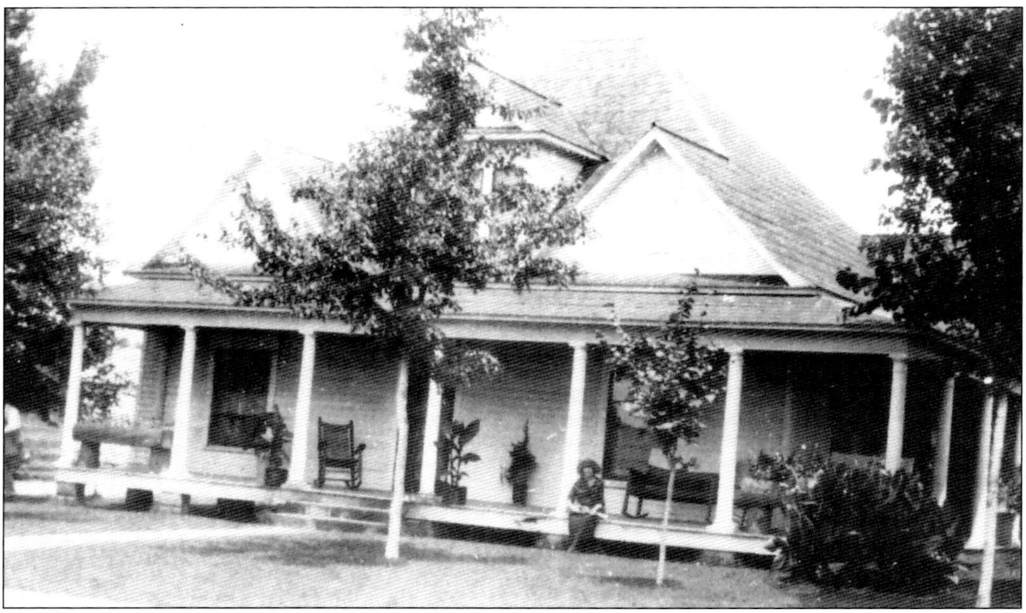

The Tom Frazier home is located on Frazier Street. Born in 1876, Mr. Frazier operated a sawmill behind his house. He also raised cattle and was a farmer. Mr. Frazier died in 1951, but the house still stands. (BCPL.)

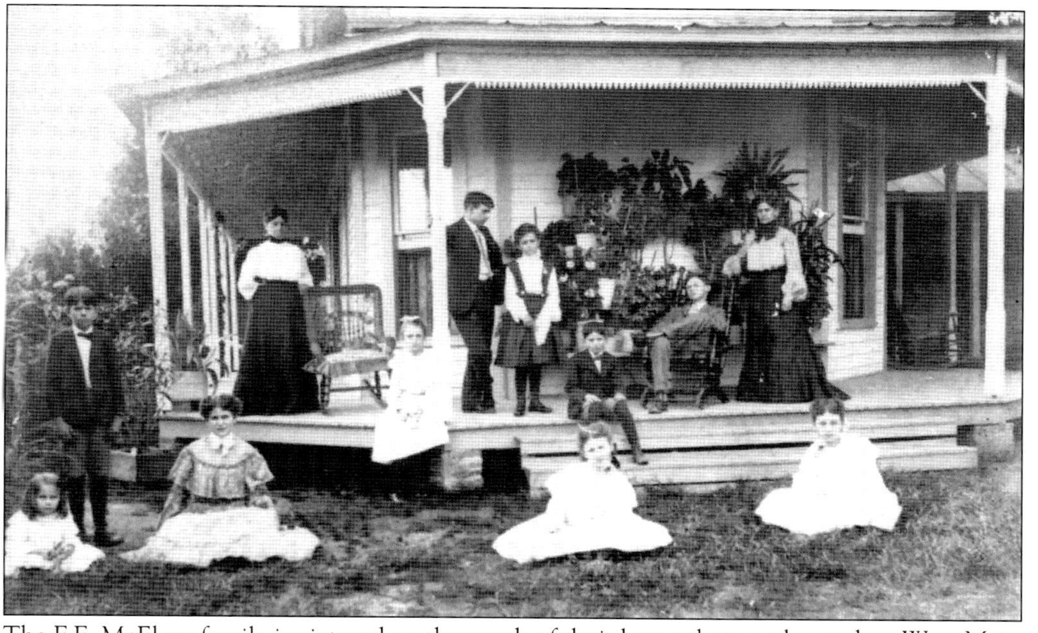

The F.E. McElyea family is pictured on the porch of their home that was located on West Main Street in Camden. Mr. McElyea was a blacksmith; he married Mary Ann Myrick. One of their daughters, Zula, married J.M. Lashlee and moved into this house, which became known in later years as the Jim Lashlee place. Only a vacant lot remains today. (BCPL.)

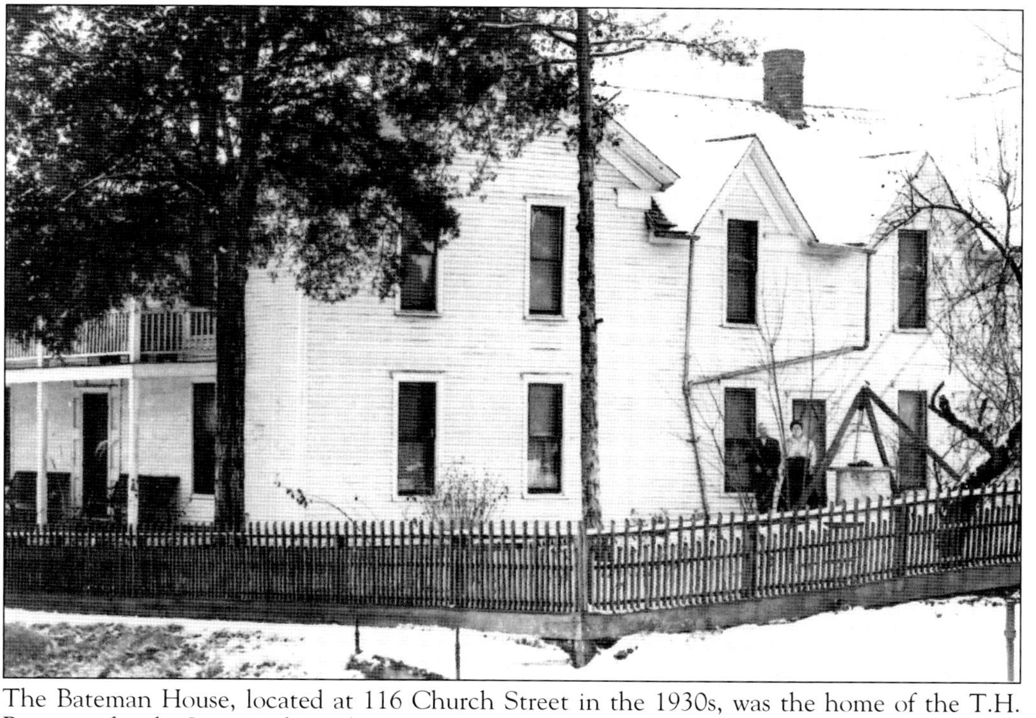

The Bateman House, located at 116 Church Street in the 1930s, was the home of the T.H. Bateman family. It was a frame house at the corner of what is now Main and Church Streets, where the Bank of Camden now stands. (BCPL.)

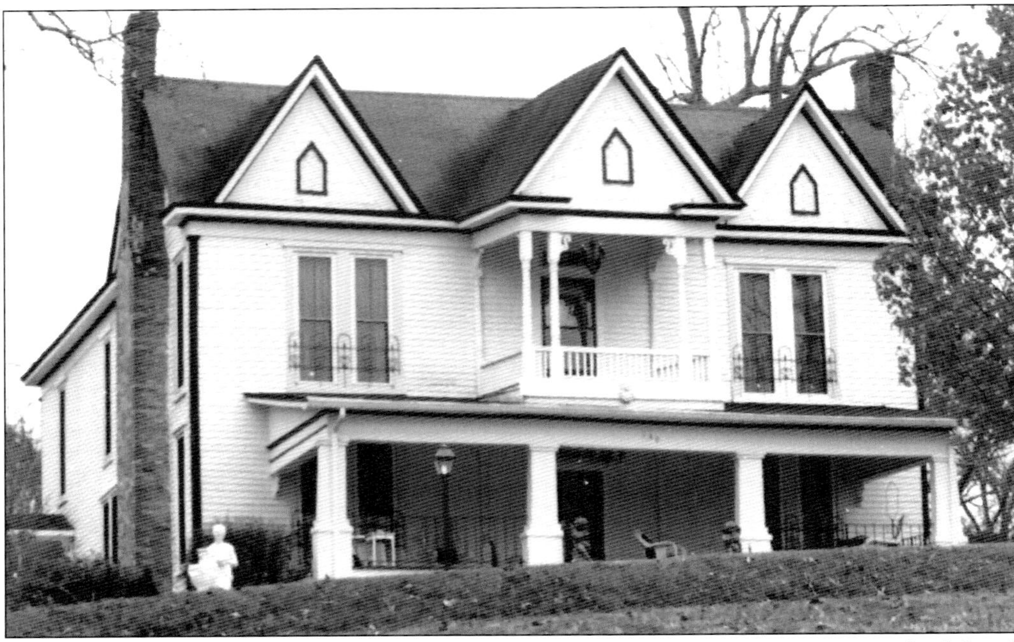

In 1902, J.F. Beaton, a saloon keeper, built this two-story residence. He apparently did well financially until anti-saloon legislation drove him out in 1903. The house became known as "the house that whiskey built." The Lashlee family lived there many years; it later served as the Camden Funeral Home and then Frank Lashlee had an insurance office there. The house is being restored by its new owners, Jack and Joyce Reynolds. (JG.)

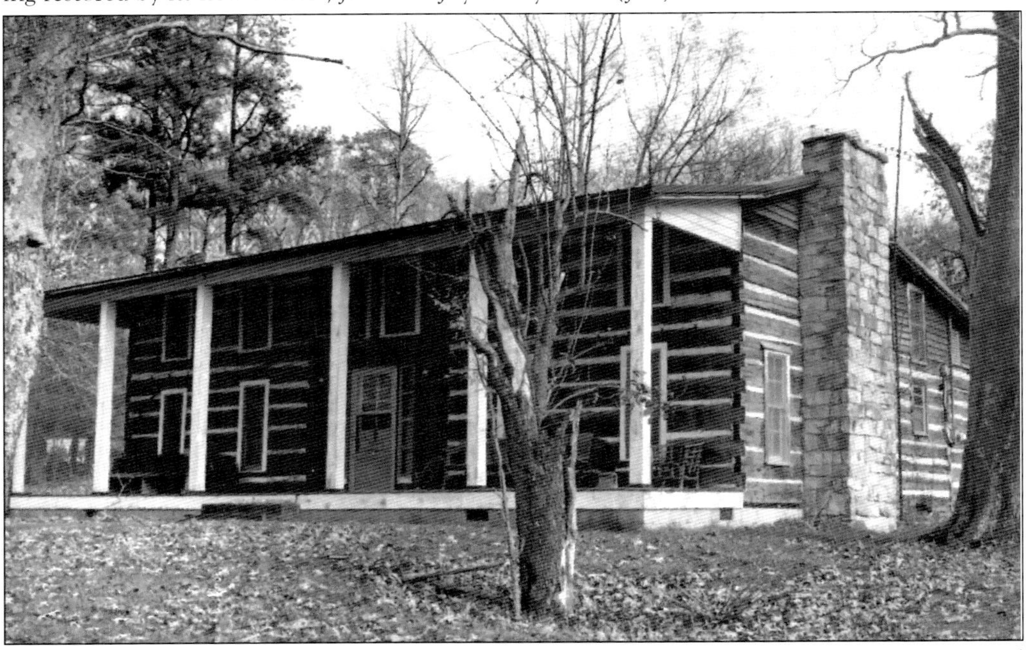

The old homestead of Sol and Belle Christopher has been restored by their children and is called "Christopher Manor." It is owned by W.C. McDaniel and located on Lick Creek Road. (JG.)

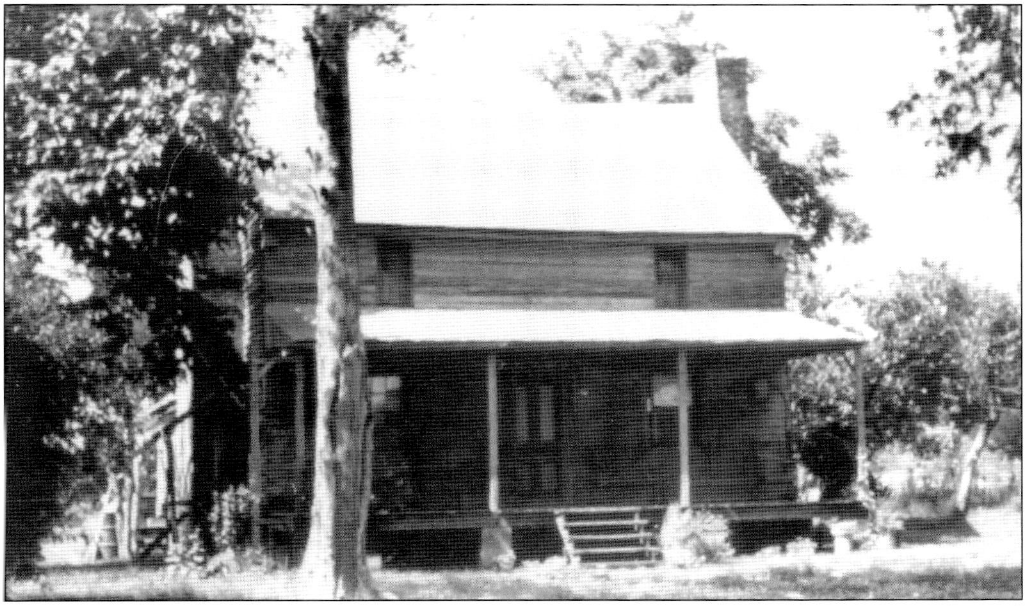

The oldest-known house in Benton County was the Joseph R. Matthews house; it was located in the small community of Chaseville. The house was well built, and it is known to have been built before 1842. In 1981, the house was sold to Bill Anderson of Nolensville, who dismantled it and moved it four miles west of Holladay on Westport Road, where it is used as a summer and hunting cottage. (CW.)

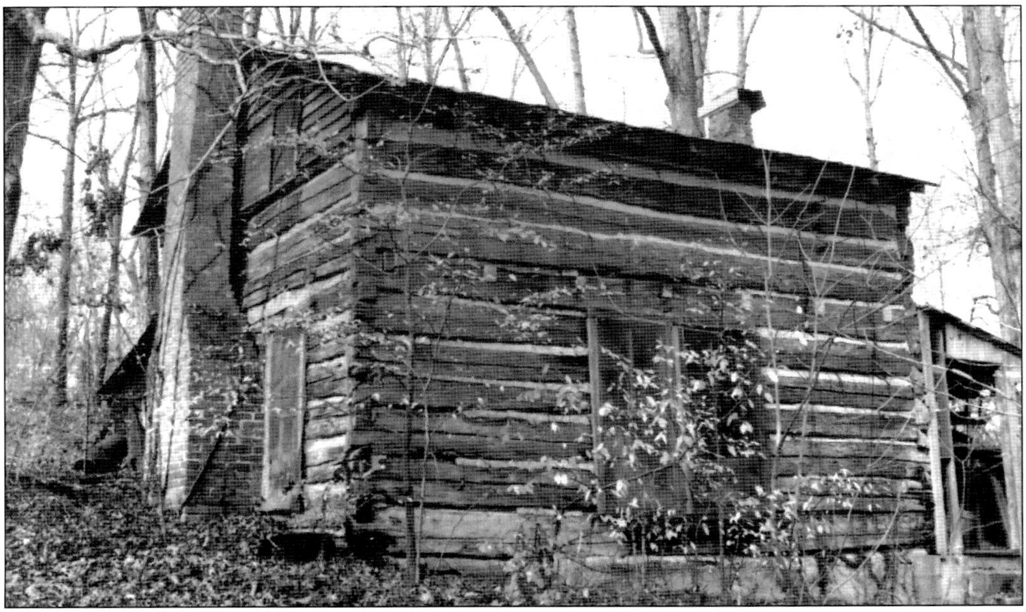

In preparation for the flooding to form Kentucky Lake (enacted by the Tennessee Valley Authority in the early 1940s), many old homes and schools were taken down and moved elsewhere. This old building was a home and post office from Gillie, Tennessee, in Henry County. It was moved from Henry County to Benton County and is owned by W.C. McDaniel. (JG.)

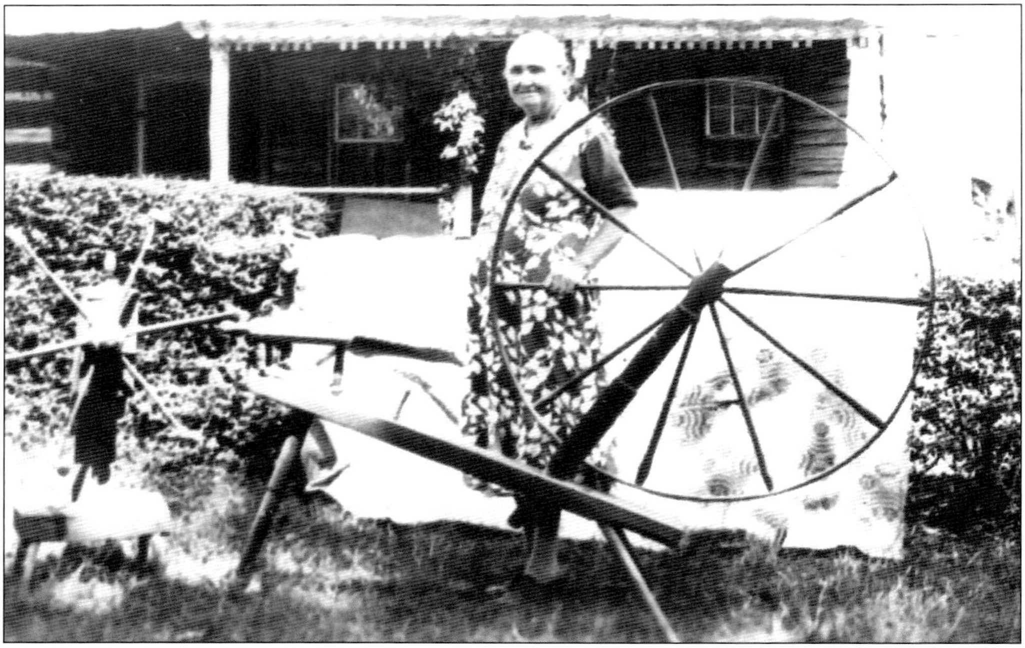

Sarah Ann Cagle is pictured standing in front of her home on Cedar Grove Road with her spinning wheel. This photograph was taken about 1940. (BCPL.)

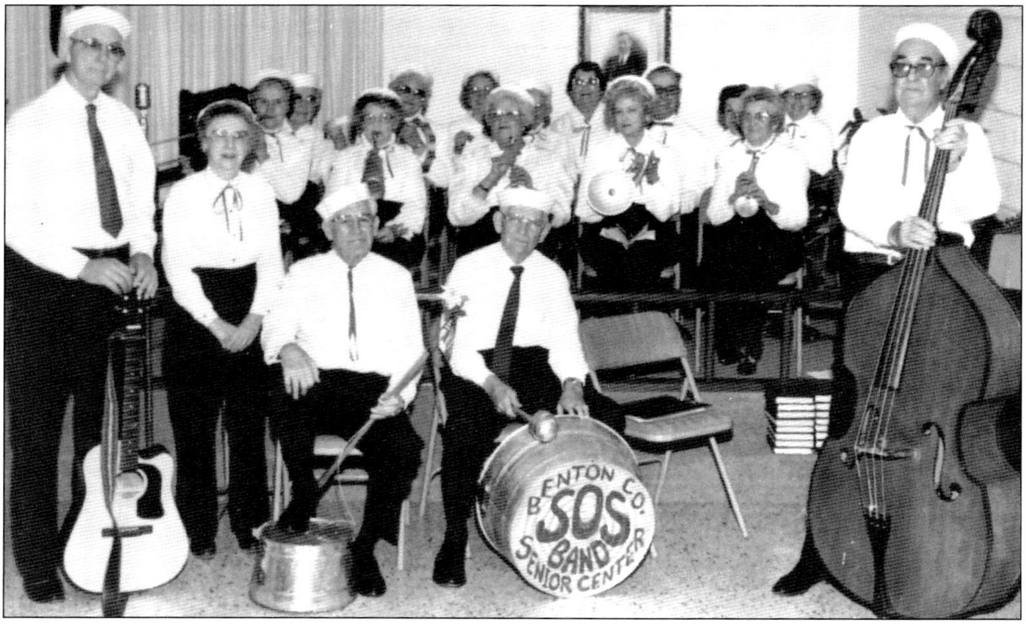

The SOS Band (Seniors Over Sixty) was created March 26, 1982, by Diane Brewer and L.V. Patterson. Those pictured on the front row, from left to right, are L.V. Patterson, Marion Holladay, Ford Hollingsworth, Glenn McGill, and Bob Hayes. Others pictured are Martha Stockdale, Ethel Kelly, Edith Pyburn, Audra Stockdale, Allie Brewer, Vera Hayes, Lorene Ott, Blossom Saunders, Daria Townzen, Annie Mae Hollingsworth, Mavis Peebles, Vonelle Wyatt, and Gus Townsen. (JD.)

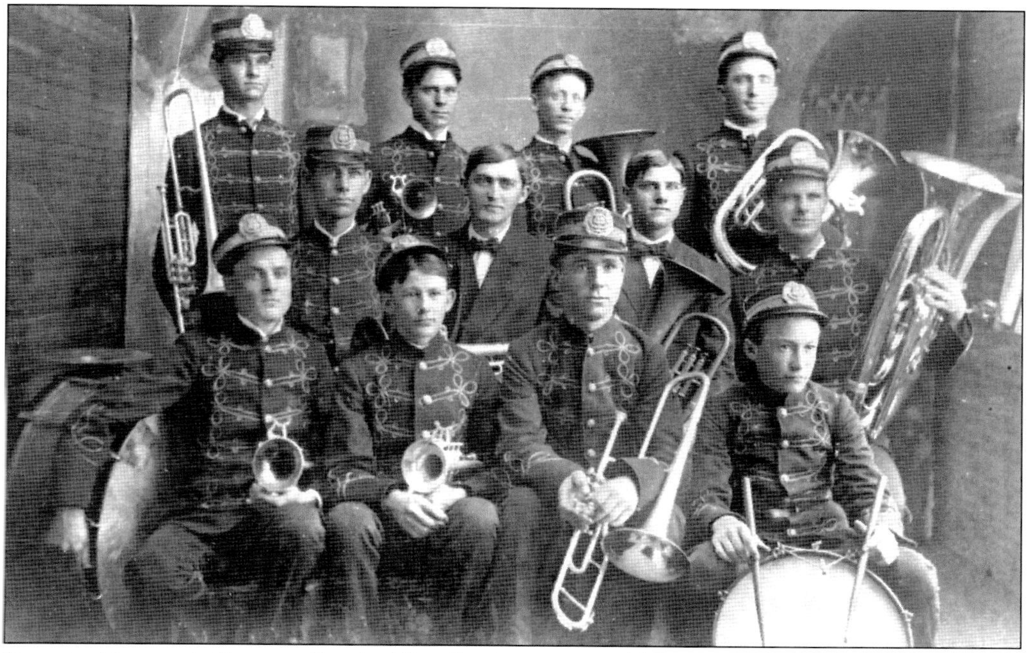

Captain Caraway's Concert Band of Big Sandy is pictured here around 1900. On the first row are Bate Akers, Pete Bowles, Perry Connell, and Leo Askew; (middle row) Hillary Hastings, Professor Ramsey, Albert Douglas, and Travis Barnes; (back row) Herman Cornell, John Connell, Will Dean, and Raymond Graham. W. Graham was also a member of the group but was unable to attend. (RD.)

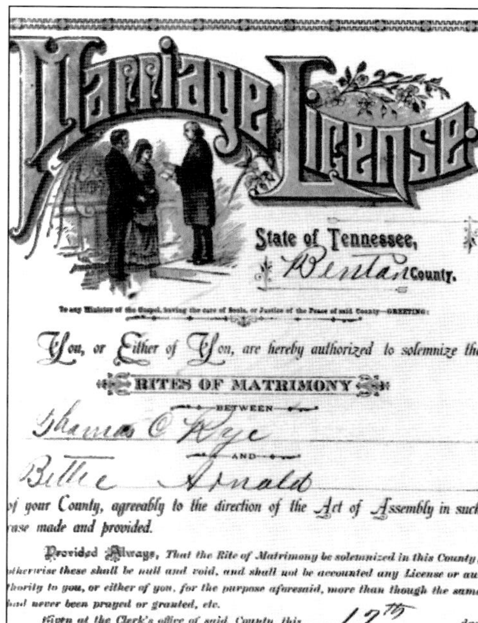

Marriage License

State of Tennessee, Benton County.

To any Minister of the Gospel, having the care of Souls, or Justice of the Peace of said County—GREETING:

You, or Either of You, are hereby authorized to solemnize the RITES OF MATRIMONY BETWEEN Thomas C. Rye AND Bettie Arnold of your County, agreeably to the direction of the Act of Assembly in such case made and provided.

Provided Always, That the Rite of Matrimony be solemnized in this County; otherwise these shall be null and void, and shall not be accounted any License or authority to you, or either of you, for the purpose aforesaid, more than though the same had never been prayed or granted, etc.

Given at the Clerk's office of said County, this 17th day of June 188

A. C. McRae
COUNTY COURT CLERK.

Thomas C. Rye (1863–1953) was born in Benton County and educated there until he was 17 years old. He went to Charlotte, Tennessee, to study law, and he applied for his license to practice on his 21st birthday. Rye returned to Camden to practice law and married Bettie Arnold in 1884. He served as mayor of Camden, and he was elected governor of Tennessee on November 3, 1914, and held two terms. (BCPL.)

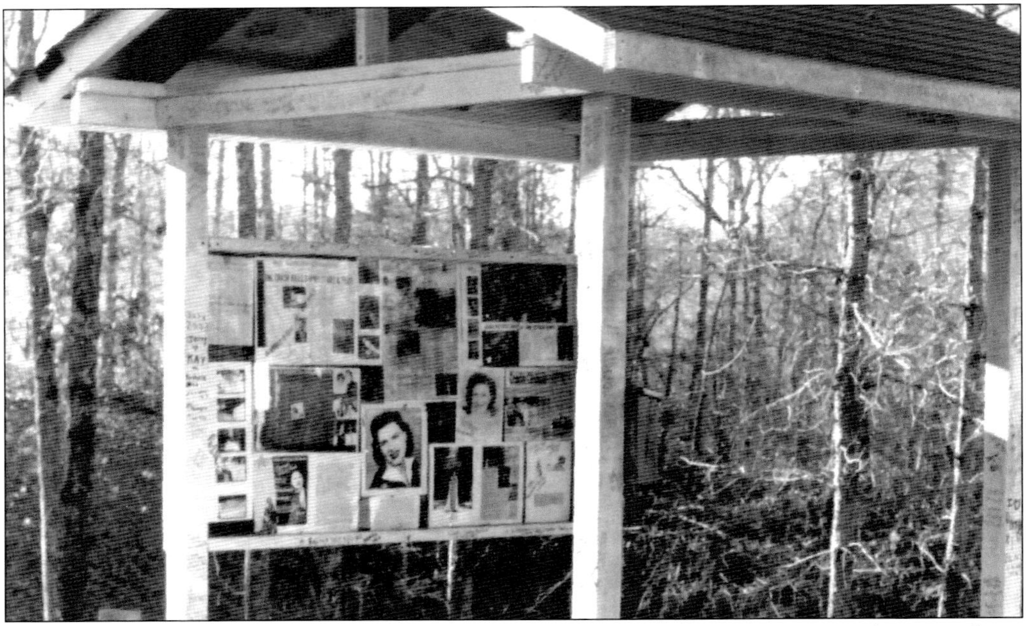

This small open building was erected near the crash site and displays newspaper clippings about the stars who died here. For many years, a Patsy Cline Sing-A-Like contest was held in the fall at The Folk Festival at Eva Beach, but it has now been changed to a time in March, closer to the time of her death. The Chamber of Commerce is working toward improving the memorial site. (JG.)

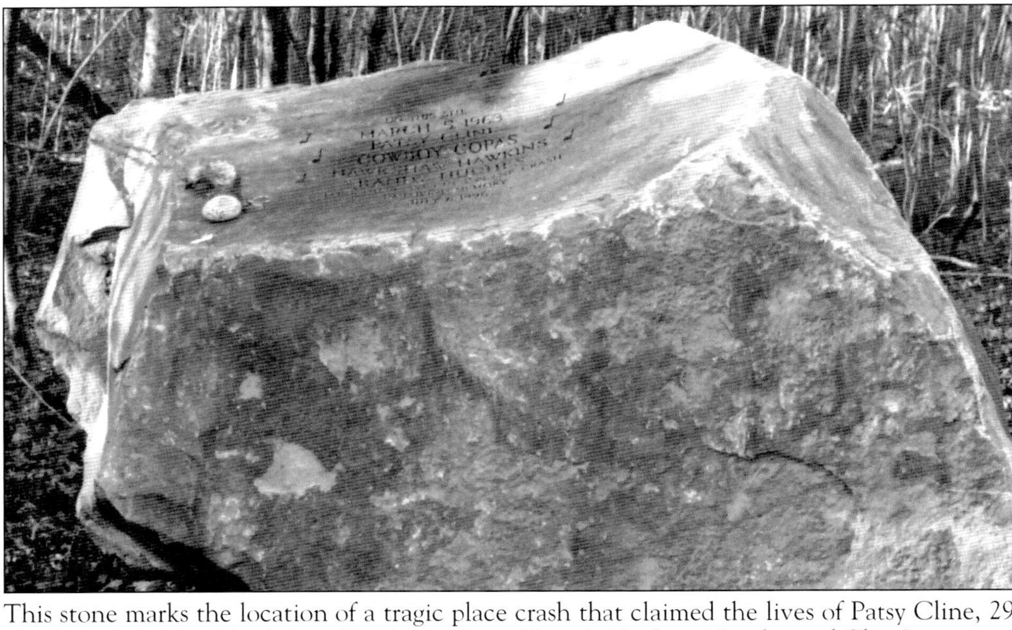

This stone marks the location of a tragic place crash that claimed the lives of Patsy Cline, 29; Cowboy Copas, 49; Hawkshaw Hawkins, 43; and Randy Hughes, 35, pilot and Cline's manager. They were returning from Kansas City, Missouri, where they had performed a benefit show for D.J. "Cactus Jack" McCall. They stopped in Dyersburg, Tennessee, refueled, and were advised of bad weather. (JG.)

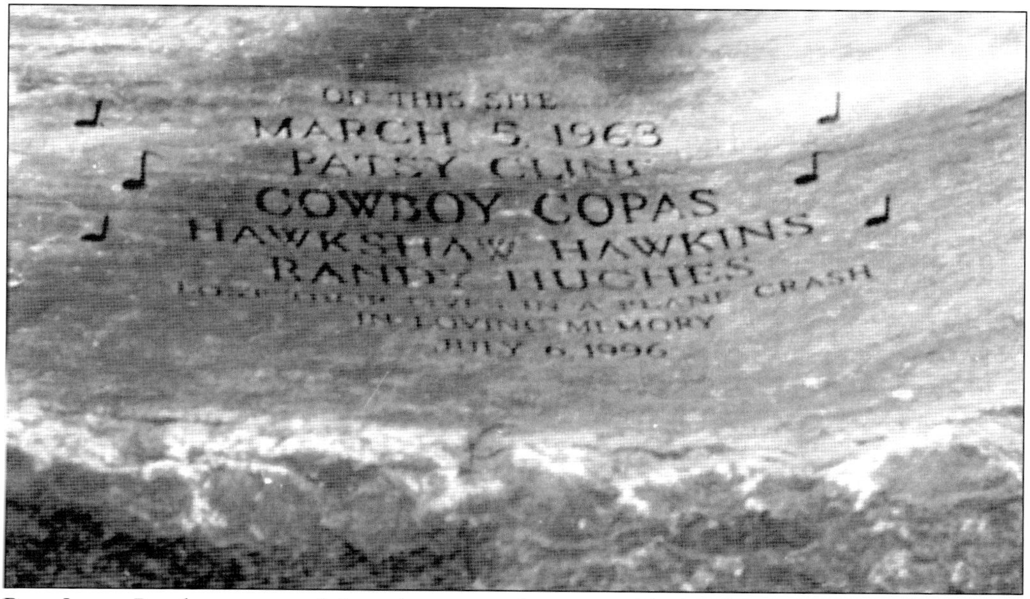

Rep. James Peach was one of the primary people responsible for the monument, which reads "On this site March 5, 1963, Patsy Cline, Cowboy Copas, Hawkshaw Hawkins, and Randy Hughes lost their lives in a plane crash. In loving memory July 6, 1996." Benton County's first music festival, which was held from July 4 through July 6, 1996, was a tribute to the stars and included a memorial at the crash site. (JG.)

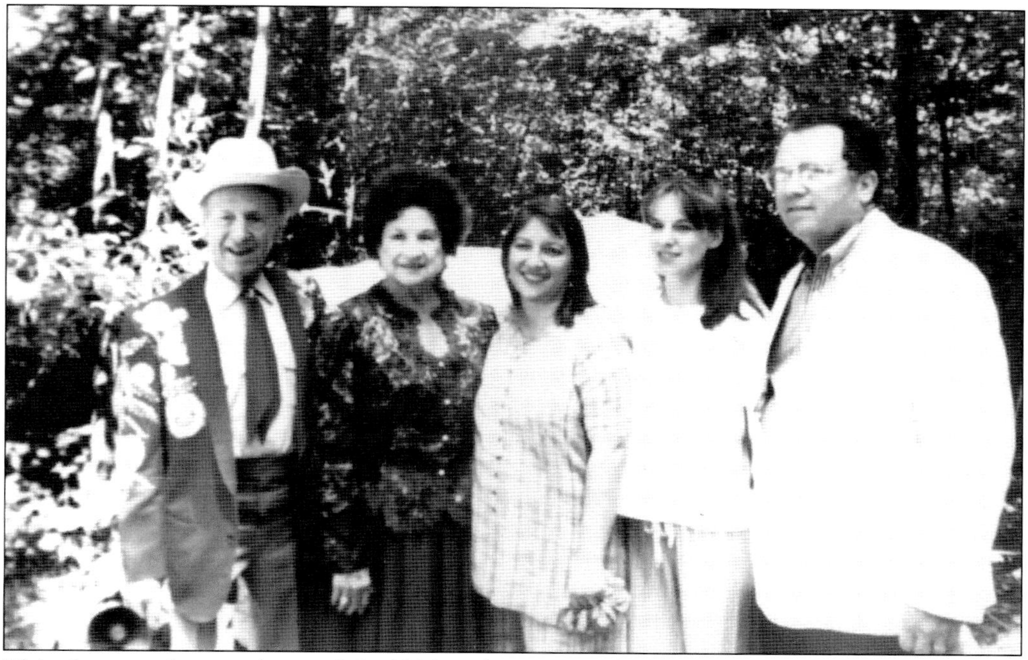

This photograph was taken in July 1996 at the memorial of the plane crash that killed Grand Ole Opry stars Patsy Cline, Cowboy Copas, Hawkshaw Hawkins, and Randy Hughes. From left to right are Jimmy Wright and wife Kitty Wells, Julie Fudge (Patsy's daughter), Michelle Fudge (Patsy's granddaughter), and State Representative James Peach on right. (RD.)

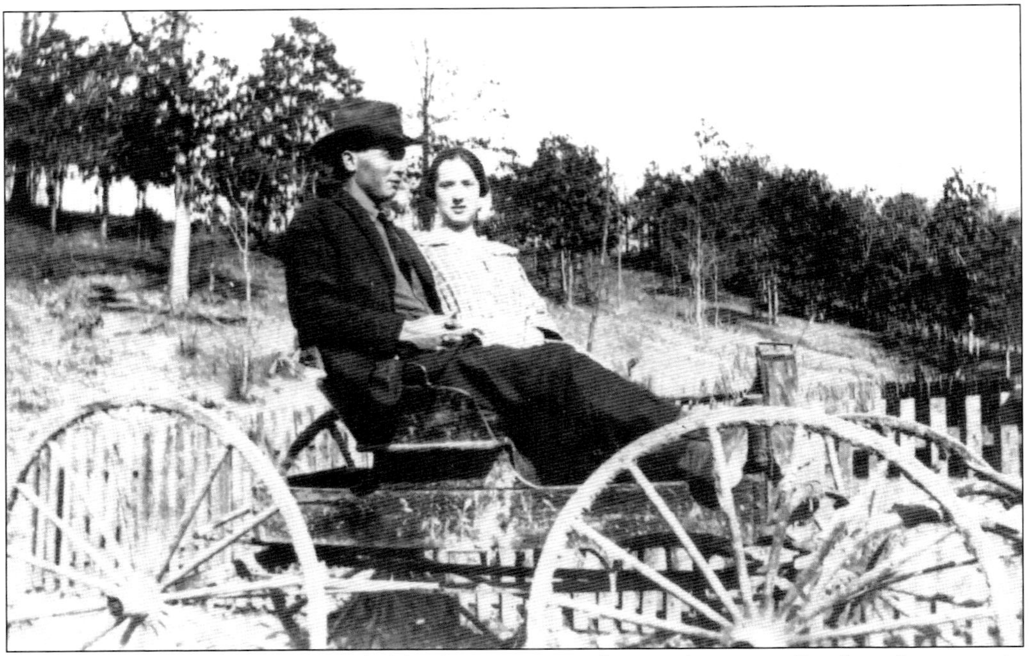

Mr. and Mrs. W.L. Hyatt traveled by buggy to visit his mother on a Sunday afternoon in 1925. (BCPL.)

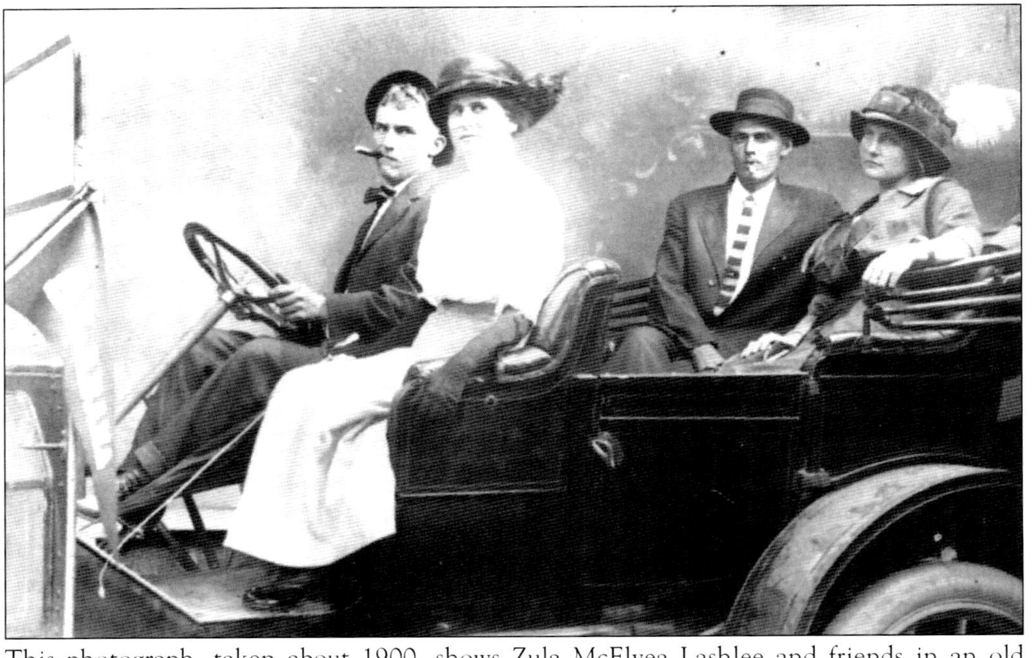

This photograph, taken about 1900, shows Zula McElyea Lashlee and friends in an old car. (BCPL.)

Six

AGRICULTURE

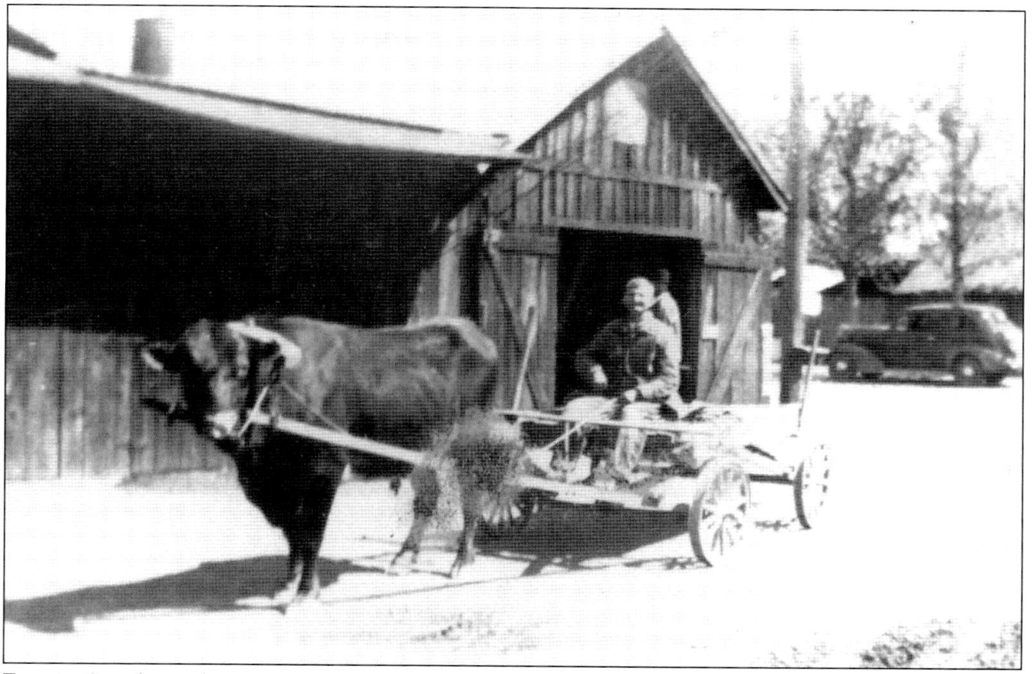

Fonzie Smith is shown in an ox wagon in front of the blacksmith shop in Big Sandy in 1938. (BCPL.)

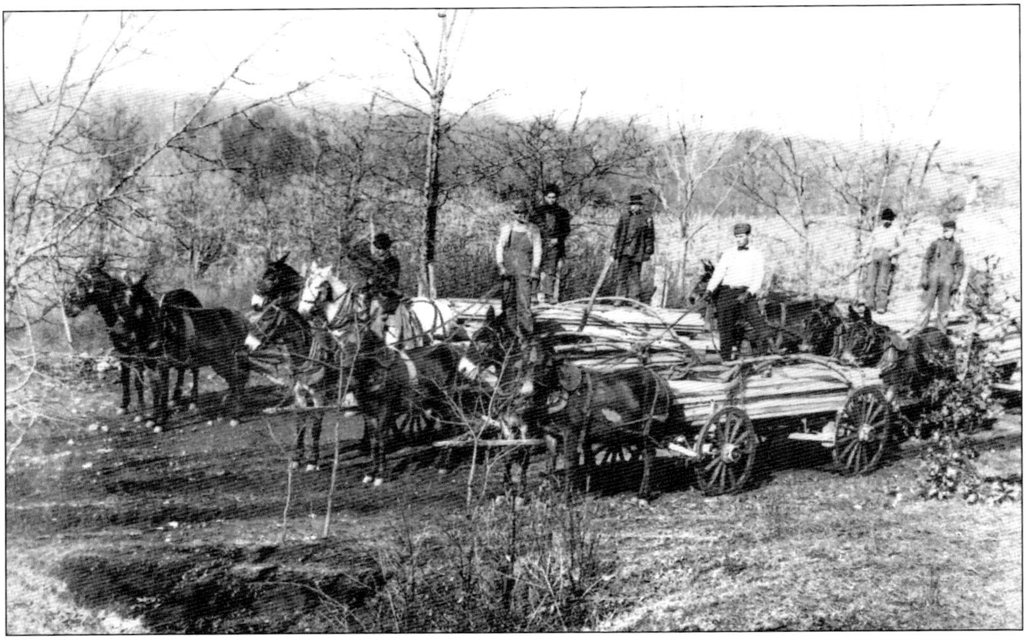

Horses are pulling a wagon loaded with lumber, about 1900. (BCPL.)

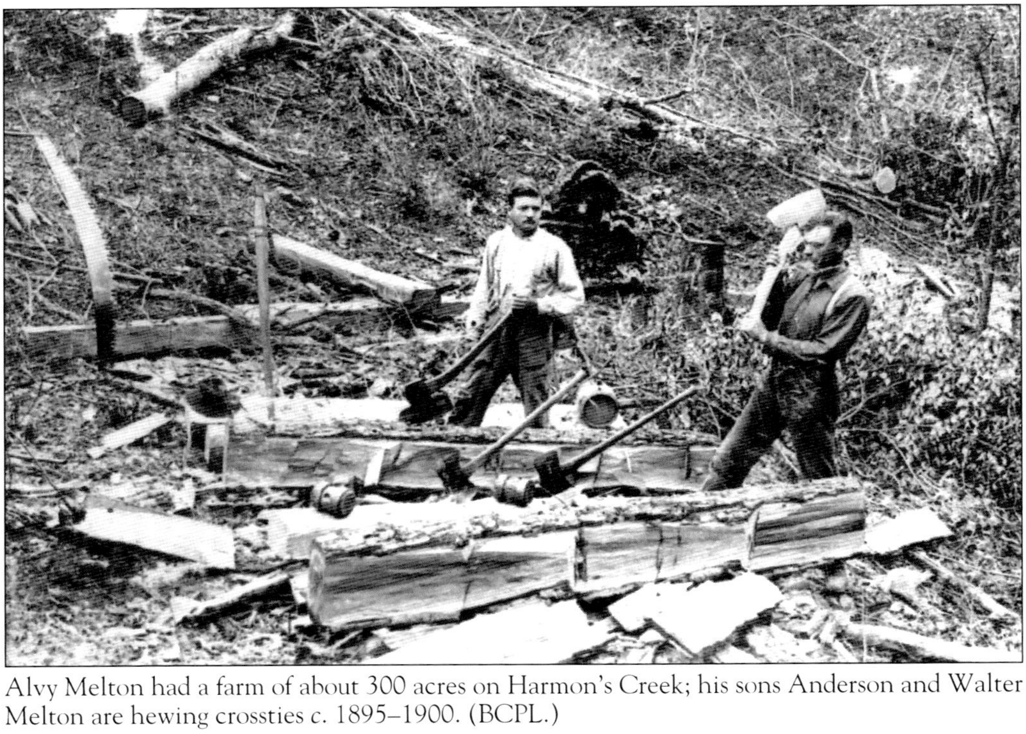

Alvy Melton had a farm of about 300 acres on Harmon's Creek; his sons Anderson and Walter Melton are hewing crossties c. 1895–1900. (BCPL.)

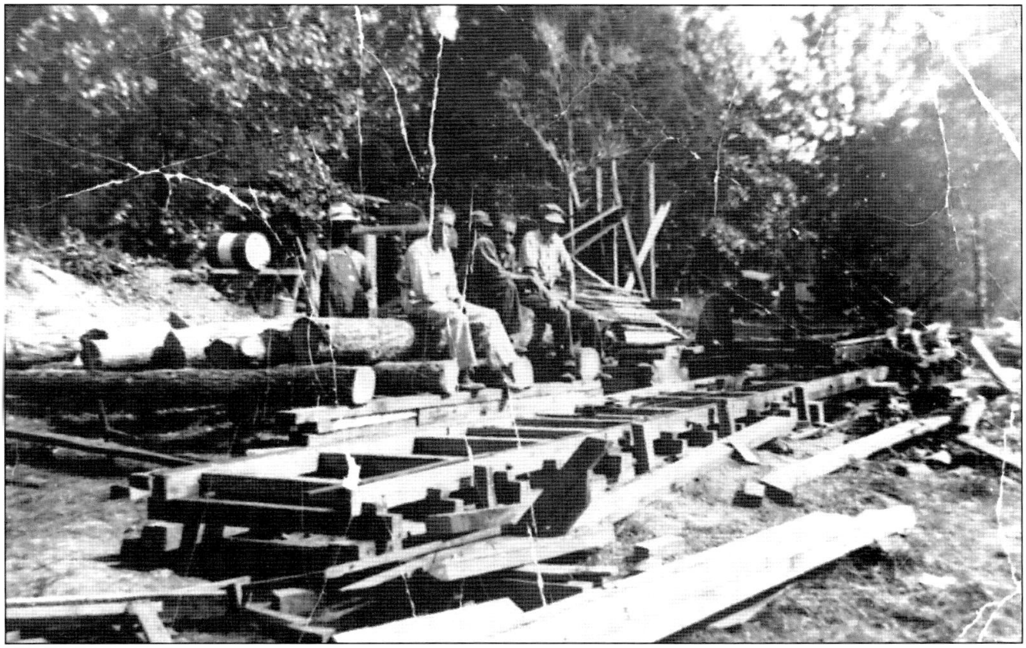

This sawmill was in operation in 1952 at Beaverdam. It probably belonged to Tye Dobson, who is believed to be the man seated second from the right. The others are unidentified. (BCPL.)

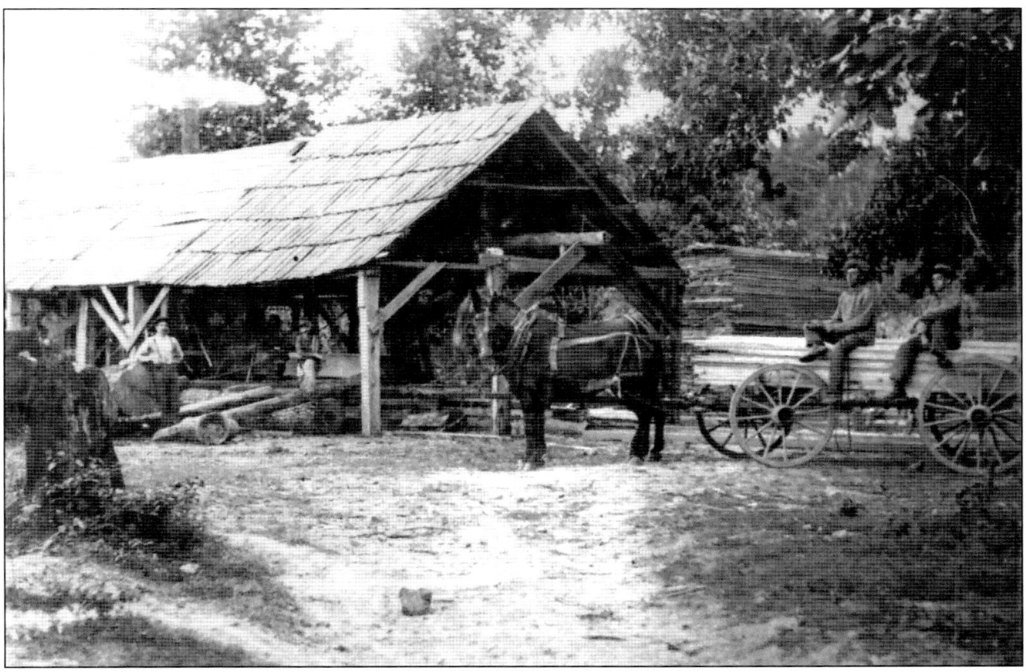

This steam powered sawmill was located at Big Sandy. The Big Sandy City Park is the site of a former sawmill, but it is undetermined if it was this sawmill or another one. (RD.)

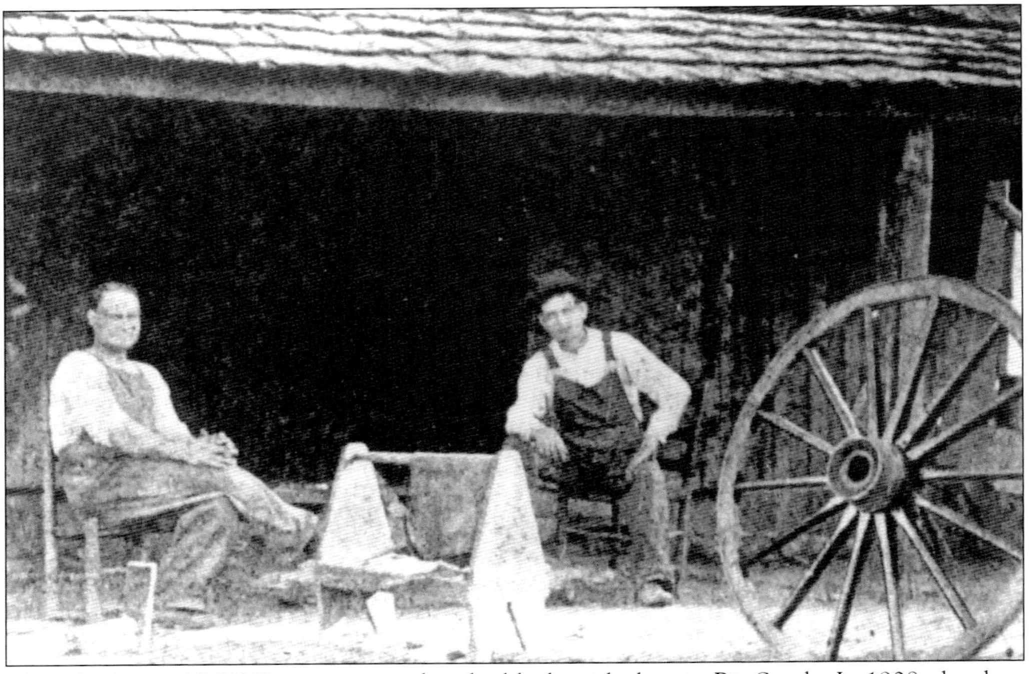

John Hawley and Will Davis are seated at the blacksmith shop in Big Sandy. In 1908, the shop was located in the area where the Feed & Grain Restaurant is now located. (RD.)

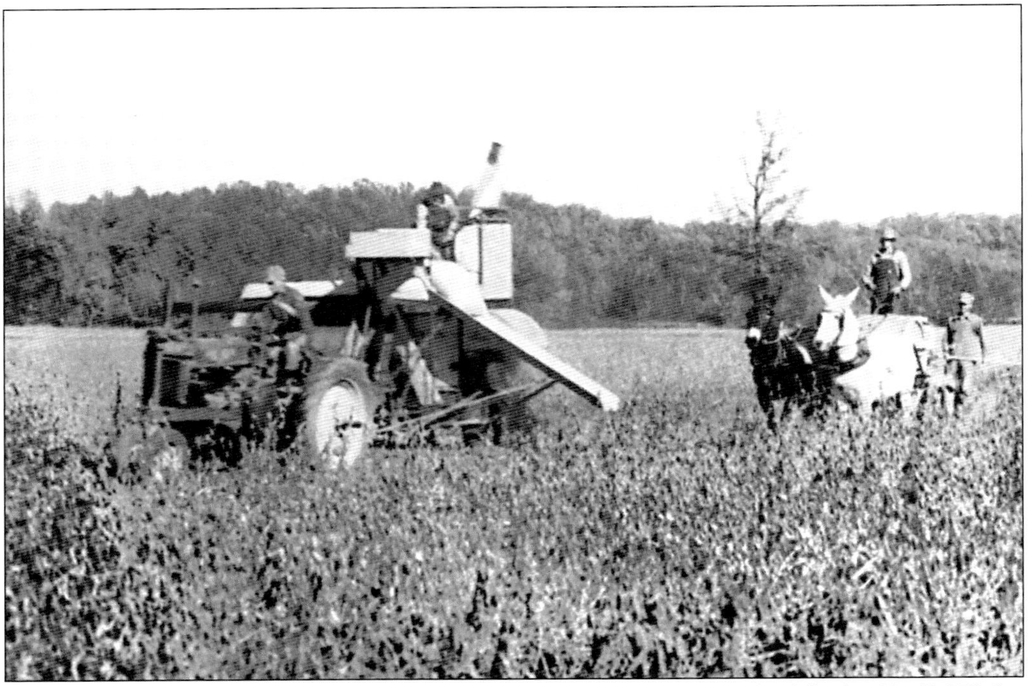

Soybeans are being harvested at the T.A. Berry Farm in Camden during the fall of 1937. (BCPL.)

Celia McKenzie and Nancy Brewer are pictured standing in cotton patch. (BCPL.)

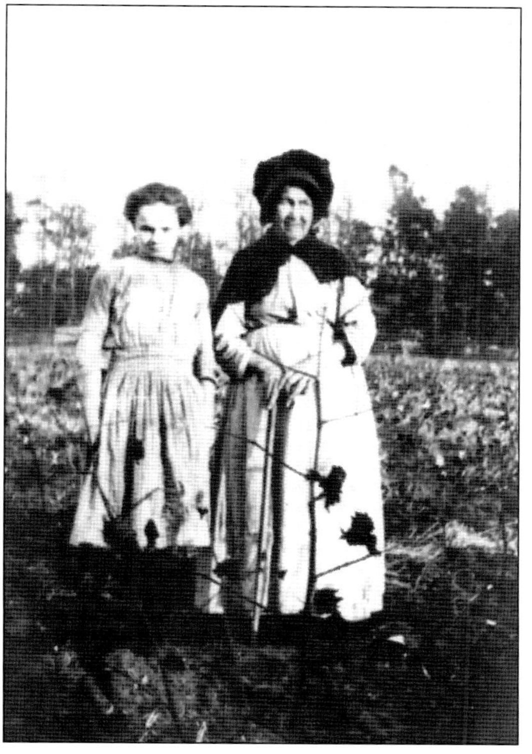

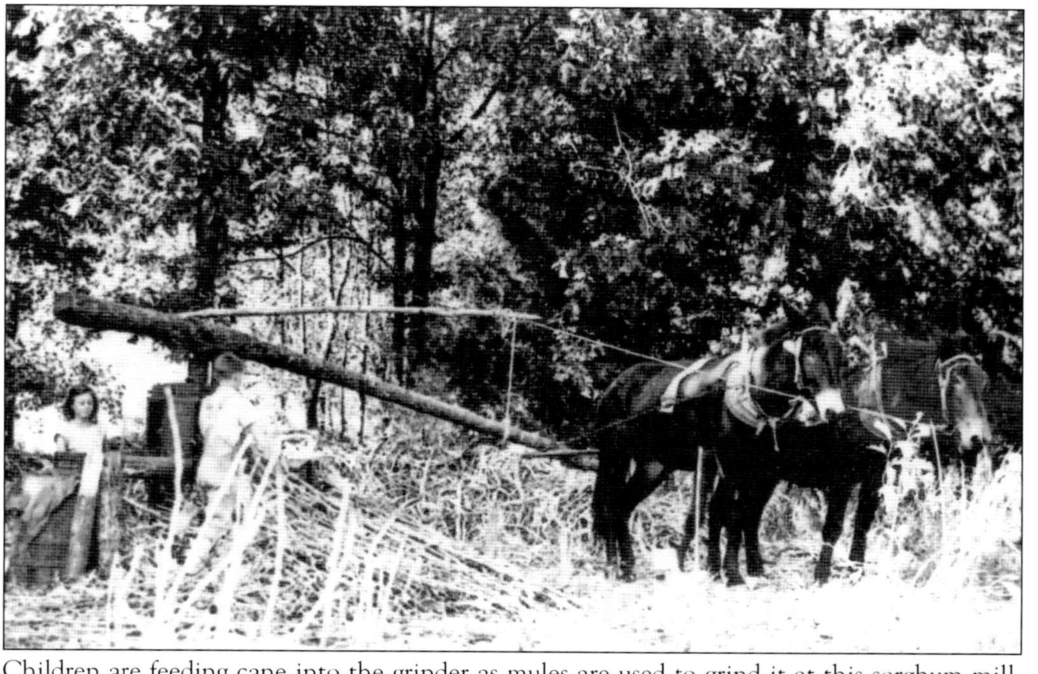

Children are feeding cane into the grinder as mules are used to grind it at this sorghum mill, located about one mile past Eva on Pilot Knob Road; the Plunket Spring furnished the water. The mill was owned by Lindell Pafford and Loranzia "Poolie" Wilson. (BCPL.)

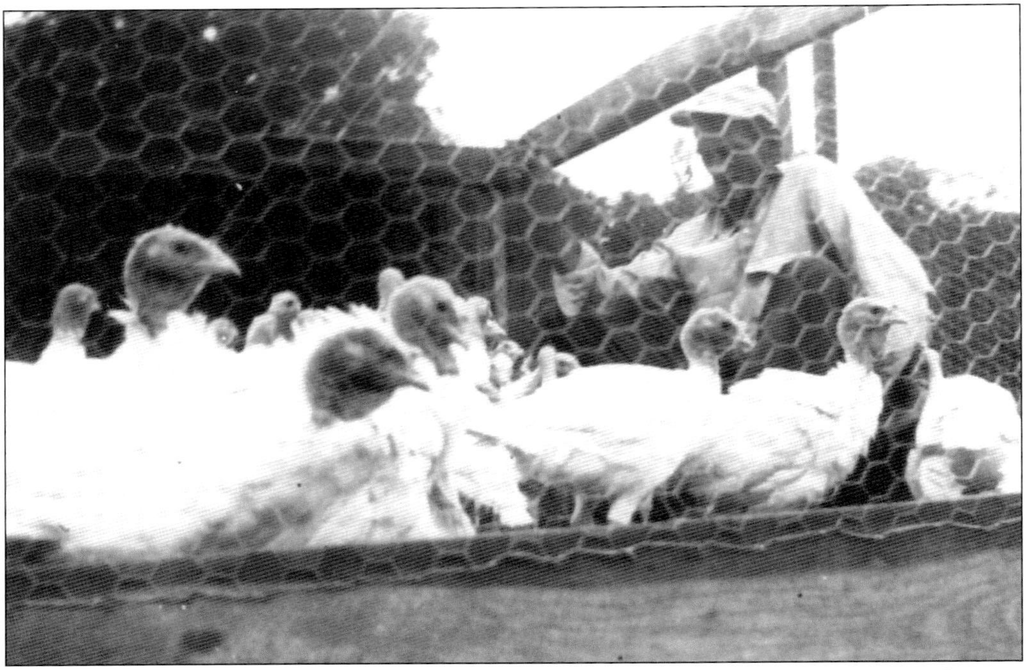

In about 1955, George McCormack raised the first Beltsville White turkeys in Benton County. Beltsville White is considered a variety of the past, but in the 1950s, they were being raised for slaughter in almost every state in the country. They were popular with consumers because of their smaller and finer-boned size. (BCPL.)

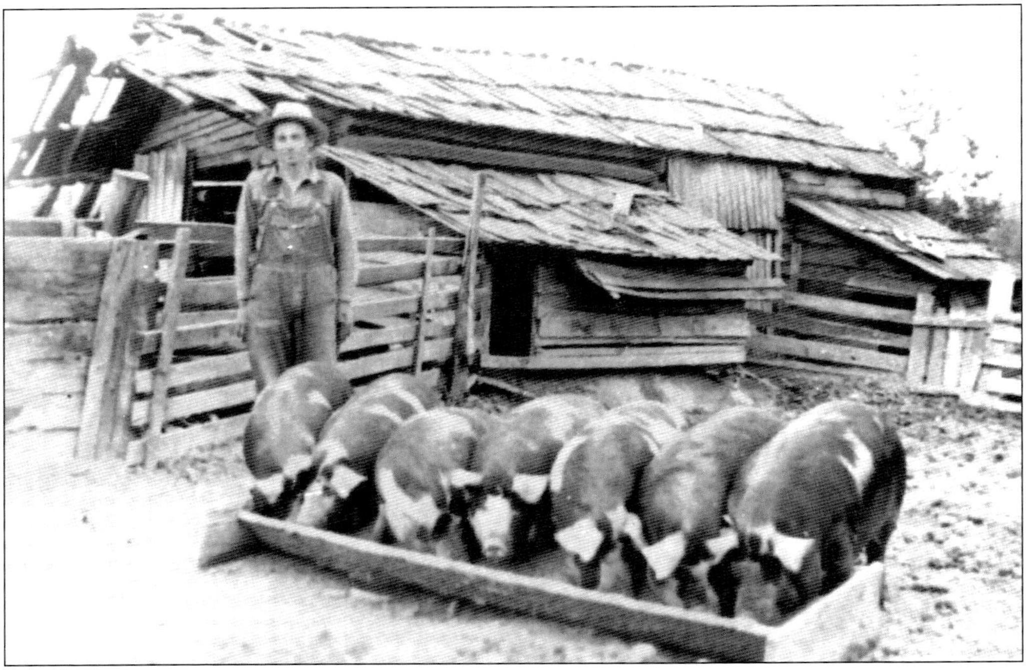

Troy Phifer is seen feeding his pigs in 1944 in the Cooper Schoolhouse area, near Camden. (BCPL.)

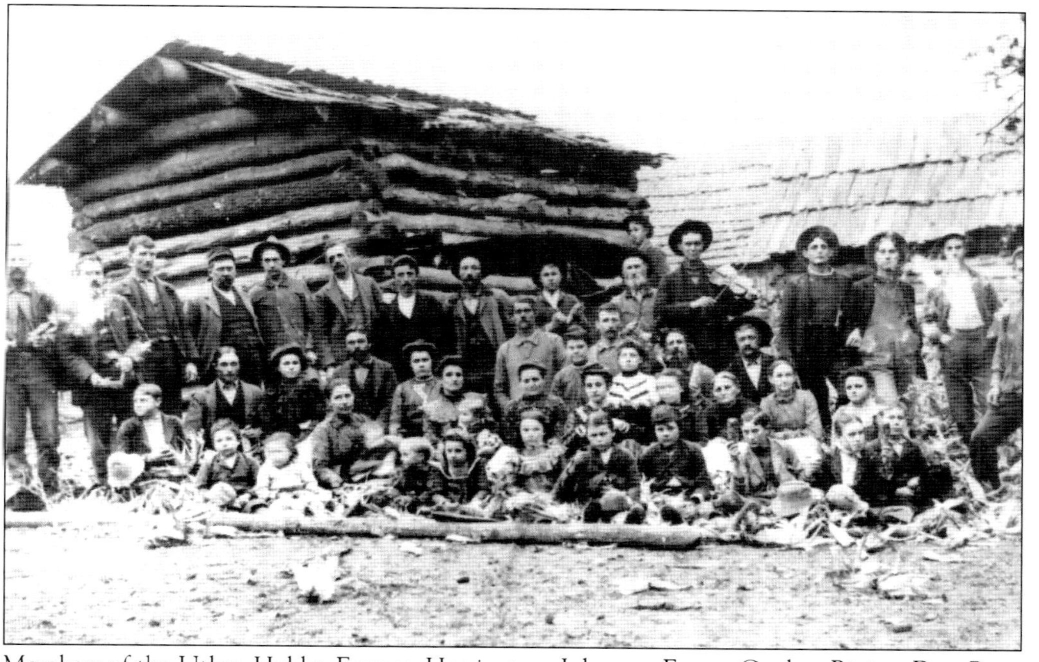

Members of the Utley, Hubbs, Farmer, Herrington, Johnson, Farrar, Cooley, Bivins, Dye, Presson, and Bishop families are gathered for this photograph of corn husking in 1899. (BCPL.)

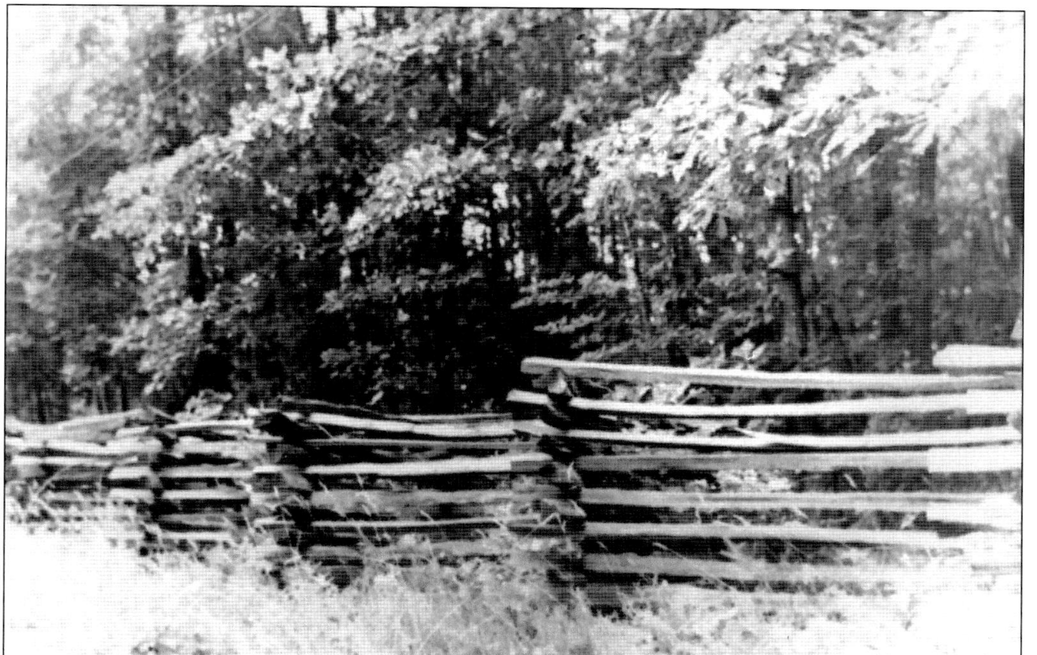

Rail fences similar to this one were a common site in Benton County. Rails were often split from chestnut trees. Much time and effort were used to make such a nice fence, and one wildfire could destroy it in short order. (BCPL.)

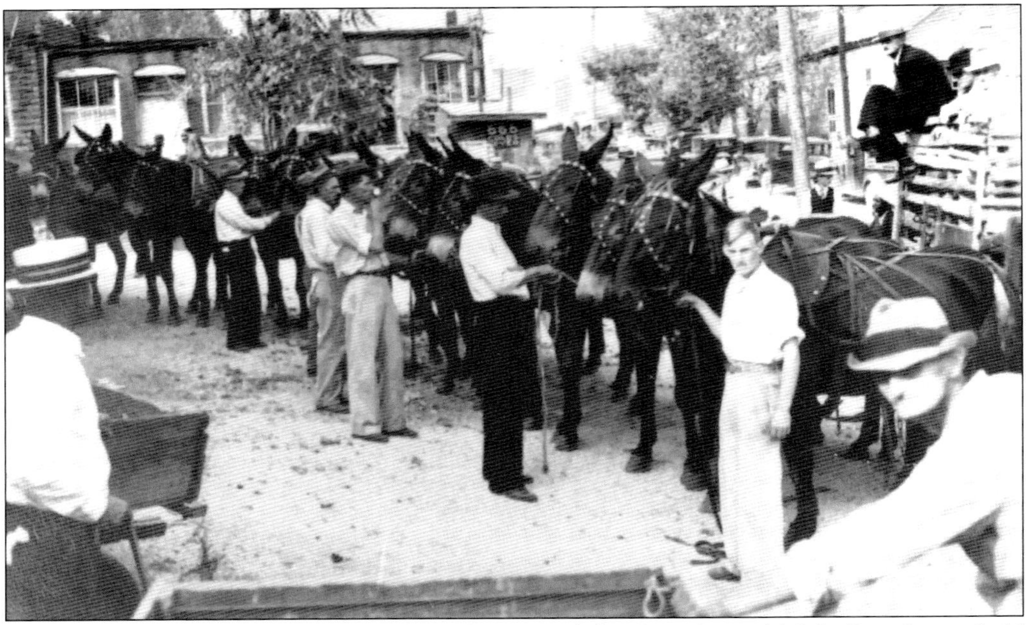

On March 31, 1939, *The Camden Chronicle* reported the First Annual Mule Day. It was held at the Mule Barn (now the Bank of Camden parking lot), behind the National Store, near Dr. McAuley's office. Shown are Lindell Crocker, John Wyly Herndon, Crof Rushing, and Marshall Harris. (BCPL.)

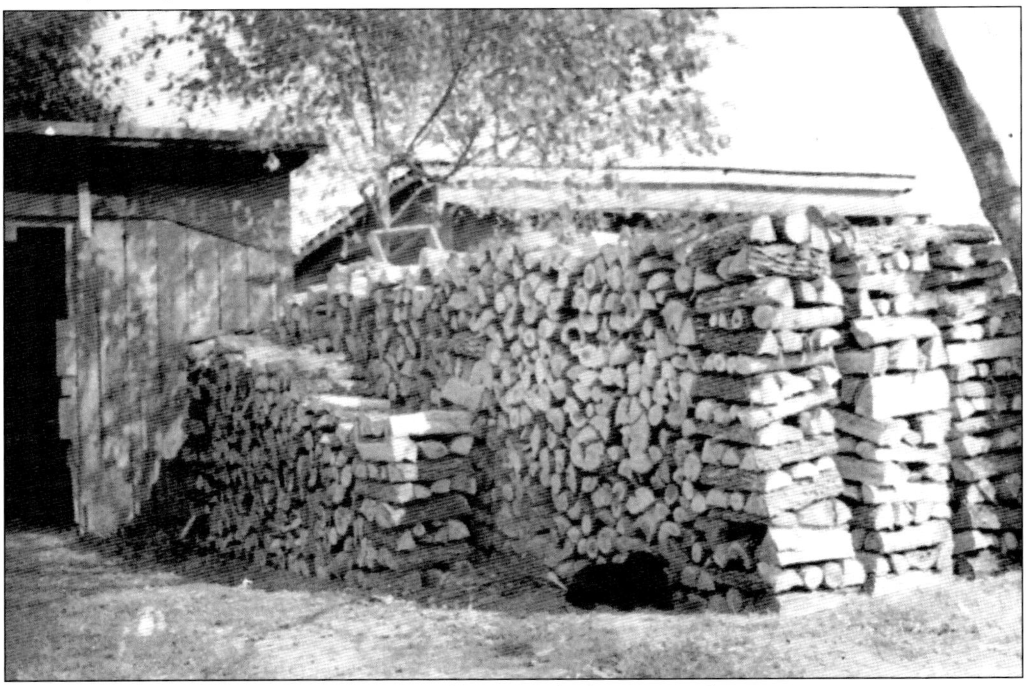

Since wood was used for both cooking and heating the home, much time was spent cutting trees and splitting wood for the winter use. This family seemed to have planned well for its winter supply with this woodpile. (BCPL.)

Seven

WATERWAYS

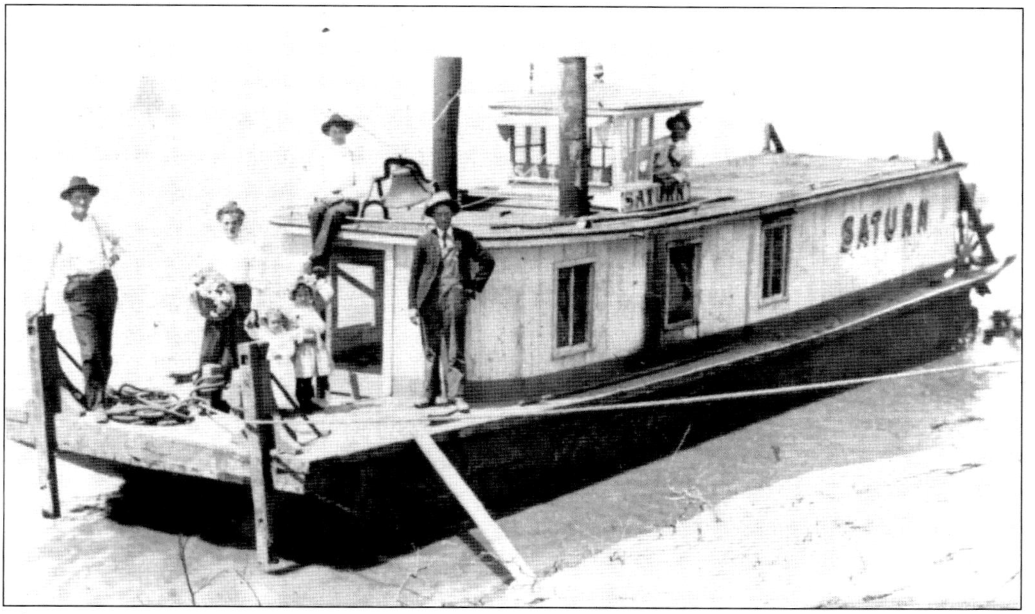

The Tennessee River was the lifeline that brought many early settlers to Benton County. It offered much easier and faster travel through the wilderness, which had few roads. This small sternwheeler steamboat was one of those that made regular stops in Benton County as it delivered mail and supplies to the river towns along the Tennessee River. (RD.)

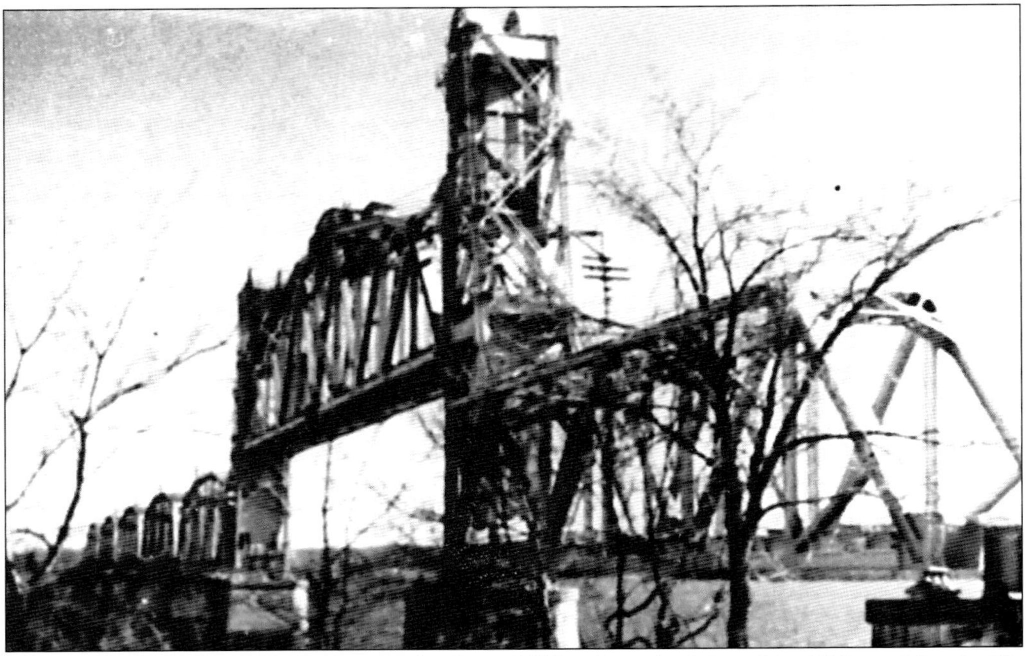

The Danville Railroad Bridge was built about 1859, when the Memphis, Ohio and Louisville Railroad built a line from Nashville through Big Sandy and on to Memphis using Irish laborers. During the Civil War, the bridge and tracks were damaged; the bridge was rebuilt in the 1870s. In 1941, when construction on Kentucky Dam started, the bridge was raised 20 feet for the higher water of the lake. In the late 1970s, the railroad through Big Sandy ceased to operate, and the bridge was dismantled and moved to Alabama. (BCPL.)

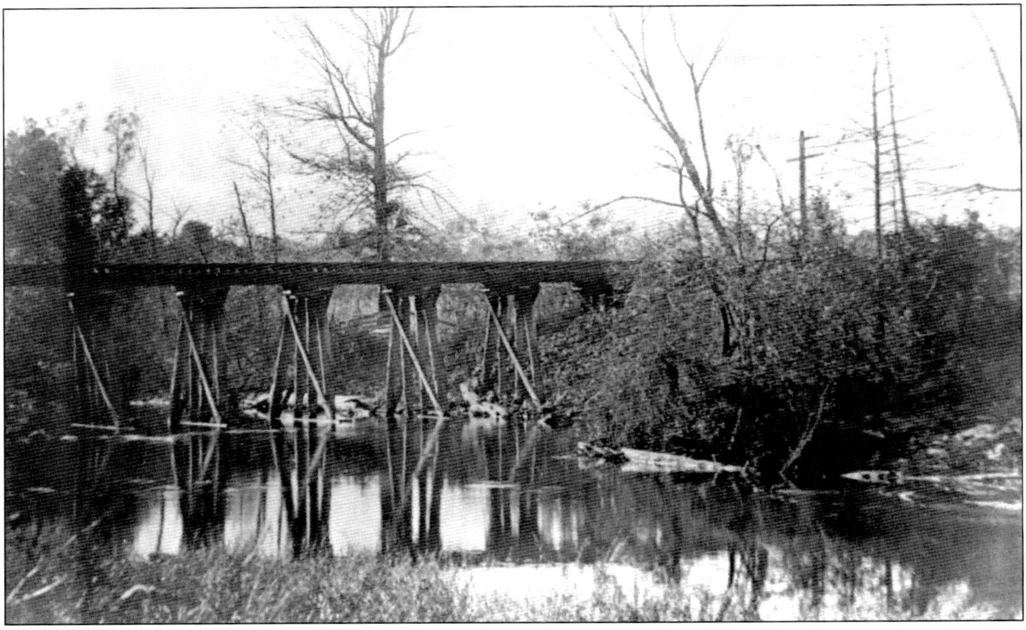

This picturesque railroad trestle was located on the west side of Big Sandy, crossing the Big Sandy River. It was 488 feet long and only 13 feet wide. (RD.)

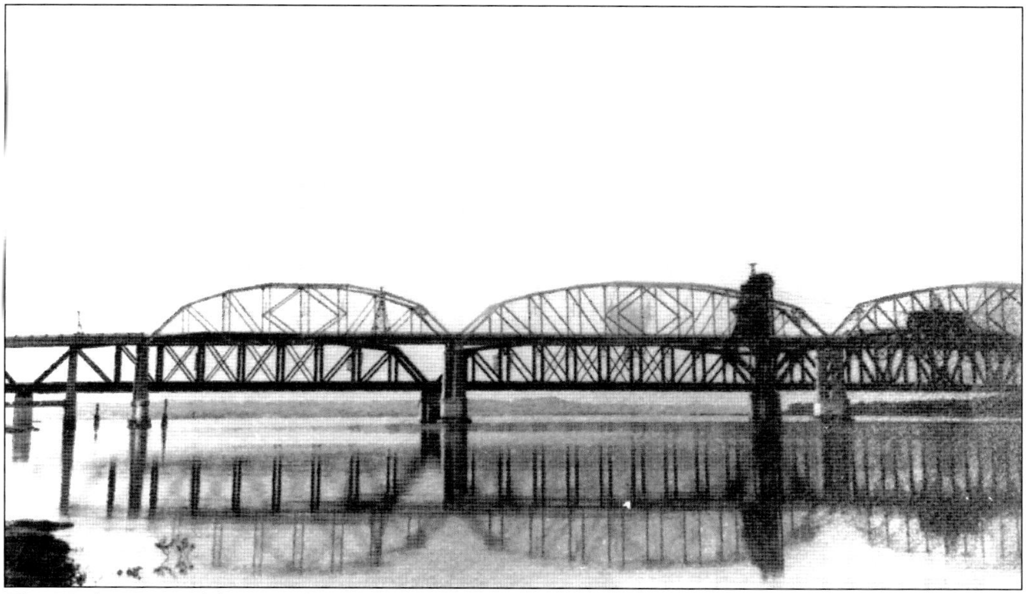

The Hickman-Lockhart Bridge crosses the Tennessee River connecting Benton and Humphreys Counties. The bridge was placed in service in May 1931 and named in honor of E.H. Hickman of Humphreys County and Edward Lockhart of Benton County. They were the first soldiers to die from each county in World War I. A toll was levied against vehicles crossing the bridge until 1947 to pay the construction cost. (BCPL.)

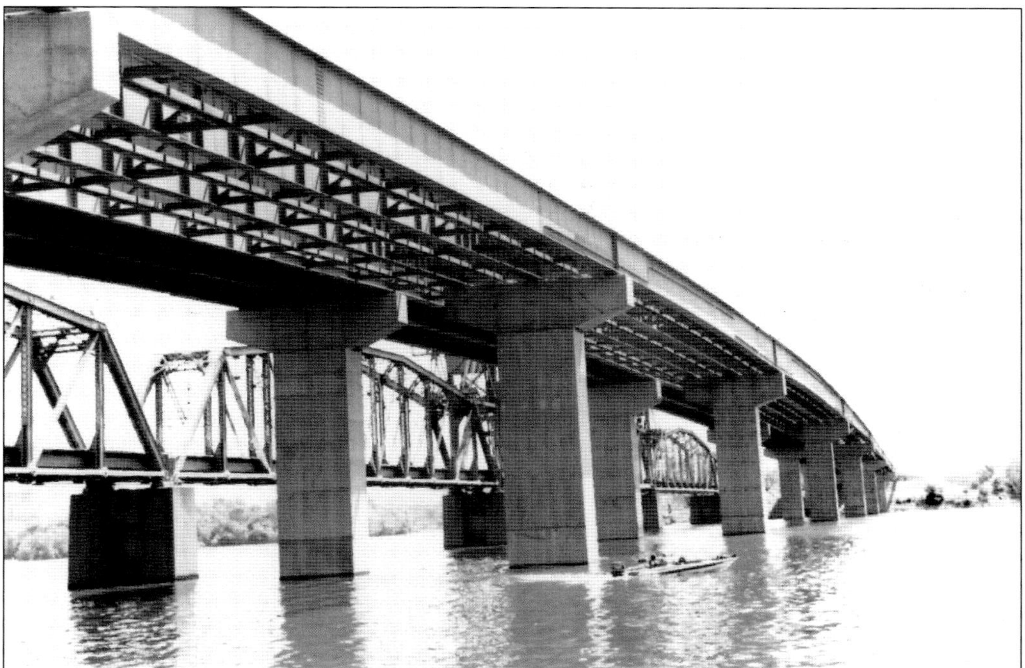

The old bridge was blown up in October 1986 to make room for a new bridge. This photograph was made during the construction of the new bridge. For a short time, the bridge was renamed, but it soon was given back its name of the Hickman-Lockhart Bridge. (JD.)

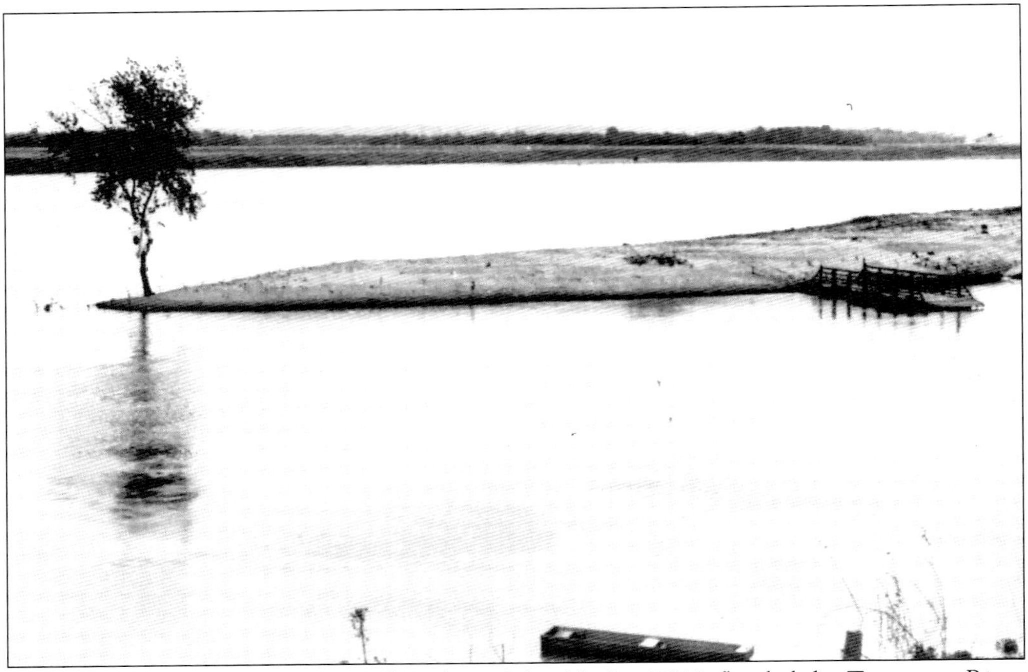

The lone tree stands at the point of Rockport Island before TVA flooded the Tennessee River in 1944. (BCPL.)

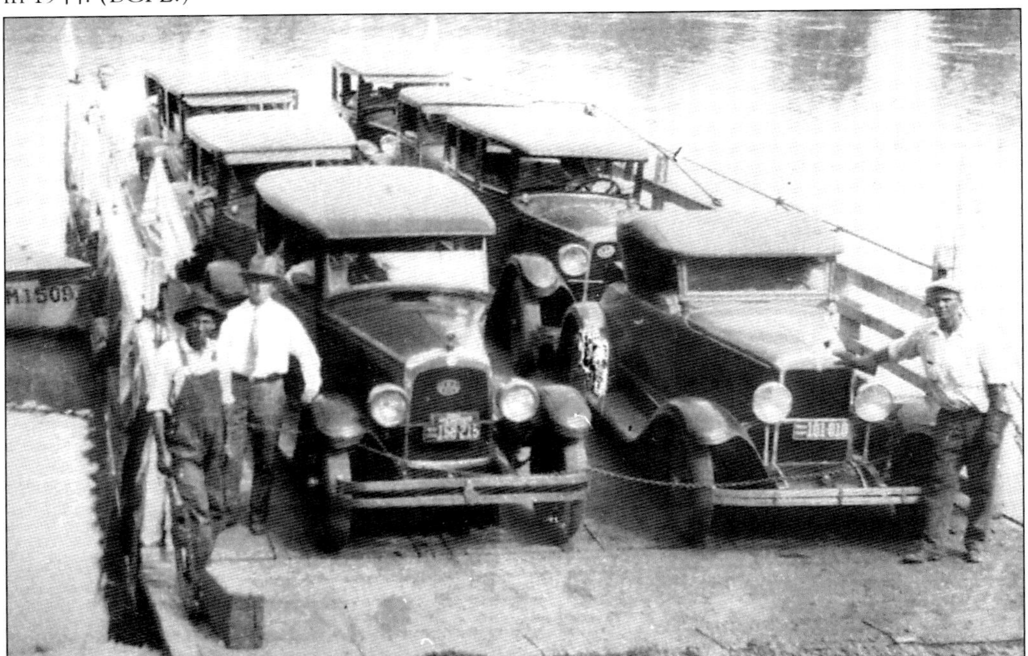

In the 1920s, Trotters Landing was a ferry crossing on the Tennessee River to get from Benton County to Humphreys County and other points east. The ferry was operated by John Wyly Lashlee, and the towboat was named *Minnie* after Mrs. O.P. Lashlee. Mack Lashlee sold colas on the boat. (JD.)

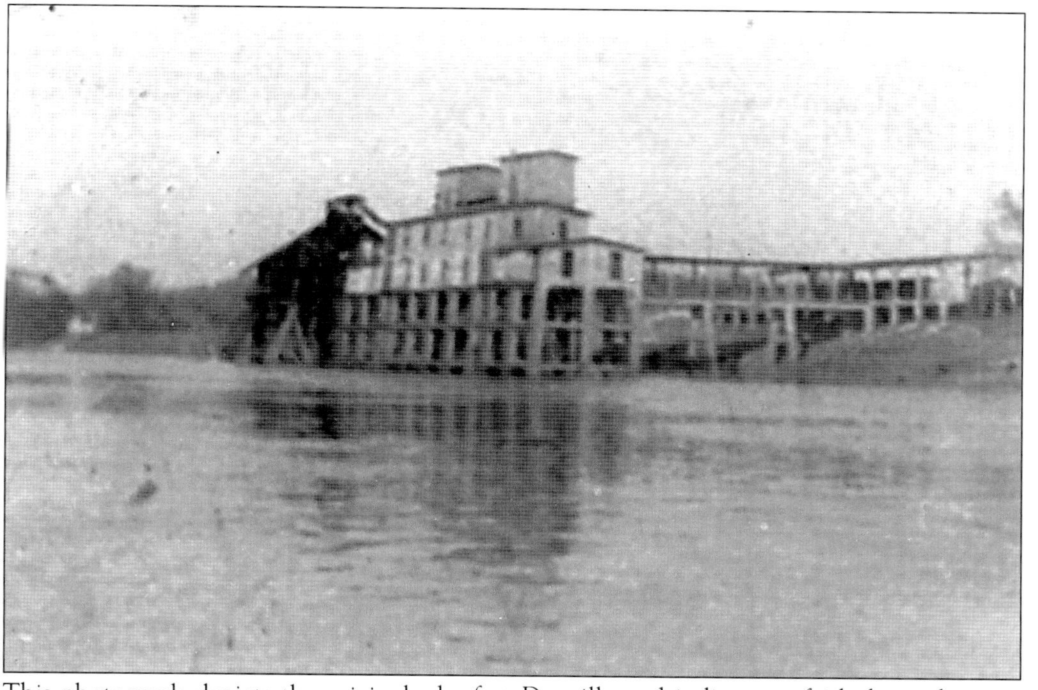

This photograph depicts the original wharf at Danville and indicates a fairly large shipping business—this was before the TVA was established by an act of Congress. (BCPL.)

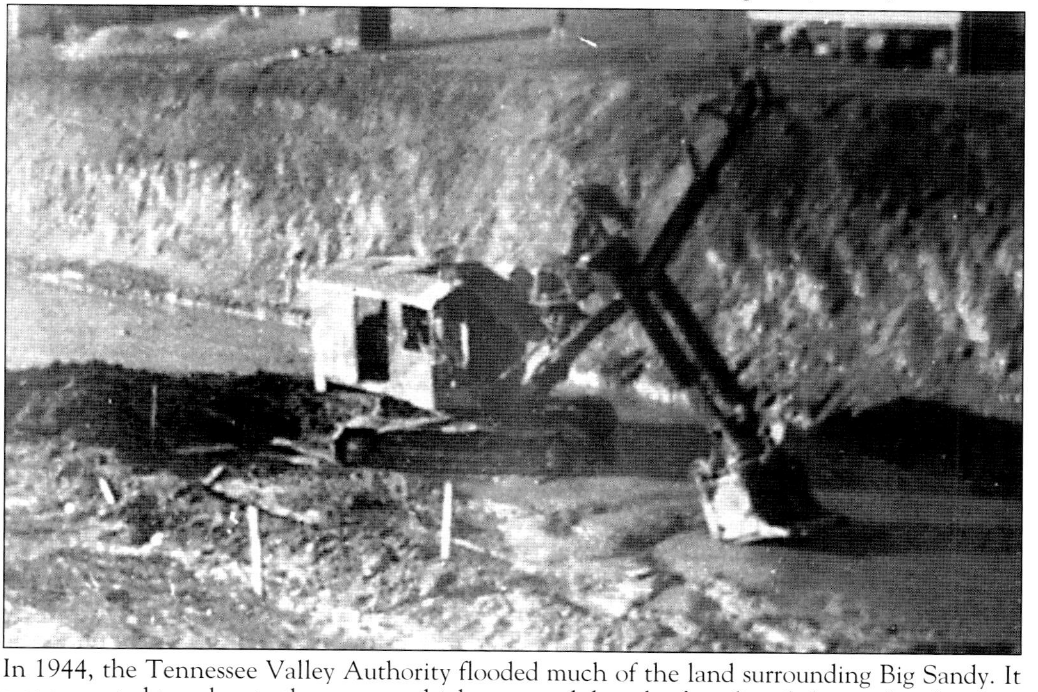

In 1944, the Tennessee Valley Authority flooded much of the land surrounding Big Sandy. It was suggested to relocate the town on higher ground, but the founding fathers refused and an alternate plan to build a levee or dike around the town was used. Pictured here is the work in progress. Among others, Ardel Watts worked on this project. (BCPL.)

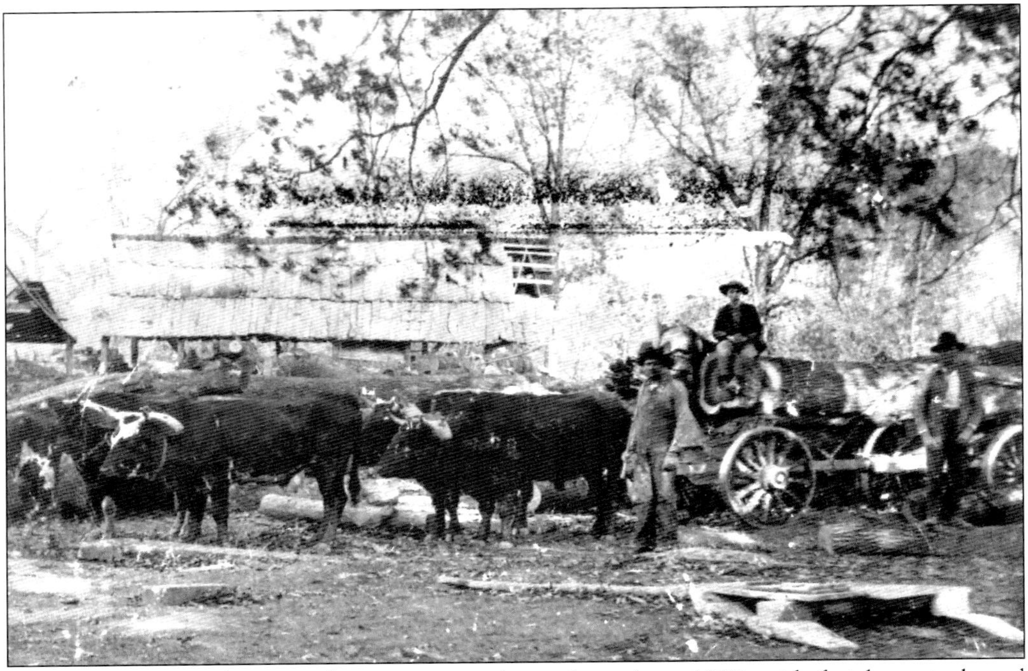

Point Mason Steamboat Landing was a very busy place about 1880, with freight arrivals and cross ties and farm products being shipped out. Pictured are Walt Lindsey in front, Ernie Lindsey on logs, and Tobe Lindsey standing by the wagon. (JD.)

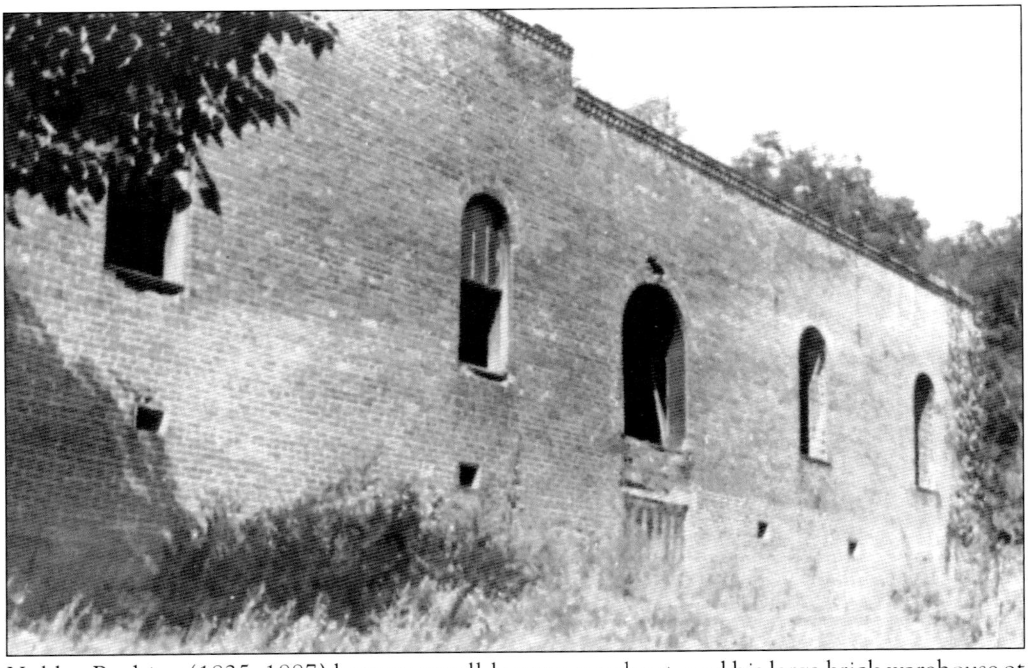

Holden Rushing (1825–1887) became a well-known merchant, and his large brick warehouse at Point Mason on the Tennessee River was a landmark for many years. (BCPL.)

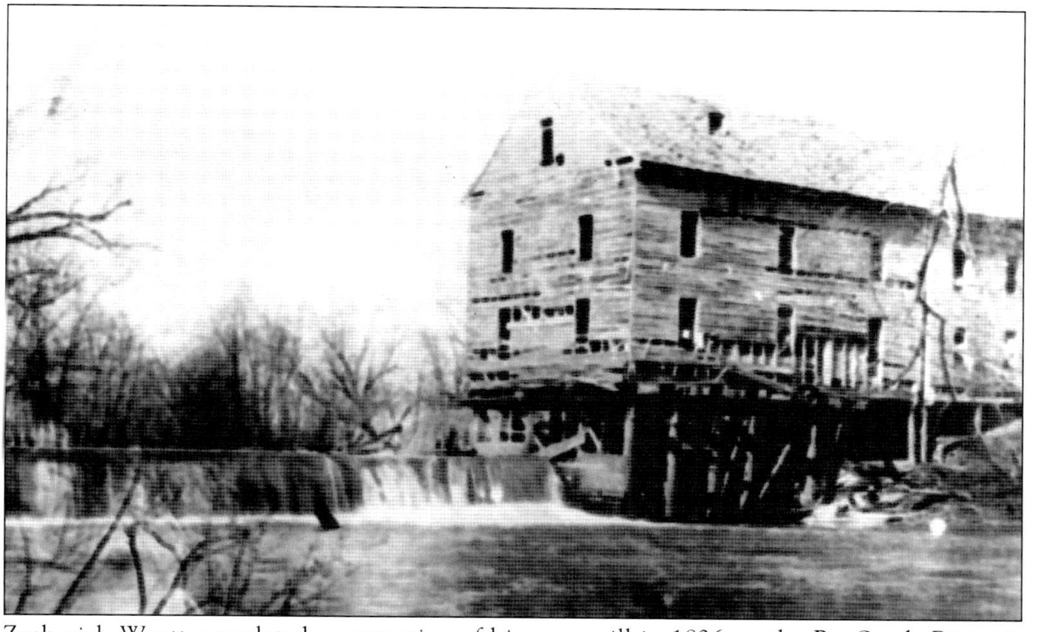

Zachariah Wyatt completed construction of his watermill in 1826 on the Big Sandy River; it was the only watermill ever constructed on Big Sandy River. It operated for nearly 100 years, and frequent references are made to it in county records although Zachariah Wyatt lived in Henry County. (BCPL.)

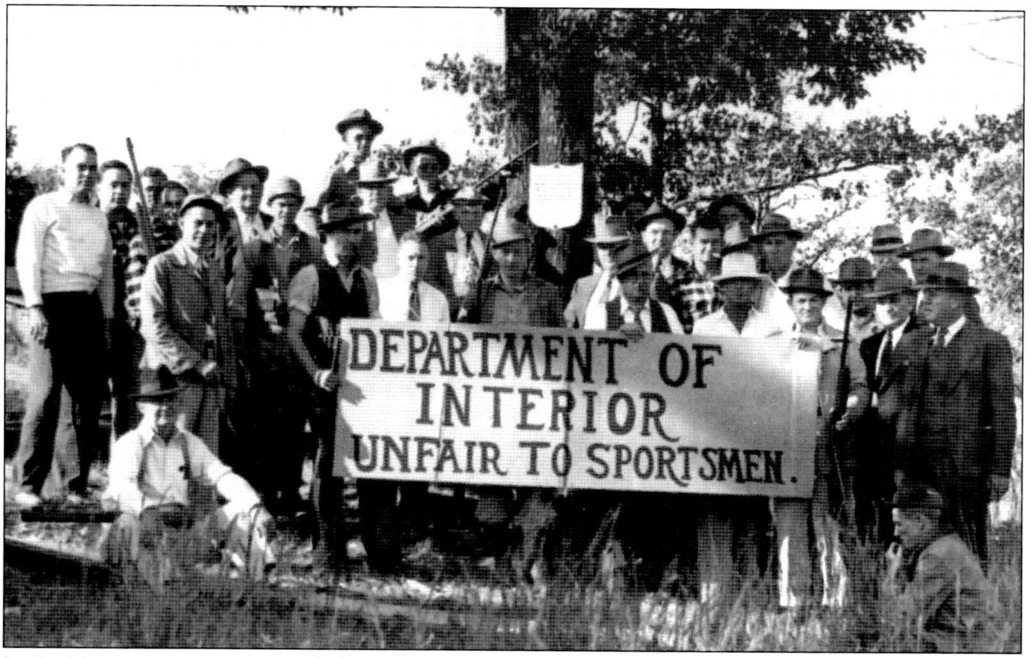

In 1946, sportsmen protested the incorporation of land into a wildlife refuge. Many had just lost land that had been in their families for generations when the Tennessee Valley Authority was formed and flooded the area. On August 30, 1944, TVA closed the gates on the Tennessee River at Gilbertsville, Kentucky, to flood the area and form Kentucky Lake. (BCPL.)

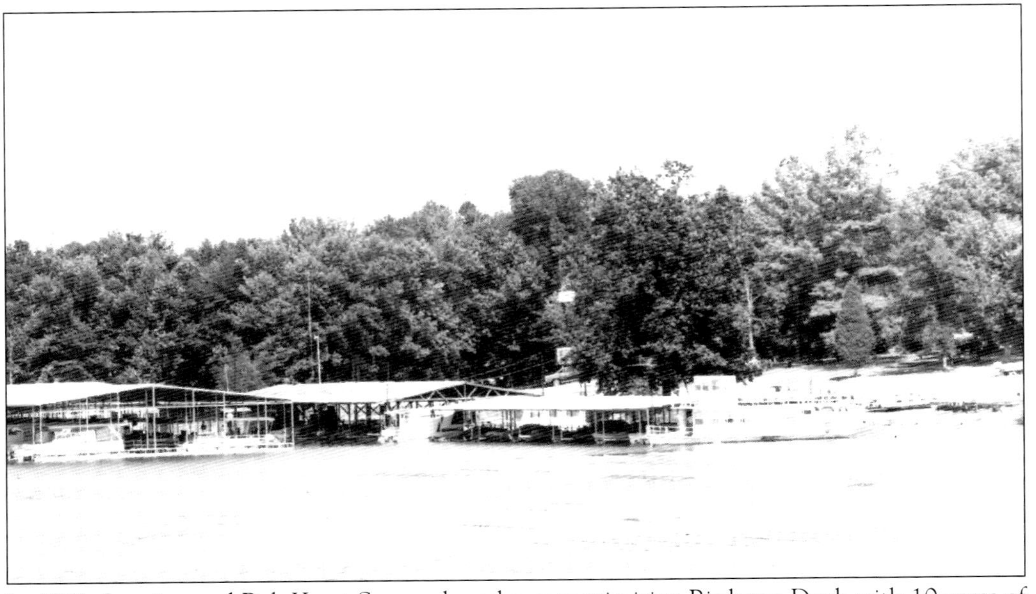

In 1961, Loraine and Bob Keast Sr. purchased a very primitive Birdsong Dock with 10 acres of land and extensive water frontage along Birdsong Embayment on Kentucky Lake. In 1964, they built the first section of 20 wet slips with roof, water, and electricity, which rented immediately. In 1968, Bob Sr. contracted for additional berthing of 30-foot and 40-foot boats. Today, it is well known as Birdsong Marina and is home to the Pearl Farm. (BCPL.)

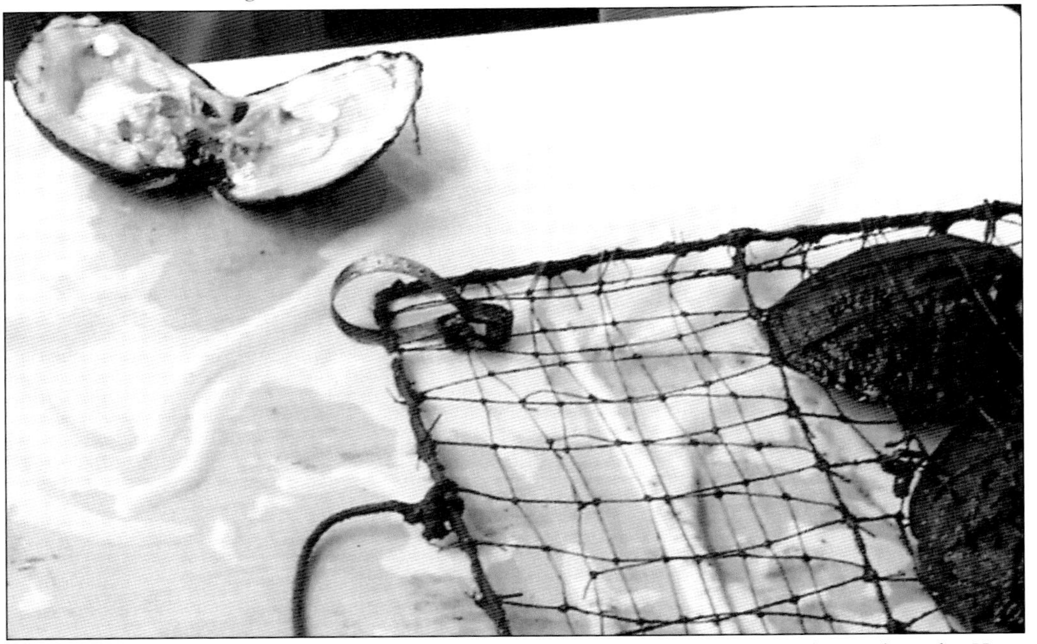

Benton County is home to the only freshwater pearl farm in America. It is located on the Kentucky Lake at the Birdsong Creek Embayment. Tours are conducted, and people come from far away to see the Pearl Farm. Some of the pearls are crafted locally into various pieces of jewelry. Shown here is a mussel that has just been opened showing several pearls, as well as two mussels in the basket in which pearls are being grown. (JG.)